WORD AND SPIRIT

*'Pray for us, that God may open a door for our message,
so that we may proclaim the mystery of Christ' (Col 4:3)*

Dedicated to the members of the New Springtime Community

Pat Collins CM

Word and Spirit
Intimations of a New Springtime

the columba press

First published in 2011 by
the columba press
55A Spruce Avenue, Stillorgan Industrial Park,
Blackrock, Co Dublin

Cover by Bill Bolger
Origination by The Columba Press
Printed in Ireland by Gemini International Limited

ISBN 978 1 85607 738 5

Copyright © 2011, Pat Collins CM

Contents

Introduction 7

SECTION ONE: EVANGELISATION

1. Mending the Breaches: A Parable for Today 12
2. Friendship, the Trinity and Evangelisation 22
3. Conversion and Evangelisation 36
4. Some Steppingstones to Faith 48
5. Contemplation and Evangelisation 59
6. Sts Vincent Ferrer and St Vincent de Paul: Extraordinary Evangelisers 66

SECTION TWO: SCRIPTURE

7. Scripture on Scripture 78
8. The Catholic Church on Reading and Praying the Scriptures 86
9. Interpreting Scripture 93
10. Claiming the Promises of Scripture 104
11. Careless Words 126

SECTION THREE: COMMUNITY

12. Christ's Presence in the Eucharistic Community 132
13. St Ignatius of Antioch on Unity in the Community 140

14. Proclamation of the Gospel and Community	147
15. Catholics and Protestants Witnessing Together	154
16. Sharing During Times of Economic Need	159

SECTION FOUR: PRAYER

17. The Teaching of Jesus on Prayer in Mark's Gospel	166
18. The Power of Prayer in Mark's Gospel	173
19. St Mark on Learning from Gethsemane	180
20. Rediscovering the Power of Praise	184
21. Group Intercessory Prayer	190

SECTION FIVE: PASTORAL

22. False Images of God and Resistance to Change	198
23. Power Encounters in Ministry	202
24. The Occult, Reiki and Yoga Evaluated	208
25. Private Revelation Assessed	215
26. Being a Loyal Catholic	224
27. The Devil's Advocate and Mother Teresa of Calcutta	235
28. Who Do Men Say I Am?	241

| Index | 248 |

Introduction

Many men and women have told me that they like to read books which help them to understand and practice their faith in a more enlightened fashion. With this in mind I have written *Word and Spirit* which consists of material drawn from different sources: articles for magazines, courses I have taught, and conference talks I have given. I have also written nine chapters specifically for this book. Some of them are short and simple and others longer and a little more difficult. In all of them I have aimed to steer a middle course between an abstract academic approach and a more pastoral and spiritual one. As a result I decided not to include footnotes. Where possible I have quoted from relevant scripture texts and the writings and sayings of the saints. There are also many quotations from ecclesial sources both papal and episcopal. The reason for this is a desire to be attuned to the mind of the church as expressed in an authoritative and reliable way through its official teachers. As you can see from the table of contents, the twenty eight chapters are divided into five different sections. While it could be argued that such a division is a bit arbitrary, it does help to organise the overlapping topics and to give the book an overall structure.

You may be wondering why the title is *Word and Spirit: Intimations of a New Springtime*. At the back of my mind were two ideas. Firstly, in Jn 6:63 there is a powerful saying of Jesus, 'The *words* I have spoken to you are *spirit* and they are life.' Secondly, it is said that shortly before his death in 1949, the well known British Pentecostal, Smith Wigglesworth predicted, in a prophetic manner, the rise and eventual demise of the Charismatic and the House Church Movements. Then he said, 'There will be evidence in the churches of something that has not been seen before: a coming together of those with an emphasis on the Word and those with an emphasis on the Spirit. When the

Word and the Spirit come together, there will be the biggest movement of the Holy Spirit that the nation, and indeed, the world, has ever seen.' His notion of an impending revival, of major proportions, is reminiscent of the New Springtime which has often been spoken about by Popes John Paul II and Benedict XVI. The former said: 'The new evangelisation, which can make the twenty-first century a springtime of the gospel, is a task for the entire People of God, but will depend in a decisive way on the lay faithful being fully aware of their baptismal vocation and their responsibility for bringing the good news of Jesus Christ to their culture and society.' In his *Pastoral Letter to the Catholics of Ireland* in 2010, Benedict XVI prayed, 'Holy Spirit, comforter, advocate and guide, inspire a new springtime of holiness and apostolic zeal for the church in Ireland.'

It is worth mentioning in this context, that in the Holy Land the farmers plant their seeds in the autumn and harvest their crops in the spring. So when Jesus said, 'The harvest is plentiful, but the workers are few. Ask the Lord of the harvest, therefore, to send out workers into his harvest field' (Lk 10:2), he was referring to the harvesting of souls by means of evangelisation in the springtime. It is also worth mentioning that in the Old Testament, the feast of Pentecost was the harvest festival referred to in Ex 23:16, 'Celebrate the Feast of Harvest with the first fruits of the crops you sow in your field.' We have reason to hope that, following a wintertime of hardship and purification, there will be a new springtime of Pentecostal grace. It will be the outcome of a new evangelisation which, hopefully, will be associated with signs and wonders.

Of course, the harvesting of souls, by means of evangelisation, will not be possible without the action of the Holy Spirit. Pope John Paul II said in par 45 of *At The Beginning of the New Millennium*, 'The Spirit is the principle agent of the new evangelisation.' Recently, I came across a delightful section in one of St Vincent Ferrer's sermons for the feast of Pentecost. He imagined that all those in the upper room were pleading with the Blessed Virgin to pray on their behalf, which she did. Then Vincent went on to say that when the Virgin Mary had finished her prayer, suddenly from heaven came a great sound like thunder, but delightful, not terrifying. It was like a voice in answer to a prayer

INTRODUCTION

of the Virgin Mary. For suddenly, in the likeness of wind the sound came down from heaven, and filled the whole house where the apostles were, and the whole house was filled with fire. This fire illuminated but did not burn, and the onlookers saw a white smoke like incense. Then the fire separated into the likeness of tongues of flame, which sat upon every one of those in the room, and they were filled with the Holy Spirit. It was an infilling with four graces: of knowledge in the mind, eloquence of tongue, charity of heart, and strength of body. Mary, star of the new evangelisation, pray for all the readers of this book that, like those in the upper room, they may proclaim the good news in word and deed by the power of the Holy Spirit.

It is my hope that this pastoral potpourri will be useful to the members of prayer groups, people who have attended Christian initiation courses such as RCIA or Alpha, and Catholics who have attended on-going formation courses who want to read books which are not only relevant in current circumstances but which also act as springboards to reflection, heartfelt prayer and efforts to establish the kingdom of God by means of evangelisation. I would like to humbly identify with some words from the end of St Augustine's magisterial book *The Trinity*, 'O Lord, may your people recognise whatever I have said in this book which comes from you, but I ask pardon from you and your people for anything that I have said that comes only from myself.'

Finally, I would like to thank the many Catholic and Protestant groups in Britain and Ireland who have invited me to talk at their respective gatherings. Besides enjoying the opportunity to share and to learn, may I say that I have a great love and admiration for the many faithful Christians I meet. I also want to thank the members of the New Springtime Community, in Ireland, to which I belong. These brothers and sisters are a constant source of encouragement, affection and edification as we seek to evangelise and train evangelisers together. Through my involvement with this new ecclesial community and its work, I have gained many insights which otherwise would have escaped me. As usual, a big thank you to Seán O Boyle for his customary expertise and encouragement in publishing this book.

SECTION ONE

Evangelisation

CHAPTER ONE

Mending the Breaches:
A Parable for Today

In the early eighties I was living in Boston, in the USA. One morning I received a mysterious word of prophecy as I travelled by train to College. It has influenced me ever since. Although I didn't understand it fully at the time, I was able to remember it and wrote it down sometime afterwards. It went as follows.

> 'Leave the city with its proud flags and go to the breach in the wall. Go and stand in the breach, the place of insecurity. Stand in the breach where the wind blows, where the jackal cries and where the enemy enters under the cloak of darkness. Stand in the breach, and intercede for yourself and for my people. Stand in the breach and listen to my word. Then call my people to the breach to rebuild the walls of Jerusalem.'

Because I was anxious to discern whether these words were inspired or not, I opted to do something that I have often advised others not to do. I decided that I would cut the scriptures with my eyes shut. Then I would put my finger on one of the open pages. If it was on the words, 'Rebuild the walls of Jerusalem,' I would presume that the word of prophecy had come from the Lord and not from myself or the evil one. After a brief prayer for help, I opened the bible at random and placed my finger on the page. It was resting on Ps 51:58, which reads, 'Rebuild the walls of Jerusalem!'

Ever since that memorable occasion I have pondered what the implications of the Lord's words might be. I felt that the church was very vulnerable and that the evil spirit would exploit weaknesses of belief and practice in the lives of its members, in order to attack it from within. In this connection I recalled something shocking which Pope Paul VI said in the course of a homily on the feast of Sts Peter and Paul in 1972.

CHAPTER ONE

'From some crevice (or breach), the smoke of Satan has entered the temple of God ... A condition of uncertainty reigns within the church. After the Second Vatican Council, we believed that the history of the church would enjoy a period of sunshine. Instead, the day became ugly, dark, cloudy and stormy. This came through an adverse power, his name is the Devil.' With thoughts like these in mind I can remember saying in a book entitled, *Unveiling the Heart: How to Overcome Evil in the Christian Life* (1995), 'I have become aware of widespread moral relativism, e.g. in the whole area of sexual values and conduct. I suspect that recent scandals, which have been widely reported in the media, may be the tip of a larger iceberg. I am also aware that in financial and business dealings there is widespread dishonesty.' A little later in the same book I surmised, 'In the coming years it is possible that, as a result of growing irrationality and moral blindness, we may have to endure a time of economic and political disruption.' Sad to say, recent scandals in the church and the world of finance have indicated that the time of trial may be immanent.

Rebuild my church

Five years ago I gained further insight about what might be involved in the re-building of the walls of Jerusalem. Toward the end of the Newman Consultation, a charismatic conference for leaders from Britain and Ireland, which was held in Birmingham in 2005, a prophetic word was spoken. It said that people from England, Ireland, Scotland and Wales should go on a walking pilgrimage to Assisi in 2007. Sometime later a Welsh woman named Margaret Thomas took the initiative. She issued an invitation for volunteers in *Goodnews* magazine. A number of people from the four countries responded, including two Anglicans. They went on a thirty-mile walking pilgrimage to Assisi from 27 September to 5 October 2007. When the group reached the town, they attended the 7.30 am Mass in San Damiano. Providentially, it was the eve of the feast of St Francis. One of the pilgrims wrote, 'The first reading that day, 3 October, was Nehemiah 2:1-8, which struck us powerfully and seemed to be the key to the pilgrimage. Nehemiah asked the king to 'send me to the city in Judah where my fathers are buried so that I can rebuild it.' The king, with the queen sitting beside him, gave permission and the necessary material help.

San Damiano was the church in which St Francis heard the Lord speak from a crucifix and say, 'Go, Francis, and repair my house, which as you can see, is falling into ruin.' Another translation puts it this way, 'Francis, don't you see that my house is being destroyed? Go, then, and rebuild it for me.' In short, 'Rebuild my church!' Francis looked around at the crumbling church of San Damiano, gathered some of his friends and rebuilt it. Then they went out and began restoring other church buildings in the vicinity of Assisi. Over a period of time, however, Francis realised that the call to 'rebuild my church' meant more than physically repairing damaged buildings. He was being asked to rebuild the institutional church from a spiritual point of view, by witnessing to the truth of the faith and calling people to renewed faithfulness to Christ and his mission.

In 2008 I joined a number of the Assisi pilgrims who met in St Non's Retreat House, in St David's, South Wales. Also present at the discernment meeting was Frances Graham, chairperson of the Welsh National Service Committee for charismatic renewal. Nearby, rather symbolically, there was the impressive ruin of a large monastery. At one point those of us who were present engaged in an extended bible study on chapters two and four of the Book of Nehemiah. In chapter two Nehemiah set the scene when he said, 'You see the trouble we are in: Jerusalem lies in ruins, and its gates have been burned with fire. Come, let us rebuild the wall of Jerusalem, and we will no longer be in disgrace' (Neh 2:17). Chapter four describes how the work was carried out. Throughout our long bible study we were very struck by the message which the two chapters contain. It was like an extended parable which is very relevant at the present time.

NEHEMIAH AND THE RE-BUILDING OF JERUSALEM

a) Nehemiah was a model leader
Nehemiah was a remarkable leader for a number of reasons. Firstly, he was a man of passion. Although he had never been in Jerusalem he was deeply disturbed when he heard that the holy city was depopulated, its walls had been breached and its gates destroyed (cf Neh 1:2-3). This awareness evoked within him a

strong desire to do something practical about the situation. Secondly, he was a man of vision. Following a time of prayer he had a divinely inspired plan for the restoration of the city (cf Neh 1:4-10). That is an important point. As Prov 29:18 says, 'Where there is no vision, the people perish.' Thirdly, he was a man of action. Having received permission from King Artaxerxes I to implement his plan to repair the walls of Jerusalem (cf Neh 2:5) he made a discreet survey of the city to see exactly what would be needed (cf Neh 2:11-16) and recruited many people to help him. The contemporary church desperately needs leaders like Nehemiah, men and women of passion, and practicality. But most of all they need a vision of a renewed church, not a vision that is based on purely human thinking but one which is inspired by the Holy Spirit. As the psalmist warned, 'Unless the Lord builds the house, those who build it labour in vain' (Ps 127:1). Sad to say, currently there seem to be very few leaders who have an inspiring vision of what the church of the future might be like.

b) The breaches in the walls
Nehemiah described how the Jewish volunteers went to the breaches in the walls of Jerusalem in order to begin the work of restoration. They said to one another, 'Let us start rebuilding.' So they began this good work. Nehemiah reassured them saying, 'The God of heaven will give us success' (Neh 2:18; 20). The breaches in the walls of Jerusalem are symbolic of the places where the present day church is weak and vulnerable. We are all too painfully aware that the walls of the Irish church have been badly damaged by sinful abuse and subsequent cover-ups that came to light in the Savi, Ferns, Ryan, Murphy and Cloyne reports. As a result, five bishops have had to resign and the church has had to pay out hundreds of millions of euro in compensation. In an article entitled, 'The Murphy Report One Year Later,' Archbishop Diarmuid Martin has said in a realistic and insightful way: 'As I look back ... I see more clearly that the catastrophic manner in which the abuse was dealt with was a symptom of a *deeper malaise within the Irish church* [my italics]. The church in Ireland had allowed itself to drift into a position where its role in society had grown beyond what is legitimate. It acted as a world

apart. It became self-centred. It felt that it could be forgiving of abusers in a simplistic manner and rarely empathised with the hurt of children. It also deluded itself about the faith of Irish people. It failed to recognise what radical evangelisation of its structures and of its people actually meant. It spoke of renewal but really did not change. It failed adequately to recognise that renewal demands conversion.' This is one striking way of identifying the breaches in the church, but there are others. One way or the other, Jesus warned in Rev 3:15-16, 'I know your deeds, that you are neither cold nor hot. I wish you were either one or the other! So, because you are lukewarm – neither hot nor cold – I am about to spit you out of my mouth.'

c) Resist the enemy firm in faith
Nehemiah was conscious of the danger of attack by enemies. In Neh 4:7-8 we are told that, 'When Sanballat, Tobiah, the Arabs, the Ammonites and the men of Ashdod heard that the repairs to Jerusalem's walls had gone ahead and that the gaps were being closed, they were very angry. They all plotted together to come and fight against Jerusalem and stir up trouble against it.' Those who opposed the rebuilding of Jerusalem are symbolic of the opposition of the devil and his demons. As St Paul said in Eph 6:12, 'our struggle is not against flesh and blood, but against the rulers, against the authorities, against the powers of this dark world and against the spiritual forces of evil in the heavenly realms.' Pope Paul VI was well aware of the assaults of the devil on the church. In 1972 he gave a long talk on the devil, in the course of which he said, 'We must fight against the demon. We do not think about this reality any more, but I now wish to draw your attention to this terrible and unavoidable subject. We must fight against this enemy, terrible and invisible, who sets snares for our life and against whom we must defend ourselves.' When he was here in Ireland in 1979, Pope John Paul II warned us about the likelihood of demonic attack when he said in Limerick, 'Satan, the tempter, the adversary of Christ, will use all his might and all his deceptions to win Ireland for the way of the world.' In many ways the prince of this world (cf Jn 12:31) has already succeeded in leading many people away from fidelity to Christ. I have also noticed that since the church and

CHAPTER ONE

financial crises kicked in, there seems to have been a big rise in manifestations of the evil one's activity and therefore an increased need for simple and solemn exorcisms.

d) Getting rid of the rubble in our lives
Nehemiah tells us that there was a great deal of rubble lying outside the walls. In Neh 4:11-12, we read, 'Meanwhile, the people in Judah said, "The strength of the labourers is giving out, and there is so much rubble that we cannot rebuild the wall." Also our enemies said, "Before they know it or see us, we will be right there among them and will kill them and put an end to the work".' Evidently, the enemies used the rubble as cover. They hid behind it, in readiness to make sneak attacks. From a symbolic point of view, the rubble represents the worldly and sinful attachments in our lives, such as an inordinate desire for things such as possessions, position, popularity, pleasure, and power, which the evil one can exploit in order to mount attacks on a vulnerable church. We need to rid ourselves of worldly attachments which nail down our spiritual energy to created things in an idolatrous way (cf Phil 3:19). We need to rid ourselves progressively of rubbish of this kind by means of on-going conversion and sensible acts of self-denial such as fasting.

We know that the members of the New Testament church fasted regularly. It served a number of purposes: to make satisfaction for sin; control bodily passions; experience solidarity with the poor; and express, in a symbolic way, a creaturely dependence on God. In the Acts of the Apostles, we are told that the believers sometimes received divine guidance following periods of prayer and fasting (cf Acts 13:2; 14:23). The *Didache*, which was written in 70 AD before the fall of Jerusalem, urged Christians to fast on Wednesdays and Fridays. Although the Lenten fast is no longer compulsory, surely Christians would do well to engage in sensible abstinence, for specified periods of time, during the year. Others fast during the liturgical seasons of Lent and Advent. In this context it is worth noting that in par 14 of his *Pastoral Letter to the Catholics of Ireland,* Pope Benedict XVI said, 'I now invite all of you to devote your Friday penances, for a period of one year, between now and Easter 2011, to this intention. I ask you to offer up your fasting, your prayer, your reading of scripture and your works of mercy in order to obtain the grace of healing and renewal for the church in Ireland.' Although some commentators in the media said that these suggestions were out of date, they were simply part of the perennial Christian notion of asceticism as a counterbalance to harmful self-indulgence (cf 1 Cor 9:24-27).

e) Intercessors and spiritual combat
Because Nehemiah was so conscious of the danger of attack, he decided to protect the city by appointing half the people to guard it and its citizens. They had the task of noticing when and where their enemies intended to attack. In Neh 4:14-15, we read, 'Therefore I stationed some of the people behind the lowest points of the wall at the exposed places, posting them by families, with their swords, spears and bows. After I looked things over, I stood up and said to the nobles, the officials and the rest of the people, "Don't be afraid of them. Remember the Lord, who is great and awesome, and fight for your brothers, your sons and your daughters, your wives and your homes".' These guardians represent the role of intercessors who engage in spiritual warfare and combat. As St Paul said in 2 Cor 10:4-5, 'We do not wage war as the world does. The weapons we fight with are not the weapons of the world. On the contrary, they have divine power to demolish strongholds. We demolish arguments and every pretension that sets itself up against the knowledge of God, and we take captive every thought to make it obedient to Christ.' In Eph 6:11, having said, 'Put on the full armour of God so that you can take your stand against the devil's schemes,' Paul described six pieces of equipment Christians should rely on, especially the sword of the word and the shield of faith 'which puts out all the fiery darts of the evil one' (Eph 6:16).

In the light of these scripture texts, it is significant that Pope John Paul II said in Limerick in 1979, 'Dear sons and daughters of Ireland, pray, pray not to be led into temptation … I ask you today for a great, intense and growing prayer for all the people of Ireland, for the church in Ireland, for all the church which owes so much to Ireland. Pray that Ireland will not fail in the test. Pray as Jesus has taught us to pray: Lead us not into temptation.' More recently, having encouraged frequent Eucharistic adoration, Pope Benedict said in his *Pastoral Letter to the Catholics of Ireland* in 2010, 'Through intense prayer before the real presence of the Lord, you can make reparation for the sins of abuse that have done so much harm, at the same time imploring the grace of renewed strength and a deeper sense of mission on the part of all bishops, priests, religious and lay faithful.' For more on the prayer of intercession see chapter twenty one.

f) Praise and the affirmation of deliverance
Nehemiah tells us that as part of the defence of the city and the workers, he appointed a trumpet player to sound the alarm during times of danger or attack. In Neh 4:19-20 we read, 'Then I said to the nobles, the officials and the rest of the people, "The work is extensive and spread out, and we are widely separated from each other along the wall. Wherever you hear the sound of the trumpet, join us there".' The trumpet symbolises the importance of praising God as an integral aspect of spiritual warfare. Ps 22:3 assures us that God lives in the praises of his people. He is greater than the enemy we face. As we nestle in his protection by means of faith-filled praise, he does battle with the evil one on our behalf. In a number of places in the Old Testament we are told that the musicians guided Jewish armies into battle (cf 2 Chron 20:21; Josh 6:8). They led the triumphant praises of the people who affirmed the fact that the Lord would be fighting for them and that victory, therefore, was assured. As Nehemiah testified, 'Our God will fight for us!' (Neh 4:19). In 2 Chron 19:15 there is a similar expression of confidence. 'This is what the Lord says to you: "Do not be afraid or discouraged because of this vast army. For the battle is not yours, but God's".' Those who want to re-build the church should engage in praise that is loud and long. For more on this see chapter twenty.

g) Re-building as the new evangelisation
In chapter three Nehemiah describes how different family groups volunteered to help with the re-building of the many breaches in the walls of Jerusalem. In contemporary terms, the builders are symbolic of the men and women who are responding to the church's repeated calls to engage in what Popes Paul VI, John Paul II, and Benedict XVI have referred to as the new

evangelisation. In his post synodal apostolic declaration on *The Word of God*, Benedict says, 'At the dawn of the third millennium not only are there still many peoples who have not come to know the good news, but also a great many Christians who need to have the word of God once more persuasively proclaimed to them, so that they can concretely experience the power of the gospel. Many of our brothers and sisters are "baptised, but insufficiently evangelised". In a number of cases, nations once rich in faith and in vocations are losing their identity under the influence of a secularised culture. The need for a new evangelisation, so deeply felt by my venerable Predecessor, must be valiantly reaffirmed, in the certainty that God's word is effective.' The message is not new, but the culture in which it must be proclaimed is different, so our evangelisation needs to be new in ardour, methods and forms of expression. The first section of this book deals with some aspects of this all important topic.

Confirmation of the Prophetic Word
On returning home from St Non's, Frances Graham opened an email from Fiona Hendy of the House of the Open Door Community in Worcestershire. She is the co-ordinator of the Network of Intercessors for the National Service Committees of the Charismatic Renewal in Britain and Ireland. They pray regularly for the renewal and the church. As a result of being led to read chapters two and four of the Book of Nehemiah, the Lord had given her and her companions a prophetic word about the importance of intercession on behalf of those who are trying to rebuild the church by means of the new evangelisation. She gave an example of such intercession from Lam 2:18-19, which reads, 'Cry aloud to the Lord! O daughter of Zion! Let tears stream down like a torrent day and night! Give yourself no rest, your eyes no respite! Arise, cry out in the night, at the beginning of the watches! Pour out your heart like water before the presence of the Lord! Lift your hands to him for the lives of your children, who faint for hunger at the head of every street.' There is an equally instructive text in Is 62:6-7, 'I have posted watchmen on your walls, O Jerusalem; they will never be silent day or night. You who call on the Lord, give yourselves no rest, and give him no rest till he establishes Jerusalem and makes her the

praise of the earth.' It seemed to those of us who were in St Non's, that Fiona Hendy's email was a remarkable confirmation of the fruits of our discernment process. Arguably, there needs to be an intercessor for every evangelist engaged in the new evangelisation! If this is so, we should make efforts to recruit and train as many intercessors as possible. For more on this subject see chapter twenty two.

Conclusion
Nearly thirty years have passed since I heard the Lord speak to my heart on the train in Boston. I feel that the time to re-build the walls of Jerusalem has finally arrived. In par 34 of the apostolic exhortation, *The Lay Members Of Christ's Faithful People*, Benedict XVI says: 'Without doubt a mending of the Christian fabric of society is urgently needed in all parts of the world. But for this to come about what is needed is to first *remake the Christian fabric of the ecclesial community itself* [my italics] present in these countries and nations.' The re-building requires a sustained and committed effort by a growing number of Catholics, clerical and lay, to evangelise the large numbers of their co-religionists who do not yet know the Lord in a personal way. As Benedict says in his letter, *Always and Everywhere* (2010), 'it is not difficult to see that what all the churches living in traditionally Christian territories need is a renewed missionary impulse, an expression of a new, generous openness to the gift of grace. Indeed we cannot forget that the first task will always be to make ourselves docile to the freely given action of the Spirit of the Risen One who accompanies all who are heralds of the gospel and opens the hearts of those who listen.'

At the present time there is no need for Christians to be either afraid or despondent. A new springtime is on the way. In the meantime we can pray with hope, 'In your good pleasure make Zion prosper; build up the walls of Jerusalem. Then there will be righteous sacrifices, whole burnt offerings to delight you; then bulls will be offered on your altar' (Ps 51:18).

CHAPTER TWO

Friendship, the Trinity and Evangelisation

Some time ago I saw Oprah Winfrey interviewing actresses Meryl Streep and Nicole Kidman on TV. At the end of their time together, Winfrey said, 'Well ladies, if you were to say that you were absolutely sure of one thing, what would it be?' Streep was the first to respond in a rather mischievous way. She said, 'I'm absolutely sure that if a woman has a baby, she never loses her stretch marks!' Kidman responded in a more thoughtful manner, 'I'm absolutely sure, because life has taught me this, that it is in giving that we receive.' As the two women were giving their responses, I found myself spontaneously answering, 'I am absolutely sure that I have a friend who really loves me.' I found this a very comforting thought, but I was a little surprised and disconcerted to find that not a single truth of faith had come to my mind. However, when I thought about my instinctive response, I suspected that these theological truths were actually implicit in the answer I gave. As St Augustine observed in *The Trinity*, book 8, chapter 12, 'If you see charity, you see the Trinity.'

Friendship
I have always admired St Thomas Aquinas. Apart from being a man of great intelligence, learning, and sanctity, apparently he had very good friends such as Theodora, one of his sisters; a niece Frances; his mentor St Albert the Great, and his colleague Reginald of Piperno. Therefore it is not really surprising to find that he was deeply influenced by books nine and ten of Aristotle's *Nichomachean Ethics*, which are about friendship.

Like the great Greek philosopher, Thomas wrote about the nature of friendship. He said there are three forms. Firstly, there is a kind of friendship which is motivated by some advantage that comes from the relationship, e.g. wealth or influence. Secondly, there is a type of friendship which is motivated by the prospect of pleasure, e.g. stimulating conversation, or sexual pleasure. Thirdly, there is genuine, reciprocal friendship which is based on benevolence, i.e. wanting in a selfless way, what is best for the other person. Writing in his treatise *On Charity*, Thomas tells us: 'Perfect friendship is not directed toward many ... but inasmuch as friendship toward one becomes more perfect as regards that one, the more perfect the love we have toward one, the better we are able to love others.' There is a wonderful description of this kind of true Christian friendship in the Office of Readings in *The Divine Office* for the feast of Sts Basil the Great and Gregory of Nazianzen. Gregory wrote, 'We seemed to have a single soul animating two bodies. And, while those who claim that all things are not readily to be believed, we, at least, had to believe that we were in and with each other. The sole ambition of both of us was virtue and a life so led in view of future hopes, as to sever our attachment to this life before we had to depart it.' Thomas, like Aristotle before him, maintained that a person will know if a friendship is genuine when the advantages and pleasures are removed, for one reason or other. If it survives those deprivations it is genuine. As the saying goes, 'A friend in need, is a friend indeed.'

Thomas also described motives people have for engaging in friendship. He said that, 'no one in his right mind would choose to live with all other external goods but without friends.' In another place he said, 'we need friends in all conditions of life because friendship is our greatest gift.' In his *Summa Theologica* he added, 'We need friends in leading lives of action and contemplation. And although the companionship of friends is not strictly necessary even in this way to the perfect happiness of our heavenly home, where a person is completely and wholly fulfilled in God, yet the companionship of friends enhances happiness.'

The Angelic Doctor also talked about means of fostering and deepening genuine friendship. Quoting Aristotle, he said that five things can be involved: 'willing the friend's good, being glad that he or she is alive, taking pleasure in living with him or her, having the same preferences, and sharing griefs and joys.' He felt that true friendship involves a reciprocal closeness and self-giving. He stated, 'All friendship consists in two-way communication, for friends have everything in common.' Because communication is so important he believed that friends would need to live together. Let's face it, most friends are unable to do so. In any case, nowadays, friends can maintain communication at a distance by means of such things as phone calls, emails, text messages, twitter, skype etc.

Friendship in marriage
According to St Thomas, Christian marriage is a form of self-giving in the context of a spousal friendship. Commenting on book eight of Aristotle's *Ethics*, he said, 'Married friendship is useful, delightful and honourable. It serves to provide for domestic life. It brings the delight of sex and physical pleasure. And if a husband and wife are attractive to one another, their friendship is expressed in virtue proper to them both, rendering it mutually agreeable.' In his *Summa Contra Gentiles*, Thomas said something similar, 'The greater friendship is, the stronger and more lasting it is. But between a man and a woman there seems to be the greatest friendship; for they are united not only in the act of intercourse, which even among the animals produces a certain sweet society, but also throughout the whole of domestic living. In sign of this it is said in Genesis that "for the sake of his wife a man leaves father and mother". Thus it is fitting that marriage be altogether indissoluble.' Of all the love relationships under God that Thomas treats it is clear that conjugal love stands at the pinnacle.

What St Thomas said about friendship in marriage seemed to be implicit in one of the central teachings of Vatican II. It was highlighted by Bishop Karol Wojtyła when he returned from the Council. He made the striking claim that par 24 of the pastoral constitution on the *Church in the Modern World* was the key to understanding the whole council. He highlighted the following sentence: 'Man, who is the only creature on earth which God willed for itself, cannot fully find himself *except through a sincere gift of himself* [my italics].' Commenting on this sentence in his book, *Sources of the Renewal: The Implementation of the Second Vatican Council*, Wojtyła wrote, 'Man resembles God not only because of the spiritual nature of his immortal soul but also by reason of his social nature, if by this we understand the fact that he "cannot fully realize himself except in an act of pure self-giving". In this way "union in truth and charity" is the ultimate expression of the community of individuals.' Pope John Paul reflected in a profound way on the theological implications of self-giving, especially in the form of spousal love.

Par 2360 of the *Catechism of the Catholic Church,* which was clearly influenced by John Paul's thinking, says that 'In marriage the physical intimacy of the spouses becomes a sign and pledge of spiritual communion ... The acts in marriage by which the intimate and chaste union of the spouses takes place are noble and honourable; the truly human performance of these acts fosters the self-giving they signify.' John Paul made the interesting point that the couple are not only made in the image of God because they are rational souls endowed with freedom, but also because 'Man becomes an image of God not so much in the moment of solitude as in the moment of communion.' Par 2205 of the *Catechism of the Catholic Church* adds, 'The Christian family is a communion of persons, a sign and image of the communion of the Father and the Son in the Holy Spirit. In the procreation and education of children it reflects the Father's work of creation.' John Paul also maintained that such communion between spouses, and within families mediated the presence of God. In a very significant sentence, he said in *Man and Woman He Created Them,* 19:4, 'The body, in fact, and only the body, is capable of making visible what is invisible, namely the spiritual and the divine. It has been created to transfer into the visible reality of the world the mystery hidden from eternity in God, and thus to be a sign of it.'

Paradoxically, people discover their innermost selves, including their God-selves, by means of self-forgetful love of others. In the words of a well known Abba song, it is a matter of 'knowing me knowing you.' So if people want to discover *who* they are as individuals, they need to know *whose* they are in and through their relationships. Pope John Paul made this point repeatedly in his writings. For instance, he observed in par 25 of *The Rosary of the Virgin Mary,* 'Anyone who contemplates Christ through the various stages of his life cannot fail to perceive in him the truth about themselves. It is only in the mystery of the Word made flesh that the mystery of our humanity is seen in its true light.' He believed that in so far as Christian couples are in communion with one another, they not only mediate the communion within the Trinity to each other, they also enable one another to relate to the God image within themselves.

It can be noted in passing that St Thomas thought that the experience of friendship, whether in or outside of marriage, was a theological template or paradigm which could be utilised to understand many Christian topics such as prayer, contemplation, grace and the Trinity. However, Pope John Paul seemed to replace the paradigm of friendship with that of spousal love as experienced in the sacrament of marriage. It is striking how few times he refers to friendship in his book *Man and Woman he Created Them*. Although this anomaly deserves further study by theologians, I suspect that they are complementary rather than contradictory points of view. Both relationships involve the crucial experience of communion, the total donation of oneself to the other as a reflection of, and participation in the communion between the persons in the Blessed Trinity.

The inner and outer Trinity
Some readers may find that this section is a little difficult, but it is included for the sake of completeness. Christian theology maintains that there are two ways of looking at the Trinity. Firstly, there is what is referred to in theology as the economical Trinity, i.e. the Divine persons as we experience them through their outer activities in creation and in the economy or plan of salvation. God the Father is the creator, Jesus the Son is the redeemer, and God the Holy Spirit is the reconciler and sanctifier. The doctrine of the Trinity is hinted at, but not developed, in the gospels and the writings of Paul. For example, at the baptism of Jesus, the Holy Spirit came upon him, and God the Father spoke to him (cf Mt 3:16-17). Before his ascension into heaven, Jesus said to the apostles that they should baptise people in the name of the three persons of the Trinity (cf Mt 28:19). In Paul's letters too, there is also an incipient doctrine of the Trinity. For instance, in 2 Cor 13:14 he wrote, 'May the grace of the Lord Jesus Christ, and the love of God, and the fellowship of the Holy Spirit be with you all.'

Secondly, there is what theology refers to as the immanent

Trinity, i.e. the Divine persons as they are in their relationships with one another within the Trinity. It is worth noting that when theology talks about the Divine persons it does not intend to say that they are like human personalities, namely individual centres of rational consciousness and freedom. The word *person* is used in a specialist sense which is deeply influenced by philosophy, especially that of Anicius Boethius (470-524). He said that a person is 'an individual substance of a rational nature'. Although he agreed with Boethius, St Thomas Aquinas also defined person as 'subsistent relation'. So, rather than saying that there are three personalities, Christians say that there are three subsisting persons, or relations in God.

The economical Trinity

While the natural mind can come to a certain limited knowledge of the existence and attributes of God, e.g. that the divine is eternal, all powerful, all knowing, perfect and unchanging (cf Rm 1:20), it cannot arrive at an unassisted knowledge of the triune nature of God. It is worth noting in passing that the God of philosophy is necessarily apathetic. This is so because God is unchanging and therefore cannot be emotionally moved by either the joys or sorrows of the human condition. The real truth about God had to be *revealed* to the human mind. As Paul testified in Rom 16:25-26, 'the revelation of the mystery hidden for long ages past, is now revealed and made known through the prophetic writings by the command of the eternal God.' Speaking of himself Paul said in 1 Cor 2:7, 'we speak of God's secret wisdom, a wisdom that has been hidden and that God destined for our glory before time began.'

The blessed Trinity was manifested in history in and through the sending of the Son of God into the world, as a human person with a divine and human nature. Instead of being apathetic, as the philosophers had asserted, the incarnation revealed that God in Christ was deeply influenced by the human condition. As Heb 4:15 says of Jesus, 'For we do not have a high priest who is unable to sympathise with our weaknesses.' This was particularly obvious when Jesus was repeatedly moved to compassion by the plight of the poor. Remember the poignant verse in Mt 9:37 where we read, 'he had compassion on them, because they were harassed and helpless, like sheep without a shepherd.' No wonder Nouwen, McNeil and Morrison could observe in their book *Compassion*, 'When Jesus was moved to compassion, the source of all life trembled, the ground of all love burst open, and the abyss of God's immense, inexhaustible, and unfathomable tenderness revealed itself.'

To relate to the humanity of Jesus, with the help of the Holy Spirit, leads the human mind and soul into the revealed truth about God as our Father. As Jesus himself said, 'the Spirit will take from what is mine and make it known to you' (Jn 16:15), and 'Anyone who has seen me has seen the Father' (Jn 14:9). Theology says that each divine person is wholly present in each of the others. For instance, par 267 of the *Catechism of the Catholic Church* says, 'Inseparable in what they are, the divine persons are also inseparable in what they do. But within the single divine operation each shows forth what is proper to him in the Trinity, especially in the divine missions of the Son's Incarnation and the gift of the Holy Spirit.' To see and experience the compassion of Jesus, is to see and experience the compassion of both the Father and the Holy Spirit.

The immanent Trinity
As a result of knowing the economical Trinity, because of the joint missions of the Son and the Spirit, we can infer something of what the immanent God is like as a trinity of persons abiding forever in undivided communion. In his masterwork, *The Trinity*, St Augustine reflected deeply on the outer life of God, as we experience it in this life, in order to infer something about the mysterious inner life of God. He concluded that the divine persons were not so much different because of their functions on our behalf, but rather in their different relations to one another. He talked about real, or subsistent relations in God. There is one divine nature, but there are also relations of opposition. For example, the Father who is unbegotten is not the Son, who is begotten. (The word begotten here does not mean created. An equivalent English word would be 'origin' or 'source'). The Spirit of love who unites the Father and Son, is equal to them, and proceeds from both. In book six, chapter five of *The Trinity*, St Augustine said, 'The Holy Spirit, whatever it is, is something

common both to the Father and Son. But that communion itself is consubstantial and co-eternal; and *if it may fitly be called friendship* [my italics], let it be so called; but it is more aptly called love.' Both St Augustine and St Thomas Aquinas felt that one could propose psychological analogies for the inner life of the Blessed Trinity which are based on the activity of the immaterial human mind. For example, speaking of the intellect in book ten, section eleven of *The Trinity*, Augustine says, 'These three, the memory, the understanding, and the will, are not three lives but one life. Not three minds but one mind, it follows that they are certainly not three substances, but one substance.' St Thomas also used the human mind's activity as an analogy for the Trinity, e.g. in pars 37-50 of his *Compendium Theologiae*.

In the spirituality of Christians, the inner and outer life of the Blessed Trinity interconnect in the giving and receiving of Christian love. As par 259 of the *Catechism of the Catholic Church* observes, 'The whole Christian life is a communion with each of the divine persons, without in any way separating them. Everyone who glorifies the Father does so through the Son in the Holy Spirit; everyone who follows Christ does so because the Father draws him and the Spirit moves him.'

God as a Trinity of Friendship Love
Echoing the insight of St Augustine, St Thomas believed that God is a Trinity of friendship love. He believed that God is triune because Christians believe that God is love! If God is love, then he must love someone. There is no such thing as love of nothing, a love that is not directed at anyone. So we ask: Who is it that God loves so that he is defined as love? How does Christian revelation answer this question? God is love in himself, before time, because there is eternally in him a Son, the Word, whom he loves with an infinite love which is the Holy Spirit. In every love there are always three realities or subjects: one who loves, one who is loved and the love that unites them. In one of his writings St Thomas observed, 'The perfect goodness of divine happiness and glory postulates friendship within God ... Perfect glory displays a certain magnificence of relationship, which charity provides. God's true and perfect happiness, therefore, requires a trinity of persons. The love of oneself alone is a pri-

vate love, not true charity. Yet God cannot supremely love another, since no creature is supremely lovable, for no creature is supremely good. It appears then that God's charity would not love to the upmost were he only one person. Not only if he were only two, for with perfect friendship the lover wills that what he loves should also be equally loved by another.' God the Father's self-communication always involves his relationship with the Son and the Holy Spirit, whom Irenaeus of Lyons referred to as 'the two hands of the Father'.

Before his ascension into heaven, Jesus said to the apostles, 'make disciples of all nations, baptising them in the name of the Father and of the Son and of the Holy Spirit' (Mt 28:19). Thomas, like all Catholics, believed that when we are born again in baptism, the Trinity lives within us. In his *Commentary on St Paul's Epistles to the Ephesians* he wrote, 'The only-begotten Son of God, wishing to make us sharers in his divine nature, assumed our nature, so that made man he makes men gods. For the human mind and will could never imagine, understand or ask that God become man, and that man become God and a sharer in the divine nature. But he has done this in us by his power, and it was accomplished in the Incarnation of his Son: "That you may become partakers of the divine nature" (2 Pet 1:4).' As a result of divinisation, Christian friendships, unlike merely human ones, take on a new significance. Not only do they reflect the inner life of the Trinity, they enable the loving friends to participate in that life.

In one of his writings, Thomas illustrated some of the links between human and divine friendship. Firstly, having said that friends converse together, he went on to say that people's conversation with God is by means of contemplation (cf 2 Cor 3:18). Secondly, he said that friends delight in each other's presence, enjoying each other's actions and finding comfort there in their anxieties. Then he went on to say that in like manner the Holy Spirit abides with us and comforts us when we experience setbacks, losses and difficulties. Thirdly, he said that friends agree together about many things such as ideals and values. Then he stated that the Holy Spirit prompts us to accept and to carry out God's will, not out of a sense of cheerless obligation, but as a result of loving conviction. No wonder St Aelred of Rievaulx

(1109-1167) said in his book *Christian Friendship*, 'God is friendship. It does sound most unusual, doesn't it? ... But I would not hesitate to attribute to friendship anything that is predicated of charity, as for instance, "he who abides in friendship abides in God and God abides in him".'

The Trinity, Creation and the Incarnation
In par 2 of the Conciliar Decree on *The Church's Missionary Activity* we read that the friendship love between the divine persons is like 'a fountain of love' which spills over in the creation of the universe and human beings. In other words, Trinitarian love is creative, generative and nurturing. As the *Dogmatic Constitution on The Church* tells us, 'The eternal Father, by a free and hidden plan of his own wisdom and goodness, created the whole world. His plan was to raise men to a participation in the divine life. Fallen in Adam, God the Father did not leave men to themselves, but ceaselessly offered helps to salvation.' In Jn 3:16-17 we read the well-known words, 'God so loved the world that he gave his only Son, so that everyone who believes in him may not perish but may have eternal life. Indeed, God did not send the Son into the world to condemn the world, but in order that the world might be saved through him.' In other words, the Word became flesh in order to carry out the saving mission of the Father in the power of the Holy Spirit. Jesus was anointed by the Spirit at his baptism in order to bring the good news to the poor (cf Lk 4:18). By so doing he wanted to restore and deepen the friendship that once existed between human beings and God.

Jesus as a Friend
Although Jesus left his parents and chose not to marry, he never renounced friendship love. In fact he said to the apostles, 'I no longer call you servants, because a servant does not know his master's business. Instead, I have called you friends, for everything that I learned from my Father I have made known to you' (Jn 15:15). A friend desires to be united as fully as possible with the person he loves. He wants to do this by means of mutual self-disclosure. However, the fact that we are separate individuals makes this well-nigh impossible. St Paul explains why this is

so: 'It is only a person's own spirit within him that knows all about him.' (1 Cor 2:11) In other words, while I have a direct awareness of myself, I can only have a partial, indirect knowledge of another person. This remains true, no matter how much s/he tells me about him or herself.

Needless to say, Jesus had a direct awareness of himself. Through the action of the Holy Spirit within his depths he also had a direct awareness of his Father. There was no barrier between them. Jesus would say: 'You, Father are in me, and I in you' (Jn 17:21). It was precisely this experience of God that Jesus couldn't convey to the apostles. They heard his words. They understood to a certain extent. But they couldn't stand inside his skin. So they couldn't share in his sense of intimacy with the Divine.

Jesus realised that his words, no matter how eloquent, would not be enough. Only the Holy Spirit would be able to lead the apostles and disciples into the truth about God. As a result, Jesus began to talk in a mysterious and paradoxical way. On one occasion he said: 'The Spirit is with you now, soon he will be within you' (Jn 14. 17). This was both a statement of fact and a promise. It was a fact in the sense that while Jesus was with the apostles the Spirit was with them. This was so because Jesus was the Christ, i.e. the One who is filled with the Spirit. It was a promise in the sense that Jesus was saying that a time would come when the same Holy Spirit would be poured out on his apostles and disciples. Then it would dwell within them and they would have 'that mind which was in Christ'. (1 Cor 2: 16) Jesus said that he would have to leave his followers before the Spirit could be given to them: 'It is better for you that I go away, because if I do not go, the Helper will not come to you. But if I go away, then I will send him to you' (Jn 16:7). In saying this, Jesus was referring to his forthcoming death and resurrection. On the cross he would give up his Spirit to the Father, 'Father, into your hands I commit my spirit' (Lk 23:46). Christ's expiration was a necessary prelude to the inspiration of the believers, in order that they could conspire to lead a Trinitarian life.

Pentecost as restoration of friendship with the Trinity
When the promised Holy Spirit was poured out on the apostles,

CHAPTER TWO

their sins were forgiven and the love of God was poured into their hearts. They had power to grasp the length and breadth, the height and depth of the love of Jesus which surpassed their understanding. It was as if he had walked through the flesh of their bodies to live within them (cf Eph 3:18). They could say, 'I no longer live, Christ lives within me' (Gal 2:20). With Jesus they could cry in the Spirit, 'Abba Father' (Rom 8:15). As a result they had been caught up into the friendship life of the Blessed Trinity.

Those who received the Spirit were one in mind and heart and had all things in common (Acts 4:32-36). There is reason to believe that in saying this Luke believed that the early Christian community fulfilled the Jewish and Greek ideals of friendship. For example, in 1 Sam chapters 18 to 20 we are told that 'Jonathan became one spirit with David and loved him as himself ... he swore eternal friendship with David because of his deep love for him. He took off the robe he was wearing and gave it to David, together with his armour and also his sword, bow and belt.' Notice the reference to unity of mind and heart expressed in shared possessions. Pythagoras, a Greek mathematician and philosopher, founded a community of friends around 500 BC. It had four guidelines, the first two of which read, 'Friends share in the perfect communion of a single spirit, and friends share everything in common.' Luke was saying that thanks to the power of the Holy Spirit the Christian community was a community of friends. In saying this he did not mean to imply that they were all sharing their most personal secrets with one another. They were one in mind in so far as they shared in the mind of Christ. They were one in heart in so far as they shared in his love. Their sharing of goods was the outward expression of their love as Christian friends. As Rosemary Radar's book *Breaking Boundaries: Male/Female Friendship in Early Christian Communities* points out, we have good reason to believe that many of the early Christians went beyond being friends in the Lord to form intimate friendships with one another.

Just as the friendship love of the Trinity led to creation, and the redemptive mission of the Son and the Holy Spirit, so the friendship love of the Christian community expresses itself in evangelisation. For more on this see chapter fourteen entitled,

'Proclamation of the Gospel and Community.' Speaking of the early Christian community, Luke said in Acts 4:33, 'with great power the apostles continued to testify to the resurrection of the Lord Jesus, and much grace was upon them all.' Luke believed that the preaching of the apostles was not only energised by the friendly love in the community, the community was the living embodiment of the good news they proclaimed, namely, the possibility of sharing in the inner life of the Trinity. In par 2 of the Decree on *The Church's Missionary Activity* we read, 'The pilgrim church is missionary by her very nature, since it is from the mission of the Son and the mission of the Holy Spirit that she draws her origin, in accordance with the decree of God the Father.' John Paul II said something similar in par 23 of his encyclical *Mission of the Redeemer*, 'The ultimate purpose of mission is to enable people to share in the communion which exists between the Father and the Son.'

Conclusion
Sr Mary Ann Fatula has written a delightful book, entitled, *Thomas Aquinas: Preacher and Friend*. In it she shows how this saintly Dominican linked, in a reciprocal way, the experience of Christian friendship, the intimate life of the Blessed Trinity and effective evangelisation. Most lay people respond to the universal call to share the good news of the saving work of Jesus Christ by engaging in one-to-one evangelisation. The most likely form it will take is what has been referred to as friendship evangelisation, i.e. where one friend shares his or her story of faith with another. In their book *Good News, Bad News: Evangelisation, Conversion and the Crisis of Faith*, authors, John McCloskey III and Russell Shaw observe, 'If there is any factor that turns up over and over in conversion stories, it is the role played by the convert's contacts with Catholic friends.' Australian born Matthew Kelly, who currently lives in the United States, says something similar in his book *Rediscover Catholicism*, 'Friendship is the original model of evangelisation, and it is the model that will triumph in the modern context. Friendship establishes trust and mutual respect, which together bring about the openness and acceptance that give birth to vulnerable dialogue. Only then can we begin addressing the questions that every human heart

longs to answer: Who am I? Where did I come from? What am I here for? How do I do it? Where am I going? Friendship is the key to evangelisation.'

As was mentioned earlier, friends share their deepest thoughts and feelings with one another. If the friendship of a believer with someone who is unchurched is to be complete, he or she would need to talk about his or her faith convictions in an empathetic and sensitive way. As par 8 of a *Doctrinal Note on Some Aspects of Evangelisation*, which was published by the Congregation for the Doctrine of the Faith in 2007, says, 'This experience of sharing, a characteristic of true friendship, is a valuable occasion for witnessing and for Christian proclamation.' The aim of such evangelisation is to draw the friend, in a conscious way, to share in the inner life of God. Speaking in a homily at Buenos Aires in 1987, John Paul linked these notions when he said, 'Truly the Father has sent his Son into the world that we, united to him and transformed by him, might be able to restore to God the same gift of love that he gave to us ... Starting from this gift of love we can better understand and realise in us the eternal life of God, which consists in participating in the total and complete gift of the Son to the Father in the love of the Holy Spirit ... I wanted to remind you of these Christian ideals in order to set before your mind and heart the final and wonderful goal of all evangelisation.'

CHAPTER THREE

Conversion and Evangelisation

In the Phoenix Park, Dublin city, there is a steel cross, 116 feet in height, which commemorates the Eucharist which Pope John Paul II celebrated for one and a quarter million people in September 1979. At the bottom of this landmark is a stone slab with the words, 'Be converted every day.' The notion of conversion is central in Catholic spirituality and evangelisation. That is made clear in par 1427 of the *Catechism of the Catholic Church* where it says, 'Jesus calls to conversion. This call is an essential part of the proclamation of the kingdom: "The time is fulfilled, and the kingdom of God is at hand; repent, and believe in the gospel".' In par 46 of *Mission of the Redeemer* John Paul II said, 'The proclamation of the Word of God has *Christian conversion* [my italics] as its aim: a complete and sincere adherence to Christ and his gospel through faith. Conversion is a gift of God, a work of the Blessed Trinity. It is the Spirit who opens people's hearts so that they can believe in Christ and "confess him"' (cf 1 Cor 12:3); of those who draw near to him through faith Jesus says: "No one can come to me unless the Father who sent me draws him" (Jn 6:44).'

In the church's preaching, this call is addressed firstly, but by no means exclusively, to those who do not yet know Christ and his gospel. In the Greek of the New Testament there are two words for conversion. Firstly there is *epistropho*, which means 'to return, to come back.' Secondly, there is *metanonia*, meaning 'a change of mind.' *Metanoia* is therefore, primarily an afterthought, different from the former thought, a change of mind accompanied by emotional regret and a subsequent change of conduct. The English word 'conversion' comes from *converses* which is the past participle of the Latin word *convertere*, which has the basic meaning of 'to turn around.' In the year 2000 Cardinal Ratzinger gave an interesting talk to catechists entitled

CHAPTER THREE

The New Evangelisation. At one point he said, 'to convert means: not to live as all the others live, not to do what all do, not feel justified in dubious, ambiguous, evil actions just because others do the same; begin to see one's life through the eyes of God; thereby looking for the good, even if uncomfortable; not aiming at the judgement of the majority, of men, but on the justice of God – in other words: to look for a new style of life, a new life.' To summarise, conversion is a change in a person's thinking about God, one that leads to a turn around in behaviour, e.g. by offering unconditional mercy and love to others.

The word repentance is often mentioned in the gospels. For instance in Mk 1:14-15 we read, 'Jesus went into Galilee, proclaiming the good news of God. "The time has come," he said. "The kingdom of God is near. Repent and believe the good news!"' The word repentance is similar to, but not quite the same as the word conversion. In Greek the word is *metamelomai* which means, 'a change with regard to something one had set one's heart on'. As such, repentance was not as radical as conversion. It referred to the correction of an error or fault. In common parlance it often refers to deeds of penance such as prayer, breaking a sinful attachment, almsgiving or fasting which a person performs as a token of good faith, e.g. during Lent or after receiving absolution in the sacrament of reconciliation.

The Prodigal son's three-stage conversion
The story of the prodigal son in Lk 15:11-32 is an archetypal description of the dynamic of conversion. There are three stages discernible in the parable.

Firstly we are told that the wayward son 'came to his senses,' and decided to return to his father. In a sense there was nothing particularly spiritual about this. In all probability it was a matter of expediency and enlightened self-interest. Even a life of slavery at home would be better than the misery he was currently enduring. The conversion of many people begins because of inner and outer problems such as stress, depression, ill-health, bereavement, financial difficulties, moral failure, addiction etc, which remind them what it means to be poor in fact or in spirit. The Easter vigil liturgy refers to problems of this kind as a *felix culpa*, (a happy fault) because they become providential steppingstones to the next stage of conversion. The implications of this point are expanded in the next chapter. That is why Carl Jung used to refer to 'sacred neurosis'. He felt that our psycho-spiritual problems, though negative in themselves, had a silver lining in so far as they gave rise to a desire for something better, such as a life of greater integration, balance, happiness and transcendence.

Secondly, when the prodigal son returned home his true conversion began when he was challenged to change his image of his father. He acknowledged that instead of offering him a harsh retributive type of conditional love which he both deserved and expected, the younger son had to accept that his father was offering him an unconditional love that he didn't deserve and had no right to expect. He was literally converted from one way of thinking to another. Whereas the first stage of his conversion was occasioned by his own experience of misery, the second stage was occasioned by the revelation of the father's love. This is an important point. True conversion as a change of behaviour is not a requirement for justification as faith-filled trust in the unconditional love of God, it is a graced consequence of it.

Thirdly, once the younger son knew what his father was really like we can presume that his behaviour changed. He would have helped around the farm, not as a matter of cheerless duty, like the elder brother, but as a matter of loving conviction. His good works would not have been a means of earning the love and acceptance of his father, but rather the grateful expression of the love and acceptance he had already received as a free, unmerited gift. Once any of us come to know what God is like there is an implicit invitation in that experience to be for others what God is for us. This dynamic is evident in the epistles of Paul. For example in Col 3:13-14 he says, 'Bear with each other and forgive whatever grievances you may have against one another. *Forgive as the Lord forgave you* [my italics].' This third stage of conversion is the discipleship one. This is when the Christian needs instruction so that he or she may learn how to lead a good life, by acting like Christ.

There is a mistaken view, which is quite common among some Catholics and Protestants, that conversion to the Lord requires a preceding renunciation of sinful behaviour. As has already been mentioned, instead of being a condition for conversion, changes in behaviour are a necessary consequence of a changed relationship with the Lord. The dramatic and sudden conversion of St Paul, as described in Acts 22:3-16, illustrates that point. Paul had not changed any of his behaviour or even indicated that he intended to change it, before his conversion. To maintain otherwise would imply that we are saved by good works – in this instance changed conduct – rather than by the power of God's grace through faith in the saving merits of Christ's death and resurrection. This is an important point for evangelists to remember. In basic evangelisation there is normally the following sequence:

1. Acknowledgement of a sense of need of one kind or another, such as material poverty, e.g. due to lack of money; or psycho-spiritual vulnerability, e.g. an addiction or a lack of purpose and meaning in life.
2. Hearing and experiencing the proclamation of the good news of the Lord's unconditional mercy and loving benevolence.
3. Conversion as humble trust in the free offer of the unmerited gift of God's saving grace. Repentance by means of changing one's way of acting, in a way that appropriately expresses one's new-found relationship as a disciple of the Lord.

There is a good example of what this kind of conversion can involve in the writings of St Justin Martyr (c. 100-160). He was a convert from paganism to Christianity. He knew, as a result of personal experience, that Christians had to let go of worldly attitudes to sex, the occult, money, and power. Speaking of sex, he observed that, 'We who once rejoiced in fornication now delight in continence alone.' Speaking of the occult he said, 'We who engaged in the magic arts have dedicated ourselves to the good and unbegotten God.' Referring to money he said, 'We who once took most pleasure in the means of increasing our wealth and property now bring what we have into a common fund and share with everyone in need.' Commenting on power he stated, 'We who hated and killed one another and would not associate with people of different tribes because of their different customs, now after the manifestation of Christ live together and pray for our enemies.'

Conversion to Christianity
The word conversion seems to be used in a number of interrelated ways in religious writing. It can refer to the way in which a non-believer becomes a Christian. It is the most radical form of conversion because it means that a person has to abandon many of his or her former beliefs, values and ways of acting, e.g. Hindu, in order to adopt new ones, e.g. Christian. The sudden conversions of St Paul on the road to Damascus (Acts 9:9-19) and of St Augustine in Cassisiacum, were classic examples of that kind of conversion.

Here is an account by St Cyprian of Carthage (d. 258) of how he experienced conversion at the time of his baptism: 'I went down into those life-giving waters, and all the stains of my past were washed away. I committed my life to the Lord; he cleansed my heart and filled me with the Holy Spirit. I was born again, a new man. Then in a most marvellous way all my doubts cleared up. I could now see what had been hidden from me before. I found I could do things that had previously been impossible. I saw that as long as I had been living according to my flesh I was at the mercy of sin and my course was set for death, but that by living according to my new birth in the Holy Spirit I had already begun to share God's eternal life ... We do not have to toil and sweat to achieve our own perfection, nor are money and influence needed to obtain the gift of the Holy Spirit. It is freely given by God, always available for us to use. Just as the sun shines and the day brings light, the stream irrigates the soil and rain waters the earth, so the heavenly Spirit pours himself into us!'

In more recent times C. S. Lewis succinctly described his conversion to Christianity in his book *Surprised by Joy*: 'You must picture me alone in that room at Magdalen (A college of Oxford University), night after night, feeling, whenever my mind lifted even for a second from my work, the steady, unrelenting approach of him whom I so earnestly desired not to meet. That which I greatly feared had at last come upon me. In the Trinity Term of 1929 I gave in, and admitted that God was God, and knelt and prayed: perhaps, that night, the most dejected and reluctant convert in all England.'

CHAPTER THREE

Conversion to another Christian Church
The word conversion is often used when a Christian belonging to one church decides to join another. When John Henry Newman was beatified in 2010 there was much talk about his decision to leave the Church of England in order to join the Roman Catholic Church. When he felt strongly attracted to the Catholic Church he remained in retirement for two years at Littlemore. There he began to study the way in which ideas develop within the Christian tradition, and gradually he came to see that the later expressions of the faith were not innovations but fuller statements of the same truth which had been present from the beginning. As time goes on, the church sees more and more clearly all that is contained in the revealed message, and she expresses this clearer vision in new formulations of doctrine which clarify but do not contradict the earlier formulations. He worked steadily on a new book. As he neared the end of it he felt that he could wait no longer. He said at the time, 'I had begun my *Essay on the Development of Christian Doctrine* in the beginning of 1845, and I was hard at it all through the year until October. As I advanced, my difficulties so cleared away that I ceased to speak of "the Roman Catholics," and boldly called them Catholics. Before I got to the end, I resolved to be received, and the book remains in the state in which it was then, unfinished.' In writing the book he had written himself into the Catholic faith. He converted to Catholicism soon afterwards.

Conversion of the un-churched
Many nominal Christians talk about the time they experienced a religious awakening when the truth about the love of Jesus Christ fell from head to heart in such a way that they moved from a rather formal to a deeply personal union with him. There are probably two ways in which this is experienced.

Paul VI said in par 56 of *Evangelisation in the Modern World*, 'There are a great numbers of people who have been baptised and, while they have not formally renounced their membership of the church, are as it were, on the fringe of it and do not live according to her teaching.' Pope John Paul II said something similar in par 47 of *The Church in Europe*, 'Everywhere a renewed proclamation is needed even for those already baptised. Many

Europeans today think they know what Christianity is, yet they do not really know it at all. Often they are lacking in knowledge of the most basic elements and notions of the faith. Many of the baptised live as if Christ did not exist: the gestures and signs of faith are repeated, especially in devotional practices, but they fail to correspond to a real acceptance of the content of the faith and fidelity to the person of Jesus.' Those engaged in the new evangelisation seek to help those who neither know the content of their faith or have an intimate relationship with Jesus as their Lord and Saviour. They can do this by means of one-to-one contact and by means of introduction to the Christian faith courses such as the Rite of the Christian Initiation of Adults, Alpha, Life in the Spirit Seminars and the Philip Retreat. Each one of them invites the participants to be converted from ignorance and apathy to heartfelt knowledge and commitment to Jesus Christ. Thankfully, many people are experiencing that kind of conversion or reversion, i.e. having left the church they return.

Here is a shortened version of a typical conversion story which was recounted by a young Australian Catholic named Carmel Brizzi: 'I was what you would call a 'cradle Catholic.' ... As a child, I was sent to a Catholic School and learned all about being a Catholic, but, like many people, never really took it seriously ... By the time I entered high school all my friends were non-Catholics and non-Christians. I wondered why they were allowed to have boyfriends and go to parties and I wasn't. I wanted to act like my friends: parties, boyfriends, and doing anything that was going on at the time ... My boyfriend, who has really been a great inspiration, helped guide me home to the Catholic Church. He explained a lot about the history of the church and I learned the truth about what Catholics believed. As I learned more, I wanted something more out of church, something that I wasn't getting ... Slowly, from my boyfriend, my own research, and my prayers, I began to learn more and more about the Catholic Church. We read books together and he gave me a lot of other information. I began feeling such satisfaction from studying the Catholic Church. For example, I began to look and find sins that I would have previously swept under the carpet. I actually felt accountable again! I actually noticed things I was doing wrong. I examined my conscience and prayed all these wonderful Catholic prayers. All this was a real eye opener and the more I explored the church, the more I felt like I was entering into a wonderful place. I felt like an excited child who was getting all dressed up and ready for a wedding! ... I recently experienced the Sacrament of Reconciliation and it was one of the most awesome experiences of my journey home. For the first time I not only felt accountable for my past sins but I had to fight back tears. I knew that I had let down God, my family and all Christians who are in the Body of Christ. However, I also knew I was forgiven! My penance gave me a feeling of peace that I have never felt in my whole life. I felt like I had a huge weight lifted off of me and that I was finally home and free. As I bowed down before the Blessed Sacrament I felt like a new person. It has never been easy for me to live as a Christian, but I have a great joy, I know that I am home and it has been worth the wait.'

Conversion of Church goers who are not fully evangelised
There are other Catholics who do practise their faith in the sense that they go to Mass nearly every week and may go to the sacrament of reconciliation occasionally. However, if you asked them about their beliefs and practices you might find that they rarely listen to the homily on Sundays, seldom if ever read the scriptures at home, and never engage in evangelisation. You might also find that there was not much difference between their sexual and financial behaviour and that of unbelievers. In a sense you could say that, while they have been sacramentalised and catechised, they have not been fully evangelised. In par 19 of his apostolic exhortation, *Catechesis in Our Time*, Pope John Paul made the interesting observation that the new evangelisation must 'concern itself ... with opening and converting the heart, and with preparing total adherence to Jesus Christ on the part of those who are *still on the threshold of faith* [my italics].'

One way of crossing the threshold of faith is by means of what some Christians refer to as baptism in the Holy Spirit. The Irish bishops have described this in-filling as 'a conversion gift through which one receives a new and significant commitment to the Lordship of Jesus and openness to the power and gifts of the Holy Spirit.' Catholics regard such adult in-fillings of the Spirit as a consequence of the graces already received in the sacraments of baptism and confirmation. As a result, scholars like George Montague and Killian McDonnell make the challenging assertion, that the in-filling of the Holy Spirit is not only an essential aspect of the sacraments of initiation, it is necessary for all Christians. This is an autobiographical example of how I experienced this transforming grace.

I was ordained in 1971. At the time my mind was full of theology and my heart was full of good intentions. Within a year or so I became disillusioned. Around that time I read the following inspiring verse in Rev 3:17: 'You say, "I am rich; I have acquired wealth and do not need a thing." But you do not realise that you are wretched, pitiful, poor, blind and naked?' I reluctantly had to admit that in spite of a good Christian upbringing and an excellent education there was something lacking in my life. From that moment onwards, instead of identifying with the Good Samaritan, as I had heretofore, I now identified with the man on the roadside (cf Lk 10:30-36). Like him I felt wounded and weak. This awareness became the birthplace of a heartfelt desire for a spiritual awakening. Desire gave way to fulfilment in February 1974 when I was invited to attend a retreat in the North of Ireland. One of the talks was given by a Protestant clergyman. He spoke about Jesus as the source of our peace. I was deeply moved and wanted to know the Lord the way he did. Afterwards a nun introduced me to him. We had a brief chat and arranged to meet privately. When we did, I told the minister that I was looking for a new awareness of God in my life. He read a memorable passage from Eph 3:16-20. Then he began to pray for me, firstly in English, then in tongues. Suddenly, and effortlessly I too began to pray fluently in tongues. I knew with great conviction that Jesus loved me and accepted me as I was. It was if the risen Lord had walked through the walls of my body to reign upon the throne in my heart. That conversion experience marked the beginning of a new beginning in my life.

Since having that experience I have occasionally tried to facilitate a similar kind of conversion in the lives of people I meet. I say something such as, 'Imagine that there is a throne room in your heart. In the centre is the king's impressive throne. Who sits on that throne, you or the king? If it is you, has Jesus any place in your life? If you say he has, is he like one of your courtiers? Are you continuously asking him to do things for you? Would you be willing to vacate the throne, so that Jesus Christ, the Son of God, might sit there as your king? Are you willing to serve him, and to do what he wants?' As *The Life in the Spirit Seminars Team Manual* says, 'To accept Jesus Christ into your life means to allow him to take the centre. It involves surrendering your life to him. When you do this, you can come to know him personally.' As I know from my own experience, when we begin to die to egocentricity so that Jesus becomes the number one in our lives, we have understood the meaning of conversion.

Gradual on-going conversion
Both Sts Paul and Augustine experienced dramatic conversions. In the case of the latter is was the final outcome of an inner conflict between the flesh and the spirit that had been going on for some time. In the case of St Paul, his conversion seemed to occur like a bolt from the blue without preceding case. However, what appeared to have been a sudden change was, in all likelihood, anticipated by many antecedent causes of an unconscious kind. For example, it is arguable that St Paul's conviction about the rightness of his Jewish faith had been progressively undermined by the obvious virtues of the first Christians. Surely Paul the Pharisee was secretly impressed by the fact that St Stephen, like Jesus before him, forgave those who were about to stone him to death, while bravely offering his soul with great trust to God. So Paul's conversion was more like a dramatic event of a conscious kind within a more long drawn out process of an unconscious nature. It is important to remember that dramatic conversions are the exception rather than the rule in the Christian life. As psychologist Michael Argyle points out in his *Psychology of Religion: An Introduction*, research indicates that for about 80% of people, especially Catholics, conversion is usually the result of a gradual process rather than a dramatic event.

Catholic spirituality talks about three stages in the Christian life: the purgative, the illuminative and the unitive. During the purgative stage especially, there is a purification process which is often punctuated by periods of desolation of spirit when the Lord helps us to move away from sin to more wholehearted commitment. As scripture says, 'Remember how the Lord your God led you all the way in the desert these forty years, to humble you and to test you in order to know what was in your heart, whether or not you would keep his commands' (Deut 8:2). Bernard Lonergan SJ, one of the great Catholic theologians of the twentieth century, maintained in his influential books *Insight* and *Method in Theology*, that Christian transformation involves a process of on-going intellectual, moral, affective and religious conversion.

It seems to me that 2 Cor 3:18 spells out an important biblical way in which one can go on experiencing these forms of conversion. In the RSV translation it reads: 'And we all, with unveiled face, beholding the glory of the Lord, are being changed into his likeness from one degree of glory to another; for this comes from the Lord who is the Spirit.' This contemplative notion of transformation is synonymous with conversion. St Paul talks about taking away the veil, i.e. those things which obscure our vision of Jesus, especially unrepented sin. He then goes on to talk about beholding or contemplating the Lord. We can do this by paying self-forgetful attention to creation and people in the belief that they can mediate the mysterious presence of God. However, it is especially in the scriptures that we can behold the Lord. Deepening relationship with the Lord leads to a progressive change in Christian behaviour. It is a matter of contemplation leading to both the desire and the ability to live in a new way. Deepening knowledge of the Lord leads to the inner imperative, 'Be for others what God is for you.' For more on this notion of gradual inner transformation see chapter twenty two.

Conversion a key to evangelisation
Those who engage in the new evangelisation aim to bring about conversion, mainly of the third and fourth kinds. I believe that the first thing that evangelists aim to do is to change people's image of God from that of a distant, demanding and punitive Father, to that of One whose heart is full of unconditional mercy and love. That image is present in many of the parables such as the prodigal Son (Lk 15:11-31). It is only when people have a heartfelt awareness of 'how wide and long and high and deep is the love of Christ, and to know this love that surpasses knowl-

edge' (Eph 3:18-19) that they will have the ability to acknowledge their sin and to turn away from it. Once people pass the threshold of faith, they will probably ask, 'What shall we do?' (Acts 2:37) It is then that they can be told about the Christian way of living. St Paul summed it up when he said in Rom 13:8-10: 'Let no debt remain outstanding, except the continuing debt to love one another, for he who loves his fellowman has fulfilled the law. The commandments, "Do not commit adultery," "Do not murder," "Do not steal," "Do not covet," and whatever other commandment there may be, are summed up in this one rule: "Love your neighbour as yourself." Love does no harm to its neighbour. Therefore love is the fulfilment of the law.'

Conclusion
The phenomenon of conversion is an important and complex one which has many interlinking aspects, theological, spiritual, psychological, social and practical. Many of them are dealt with in a book Walter Conn edited. It is entitled, *Christian Conversion: A Developmental Interpretation of Autonomy and Surrender* (1986 & 2006). A similar volume *Handbook of Religious Conversion* (1992) was edited by Newton Maloney and Samuel Southard. By way of conclusion it has to be said that instead of trying to convert people to Christ, sadly, many modern day Christians seem to content themselves with helping them in practical, developmental ways. They may talk about spirituality and religion in a general manner without courageously sharing their faith in Jesus Christ and inviting their listeners to a change of mind and heart, one that would lead them to make a conscious commitment to Jesus as their Saviour and Lord.

CHAPTER FOUR

Some Steppingstones to Faith

A number of years ago I conducted a retreat in Ilkley, Yorkshire. During a free afternoon I visited Bolton Abbey which was a few miles away. The ruins of this pre-Reformation monastery are still standing in an idyllic rural setting. Like so many other religious houses of that era it became a victim of King Henry VIII's suppression of the monasteries. I felt really sad about the desecration of such impressive buildings and the religious purpose they once served. A green, undulating slope stretched downwards from the stone walls to a wide meandering stream below. When I walked the few hundred yards to its banks I noticed that there were stepping stones placed strategically in the fast running water. They enabled people to cross from one side to the other. This chapter will look at symbolic stepping stones which can enable people in our fast changing culture to cross from unbelief to Christian faith.

We are living in a society where the cause of God and religious faith are increasingly being sidelined. In par 55 of the apostolic declaration on *Evangelisation in the Modern World* Paul VI observed: 'One is forced to note in the very heart of this contemporary world the phenomenon which is becoming almost its most striking characteristic: secularism ... a concept of the world according to which the latter is self-explanatory, without any need for recourse to God, who thus becomes superfluous and an encumbrance. This sort of secularism, in order to recognise the power of man, therefore ends up by doing without God and even by denying him.' This secularising attitude has all kinds of effects.

In his encyclical *Lord and Giver of Life*, John Paul II noted the fact that due to the separation of religion from life, there is a growing suspicion in Western culture that instead of being the friend of man, God is our enemy. When I was teaching psychology of religion courses, it was clear that thinkers such as Freud, Fromm and Maslow propounded this point of view in their own individual ways. In par 38, John Paul wrote, 'God the Creator is placed in a state of suspicion, indeed of accusation, in the mind of the creature.' The Pope then went on to observe, 'Man will be inclined to see in God primarily a limitation of himself, and not the source of his own freedom and the fullness of good. We see this confirmed in the modern age, when the atheistic ideologies seek to root out religion on the grounds that religion causes the radical alienation of man, as if man were dispossessed of his own humanity when, accepting the idea of God, he attributes to God what belongs to man, and exclusively to man! Hence a process of thought ... in which the rejection of God has reached the point of declaring his death.'

There are many other people who are simply indifferent to God and religion. They adopt a this-worldly, scientific and materialistic attitude to life. As John Paul II said in par 9 of the apostolic exhortation *The Church in Europe*, humanistic secularism 'is an attempt to promote a vision of man apart from God and apart from Christ ... it is therefore no wonder that in this context a vast field has opened for the unrestrained development of nihilism in philosophy, of relativism in values and morality, and of pragmatism – and even a cynical hedonism – in daily life. European culture gives the impression of "silent apostasy" on the part of people who have all that they need and who live as if God does not exist.' Let me offer an example of what John Paul meant.

Recently I read a bestselling science book by Christopher Potter, entitled, *You are Here*. The author argues that the Darwinian notion of natural selection, by means of random genetic mutations and the survival of the fittest has not only been confirmed by empirical research, it puts paid to the notion that there is any ultimate meaning or purpose in the universe or in our lives. The book ends with these stark words: 'In a modern world obsessed with certainty and things eternal, we might learn to live in the uncertainty of an unending scientific process. We want to believe that things last forever, whether it is love, God or the laws of nature ... Perhaps the best we can hope for is to live in uncertainty as long as we can bear it.' I worry about people who live within such a meaningless, pointless and hopeless worldview. When the activity of the psyche is no longer locked on to any ultimate purpose it becomes dysfunctional. As a result, all kinds of negative forces become active in the unconscious and threaten to spill over in disruptive attitudes and behaviours.

In the light of Potter's despairing words it is worth quoting what Pope Paul VI said in par 55 of *The Church in the Modern World*: 'One cannot deny the existence of *real stepping-stones to Christianity* [my italics], and of evangelical values at least in the form of a sense of emptiness or nostalgia. It would not be an exaggeration to say that there exists a powerful and tragic appeal to be evangelised.' Years later Pope John Paul II echoed Paul's observation when he wrote in par 45 of *The Church in Europe*: 'Even if it remains unexpressed or even repressed, there is the most profound and genuine plea rising from the hearts of Europeans today, who yearn for a hope which does not disappoint.' The notion of steppingstones to faith would correspond with the first of the four stages of conversion mentioned in the previous chapter.

Inculturation
In its documents on evangelisation, the church talks about the importance of inculturation. As par 52 of the encyclical *Mission of the Redeemer* explains, 'Inculturation means the intimate transformation of authentic cultural values through their integration in Christianity and the insertion of Christianity in the various human cultures.' To do this evangelisers need to discern where there are signs of a conscious or unconscious longing for transcendence in people's lives. John Paul II repeatedly recommended St Paul's speech at the Areopagus in Athens as a model of evangelisation as inculturation (cf Acts 17:16-34). Paul entered into 'dialogue' with the cultural and religious values of the Athenians. He appealed to the Greek world's belief in divinity as responsible for the origin and existence of the universe. In doing so, he attempted to show his listeners that God was already present in their lives as Creator and Sustainer. But to recognise him as he really is, the Athenians would need to abandon their false gods and believe in the Lord Jesus Christ. As he

said in 1 Cor 20-2, 'Where is the wise man? Where is the scholar? Where is the philosopher of this age? Has not God made foolish the wisdom of the world? For since in the wisdom of God the world through its wisdom did not know him, God was pleased through the foolishness of what was preached to save those who believe.'

As Pope John Paul II so rightly observed in par 57 of his apostolic letter *As the Third Millennium Approaches*, 'Today there are many "areopagi," and very different ones: these are the vast sectors of contemporary civilisation and culture, of politics and economics. The more the West is becoming estranged from its Christian roots, the more it is becoming missionary territory, taking the form of many different "areopagi".' Pope John Paul employed the Areopagus as a symbol of the new 'places' in which the good news must be proclaimed, and to which the mission of Christ is to be directed. He said on one occasion, 'Today these areopagi are the worlds of science, culture, and the media; these are the worlds of writers and artists, the worlds where the intellectual elites are formed.' I published one article entitled 'Postmodernism and Religion,' in *Doctrine and Life* (Jan 1999), 22-31, and another entitled 'Evangelisation as Inculturation in the Christology of Teilhard de Chardin' in *Milltown Studies*, no 64 (Winter 2009): 76-99. In both, there is an attempt to makes sense of the Christian message in the context of a scientific and postmodern worldview. At this point, we will look at some of the steppingstones to Christ and his gospel which are discernible in modern culture.

Transcendental Longings
Karl Rahner suggested that a vague unconscious openness to God and his justifying grace remains in the lives of people. He used to refer to a person's 'obediential potency'. This technical term refers to the disposition of a person to receive and accept the gift of God's self-communication, which leads to the fulfilment of his or her spiritual nature. In some ways Rahner's notion is borne out by empirical evidence. In a *Tablet* article entitled, 'Is Britain's Soul Waking-Up?' David Hay and Kate Hunt referred to the results of interesting research conducted in the UK. While it confirmed that fewer people go to church, nevertheless there

has been a dramatic rise in the numbers claiming to have had religious experience. In his earlier writings, Hay used to describe religious experience a little vaguely as 'a sense of a presence or power beyond one's everyday self'. That could include occult type experiences which would not be genuinely religious. Nowadays he uses the more precise and helpful phrase, 'relational consciousness'. It is virtually synonymous with religious consciousness, when one takes into account the fact that the word religion is derived from the Latin *religare*, meaning 'to bind'. Relational consciousness understands religious experience as a sense of ultimate belonging.

I may say in passing to those who are interested in the philosophy of religion, that two twentieth-century thinkers, Karl Jaspers and Karl Rahner, spoke in their different ways about this notion. The former talked about 'the Comprehensive' in his book *Way to Wisdom: An Introduction to Philosophy* (1954). He explained: 'We inquire after the Being which, with the manifestation of all encountered appearance in object and horizon, yet recedes itself. This Being we call the Encompassing. The Encompassing, then, is that which always makes its presence known, which does not appear itself, but from which everything comes to us.' For his part, Rahner spoke about the *vorgriff* in his book *Hearers of the Word: Laying the Foundation for a Philosophy of Religion* (1941). The *vorgriff* is an epistemological phenomenon whereby a particular object of knowledge in each act of cognition is grasped in its limitation against a background of an infinite, unlimited horizon.

Over the past 25 years there has been a startling 110% rise in the number of men and women reporting a sense of a mysterious Power or Presence, beyond their everyday selves. Hay and Hunt remark: 'We are in the midst of an explosive spiritual upsurge.' They go on to say: 'We know, from the research we have done, that most people's spirituality is a long way away from institutional religion. This spirituality has little doctrinal content, and few people have more than the vaguest remnants of religious language to express their experience of God. The phrase we commonly hear is "I definitely believe in Something; there's Something there." Their spirituality is based upon a longing for meaning.'

That last statement is a significant one for a number of reasons. Firstly, the incidence of religious experience is backed up by the fact that modern science has clearly demonstrated the fact that the brain is hardwired for such experience. Secondly, Hay's findings confirm Viktor Frankl's contention that the deepest longing of the human heart is for meaning of an unconditional kind, i.e. God. Thirdly, Hay's research implies that even at a conscious level of experience, postmodern men and women are looking for meaning rather than forgiveness. So the Alpha course is spot-on when it focuses on meaning of life issues. In all probability the issue of sin and forgiveness will only surface when evangelisers help the spiritual pilgrims of our time to explore what it is that blocks or alienates them from the meaning they seek. In spite of his atheism, it is worth noting that Christopher Potter acknowledges the longing of people today 'to believe that things last forever, whether it is love, God or the laws of nature'.

Silence and religious aspirations
In *The Perennial Philosophy*, Aldous Huxley said that there are three kinds of silence, silence of the mouth, silence of the mind, and silence of the will. But Huxley observed, 'Our era is among other things, the Age of Noise. Physical noise, mental noise and the noise of desire.' During an Advent homily in 2002, John Paul II maintained that as a result of noisy distractions many people were losing touch with God. It is not surprising, therefore, that nowadays numerous men and women complain about the silence of God. In his book *Crossing the Threshold of Hope*, John Paul wrote: 'It is truly difficult to speak of the silence of God. We must speak, rather, of the desire to stifle the voice of God.'

Those points were well illustrated in *The Big Silence*, three programmes which were devised by Abbot Christopher Jamison of Worth Abbey. Commenting on the need for silence, the Abbot said, 'Silence is something that people today avoid or even fear … Our busy culture prevents us being still. Daunting as it may be, we all need silence. When we enter regularly into silence, we start to see things with greater clarity. And especially, I come to know myself and I come in touch with that part of myself which is the deepest part: my soul. Silence is the gateway to the soul and the soul is the gateway to God.' In October 2010 the three BBC2 programmes showed that when five volunteers, most of whom were unchurched or unbelievers, became silent, especially over a period of eight days in St Beuno's Retreat and Spirituality Centre in North Wales, they not only became aware of the deeper things of their own hearts, some of them went on to experience a vivid sense of God.

While many people, like those retreatants, normally fail to have quiet times, sometimes providence takes a hand. It does so in the form of such things as sickness, unemployment, separation from loved ones, travel alone etc. During these periods of quiet and greater introspection the deeper things of the heart are inclined to surface, such as a vague ache for meaning, and ultimately for God. As Pope John Paul II observed in par 4 of the apostolic exhortation, *On the Vocation and Mission of the Lay Faithful*, 'Human longing and the need for religion, however, are not able to be totally extinguished. When persons in conscience have the courage to face the more serious questions of human existence – particularly questions related to the purpose of life, to suffering and to dying – they are unable to avoid making their own the words of truth uttered by Saint Augustine: "You have made us for yourself, O Lord, and our hearts are restless until they rest in you".'

Crises and desire for meaning
Speaking about a common lack of self-awareness, St Augustine once wrote: 'People travel to wonder at the height of mountains, at the huge waves of the sea, at the long courses of rivers, at the vast compass of the ocean, at the circular motion of the stars; and they pass by themselves without wondering.' It is an ironic fact that many of us know a lot about the world and surprisingly little about ourselves. 'The longest journey,' as the saying goes, 'is the journey inwards.' Divine providence helps us to make that journey and so to grow in self-awareness.

In Jer 17:9-10 we read, 'The heart is deceitful above all things and beyond cure. Who can understand in it? I the Lord search the heart and examine the mind.' One way the Lord does this is by means of life crises. Development psychologists have suggested that our lives are made of a succession of times of relative stability and security (usually about ten years), and times of transitional crisis (usually about three years). There are two main types of crisis, predictable and unpredictable. Predictable crises occur regularly throughout our lives. They precede the main developmental phases, e.g. before the onset of early, middle and late adulthood. The purpose of these crises is to urge us to tackle some specific developmental task. By doing so we grow into a new depth of maturity. Unpredictable crises occur when 'the slings and arrows of outrageous fortune' come our way. People can be pitched into a period of turmoil and soul-searching by the death of a close relative, the news that they have cancer or have lost their job. Often a predictable crisis, such as mid-life, will occur at the same time as one or two unpredictable ones.

Transitional crises of either kind have a threefold structure: (1) There is the onset and restlessness. (2) It is followed by a longer time of darkness and exploration, often accompanied by feelings of anxiety, stress, depression and spiritual desolation. (3) They come to an end with a sense of resolution and re-stabilisation. When people are going through life crises, they are likely to become more aware of their vulnerability and to seek sustaining values and meanings, including those of a religious kind, to replace the ones they have found to be inadequate.

The three stages involved in transitional crises were reflected in the drama of the thirty three Chilean miners who in 2010 were entombed for 63 days in a cavern, nearly half a mile underground. Their liberation had an archetypal quality. In the mirror of their ordeal, many people saw something of their own life experience being reflected. From a symbolic point of view, the notion of the miner's descent represented a journey from external security to inner insecurity, from the everyday clarity of conscious awareness and control into the darker, more mysterious realms of the unconscious where one encounters all kinds of unsettling emotions, desires, memories, fears and temptations, prior to a subsequent ascent to a new found self-knowledge. Mario Sepulveda, one of the Chilean miners, spoke for many men and women in modern society when he said, 'I think I had extraordinary luck. I was with God and with the devil. And I reached out for God.' There are many metaphorical caves such as negative emotions, ennui, and addiction to things like drugs and pornography.

Longing for the joy of belonging
Sociologists tell us that modern society is moving from tightly-knit communities to individualistic more loosely-knit ones. They say that, as a consequence, social capital, i.e. the nurturing aspects of supportive relationships and networks, is in decline. Christian communities are countercultural in so far as they are genuinely loving and accepting. Fellowships of that kind provide spiritual seekers with a sense of belonging which is already the good news in action. That is why Alpha is wise to encourage those who run its courses to begin with a meal. Once people experience warm, friendly relationships, not only will a deep human need be satisfied, many of them will be curious to find out what beliefs and values animate such a warm sense of communion. As a result, many of them may be receptive to the testimony of Christian evangelisers who respond to their heartfelt questions rather than trying to indoctrinate them. Hopefully, they will move from a sense of belonging to the community, to experience the ultimate joy of belonging to God. For more on this topic see chapter twenty two.

Focus on the deepest desire
It follows from what has been said that one of the most important questions evangelists can ask people in contemporary culture is 'what do you deep-down want?' (cf Jn 1:37; Mk 10:36). The emphasis on deeper desires as the expression of people's inner sense of need, whether material or spiritual, is a crucial one for those who wish to engage in basic evangelisation. The God of the word and the word of God can only be received by those who in their vulnerability and poverty of spirit are open to receive them. As Jesus said, in Jn 6:44, 'No one can come to me unless the Father who sent me, draws him.' The Father draws us to Jesus by means a transcendental desire for meaning which is expressed in phrases such as, 'I still haven't found what I'm looking for,' 'Is that all there is?,' 'My heart is restless no matter what I have, or experience,' 'I know I need something, but I don't know what it is.' Like our Lord, evangelists need to have a

metaphorical towel of service wrapped around their waists. They need to tune in to people's deepest needs, those that are rooted in their sense of creaturely contingency, by paying empathic attention to their verbal and non-verbal communication.

I can remember going to a *Peregrinatio Pro Christo* (travellers for Christ) conference which was organised by the Legion of Mary in the nineteen sixties. Frank Duff, founder of the Legion, gave a talk in the course of which he quoted a line from the *Legion Handbook*. I have never forgotten it, 'A man will meet you in the street and ask you for a match. Talk to him, and in no time he will be asking you for God.' In other words, in the course of casual conversations about mundane issues there may be a an unexpected switch to meaning of life issues. It has to be said that often people will begin by telling us about their immediate problems such as a concern for a sick child, coping with bereavement, overcoming depression, etc. These presenting needs are often the expressions of a deeper, but usually less articulate sense of spiritual need and a longing for happiness, truth, hope and meaning, and as such they are steppingstones to faith. The Spirit will help evangelists to discern what those deeper needs might be. It will also help them, not only to assist people to name and express their deepest desires, but also to respond to them in a sensitive and understanding manner in the belief that the poor in spirit are blessed and that the kingdom of God is theirs (cf Mt 5:3).

Conclusion
It is arguable that the current long drawn out recession in the Western world involves a blessing in disguise. Just as the experience of famine and hardship helped the prodigal son to come to his senses and to return to his father, so the contemporary experience of things like the collapse of the stock market, the threat and actuality of unemployment, debt, and poverty may prompt many disillusioned people to question their secular beliefs and values. They may discover within themselves a certain nostalgia for God, one that floats into their minds from the depths of their unconscious. As a result they will 'seek the Lord while he may still be found' (Is 55:6). Not only should Christian evangelisers empathise with people who have to endure such

hardship and purification, they need to discern what stepping stones to faith are implicit in their experience, in order to speak to them in a sensitive and relevant way, about the good news of Jesus Christ.

CHAPTER FIVE

Contemplation and Evangelisation

Nowadays you will often hear people talk about the importance of 'being in the moment,' and 'living in the now'. In other words, instead of remembering past events, or anticipating future ones, the person gives his or her complete attention to whatever is happening in the present. Children are good at doing this. I have noticed how a child can look through a window at a little bird which is hopping around outside, or at a stray leaf that is being tossed about on a gentle breeze. The baby is fascinated and gives the bird or the leaf his or her rapt attention. One of my colleagues told me how his young nephew spotted a tulip in a flowerbed. He looked at it for some time. Then he approached, knelt beside it, cupped the flower in his two hands and declared, 'You are beautiful!' That type of wonder and contemplation enables those who have such a capacity, to have intimations of God's presence as mediated by the goodness and beauty of the world. As William Blake wrote in his *Auguries of Innocence*, 'To see a World in a Grain of Sand, And a Heaven in a Wild Flower, Hold Infinity in the palm of your hand, And Eternity in an hour.'

Credible witness and personal experience
In Acts 1:8 we are told that Jesus said to the apostles before his ascension, 'You shall receive power when the Holy Spirit has come upon you; and you shall be my witnesses in Jerusalem and in all Judea and Samaria and to the end of the earth.' A witness is someone who speaks with authority on the basis of personal experience. The apostles were able to be credible witnesses because they had accompanied Jesus in his ministry, heard what he said, and saw what he did. In his parting words to them he promised that the Holy Spirit would lead them more profoundly into the truth of who he was and the deeper meaning and signif-

icance of his ministry and message. As a result they would be empowered to evangelise in a fruitful way. From the New Testament onward, evangelists are those who speak of what they know as a result of Spirit-prompted religious experience. As Pope Paul VI said in par 76 of *Evangelisation in the Modern World*, 'This world is looking for preachers of the gospel to speak to it of God whom they know as being close to them, as though seeing him who is invisible.' In 2010 Benedict XVI said something similar in his letter, *Everywhere and Always*: 'To proclaim fruitfully the Word of the gospel one is first asked to have a profound experience of God.'

How do modern day Christians share in the New Testament experience of Jesus Christ? Luke, who like us never met the earthly Jesus, gave a nuanced answer in his story of the meeting of the disciples with the risen Jesus on the road to Emmaus (cf Lk 24:13-35). As chapter twelve of this book indicates, the story has a liturgical structure and seems to say that Christ's mystical presence can be contemplated in the gathering of the people, the priest who presides, the readings from scripture, the homily, and in the consecrated bread and wine. Like those first disciples, modern day Christians sometimes find that their hearts burn within them as they contemplate the mysterious presence of the Lord in the eucharistic community. The truth is, God's presence can be mediated by people and any aspect of the natural world. Speaking about the former, Gerard Manley Hopkins wrote in his poem *As Kingfishers Catch Fire*, 'Christ plays in ten thousand places, Lovely in limbs, and lovely in eyes not his, To the Father through the features of men's faces.' Speaking about the latter, a hymn in the *Divine Office* says, 'The Father gives his children the wonder of the world in which his power and glory like banners are unfurled.'

Contemplation

The English word 'contemplation' is derived from the Latin, *contemplare* 'to gaze at,' 'to view attentively,' 'to behold.' The word contains the Latin, *templum*, i.e. 'temple,' because Greek holy men and women used to observe the presence of God within its sacred precincts. Contemplation is sustained by the belief that one can enter, not only the reality of the created things being contemplated, but also that one can have intimations of the reality of the Creator, whose presence is mediated by the things God has made. As St Paul said in Rom 1:20, 'For since the creation of the world God's invisible qualities – his eternal power and divine nature – have been clearly seen, being understood from what has been made.'

St Bernard wrote, 'Contemplation may be defined as the soul's true unerring intuition, or as the unhesitating apprehension of truth.' In his *Treatise on the Love of God*, St Francis de Sales wrote, 'Contemplation is simply the mind's loving, unmixed, permanent attention to the things of God.' Par 2724 of the *Catechism of the Catholic Church* describes contemplation in more specifically Christian terms: 'Contemplative prayer is the simple expression of the mystery of prayer. It is a gaze of faith fixed on Jesus, an attentiveness to the Word of God, a silent love. It achieves real union with the prayer of Christ to the extent that it makes us share in his mystery.'

In brief, here are some of the characteristics of the contemplative attitude.

1. Contemplation as sustained attention is other orientated. It is worth noting that etymologically the word attention is derived from the Latin, *tendere*, meaning 'to stretch.' In other words the mind stretches toward the object, whatever it might be.

2. Contemplation is self-forgetful in so far as it breaks free of the gravitational pull of self-absorption and brackets out distracting thoughts, feelings and memories while abstaining from projecting them on to the object of attention.

3. Contemplation is intuitive. Etymologically, the word is derived from the Latin, *intueri*, meaning to 'look into'. In other words intuition seeks to go beyond external appearances to know the essential nature or 'isness' of things and persons.

4. Contemplative attention is empathic when beholding other people by recognising at an emotional level what their feelings might be, and at a cognitive level why they might feel the way they do.

5. Contemplation is a state of dynamic passivity. It is dynamic in so far as it is energised by a desire to know, while at the same time being passive in so far as it is open and receptive to the gift of revelation.

6. Religious contemplation involves mediated immediacy in so far as created things mediate something of the mysterious presence of the unseen God who created them. This point is illustrated in Patrick Kavanagh's poem, *The Great Hunger*. Speaking of Christian farmers he says, 'Yet sometimes when the sun comes through a gap , these men know God the Father in a tree: the Holy Spirit is the rising sap and Christ will be the green leaves that will come at Easter from the sealed and guarded tomb.'

In contemplation, especially during times devoted to scriptural forms of prayer, we may have a graced awareness of the presence and the purposes of Christ. As Pope John Paul II reminded us in par 20 of *At the Beginning of the New Millennium*, 'We cannot come to the fullness of contemplation of the Lord's face by our own efforts alone, but by allowing grace to take us by the hand.' In 1981, the Sacred Congregation for Religious published *The Contemplative Dimension of the Religious Life*. In par 30 it said that, 'The contemplation dimension ... renews the following of Christ because it leads to an experiential knowledge of him.' In the light of these quotations, it is clear that contemplation enables a person, who desires to know the Lord, to go beyond thought and talk about God to have a more direct awareness of the divine.

Here is an example of what can be involved. It is taken from a book by Meg Maxwell and Verena Tschudin, entitled, *Seeing the Invisible: Modern Religious and Other Transcendent Experiences*. 'I was standing one morning in the shower, using the time for a period of thanks and praise addressed to my God. Suddenly and quite involuntarily I said aloud, "If only I might see you as you are rather than in images." Before I could reflect upon what I had dared to say, a clear voice broke through the sound of rushing water: "Read the first chapter of Corinthians again, verses 4 to 7." I was very familiar with those words. As I reread them, a flash of insight revealed my God and I knew that to see him face to face would mean death. God I saw more clearly than anything I had ever been shown of him before, a God who is Love, the absolute essence of patience and kindness, the complete antithesis of jealousy and conceit, neither proud, ill-mannered, selfish or irritable. Further, contrary to what some theologians teach, he does not keep a record of my wrongs. He is not happy with evil but happy with truth. He never gives up. His faith in me, his hope for me and his patience with me will never fail ... I hope the foregoing will be of encouragement to the increasing number of men, women and children who are in this age learning that when man listens, God speaks, when man obeys, God acts; when God acts, miracles happen.'

Evangelisation a fruit of contemplation
As a member of the Order of Preachers, it is not surprising to find that St Thomas Aquinas saw a clear link between contemplation and evangelisation. His motto for the Dominicans was, 'to contemplate, and to give to others the fruit of what has been contemplated.' He said that, 'The life that comes from the fullness of contemplation, such as teaching and preaching, is more excellent than simply contemplating God. Just as it is better to enlighten others than merely to shine, it is better to give the fruits of our contemplation to others than merely to contemplate.' St Vincent de Paul echoed St Thomas's point when he encouraged the members of the Congregation of the Mission, which he founded, to be 'contemplatives at home and apostles abroad'.

In the light of the foregoing points, it is interesting to hear what Pope John Paul II had to say in par 91 of *The Mission of the Redeemer*: 'The missionary must be a "contemplative in action". He or she finds answers to problems in the light of God's word and in personal and community prayer ... the future of mission depends to a great extent on contemplation. Unless the missionary is a contemplative, he cannot proclaim Christ in a credible way. He is a witness to the experience of God, and must be able to say with the apostles: 'that which we have looked upon ... concerning the word of life ... we proclaim also to you (1 Jn 1:1-3).' On another occasion Pope John Paul II said to The Catholic Fraternity of Covenant Communities and Fellowships (2001): 'Contemplation which does not give life to mission is condemned to frustration and failure ... because contemplation engenders evangelisation.' In saying these things, the Holy Father was echoing something St Thomas Aquinas wrote in the forth lecture of his commentary on chapter one of John's gospel, 'for we can testify about something only in the manner in which we have shared (in) it', i.e. by means of contemplation.

Some practical possibilities
A number of practical points follow from the preceding ones. In 2 Cor 3:18, St Paul stated: 'And we all, with unveiled face, beholding the glory of the Lord, are being changed into his likeness from one degree of glory to another; for this comes from the Lord who is the Spirit', as was noted in another chapter. We behold, or contemplate the Lord, first and foremost, by reading and praying the scriptures. To do this we need to spend time each day in heartfelt prayer. *Lectio Divina* is an excellent way of doing this. At the centre of this Benedictine method is contemplation, those precious moments when, having expressed our desire to see the face of God by reading, meditating and praying, the Lord responds by revealing something of the divine presence, attributes and intentions. These are mildly mystical moments when we touch, taste, and apprehend a little of the mystery of the divine. It may be that one enters a biblical scene in an intensely real way, or one has a revelatory vision of the Lord, or hears him speaking interiorly to one's spirit. For more on *Lectio Divina* see chapter eight.

The church also recommends the recitation of the rosary – the gospel in miniature – as a contemplative form of prayer. In par 3 of *The Rosary of the Virgin Mary,* Pope John Paul II said, 'The Rosary, reclaimed in its full meaning, goes to the very heart of Christian life; it offers a familiar yet fruitful spiritual and educational opportunity for personal contemplation, the formation of the People of God, and the new evangelisation.' However, in par 12 he warned, 'Without contemplation, the Rosary is a body without a soul, and its recitation runs the risk of becoming a mechanical repetition of formulas.' Speaking about the rosary in Pompeii, 28 October 2008, Pope Benedict XVI said: 'If Christian contemplation cannot do without the Word of God, even the Rosary, to be a contemplative prayer, must always emerge from the silence of the heart as a response to the Word, on the model of Mary's prayer.'

Many Charismatic Christians have found that besides being a form of intercession or praise, the gift of tongues can gently lead a person beyond concepts and images into the conscious awareness of the God who dwells in a cloud of unknowing. I know from personal experience that this can be a form of contemplative prayer. By God's grace, head knowledge becomes heart awareness, in such a way that it illumines the inner self as a result of inspirations, while motivating and empowering the person to share what has been experienced by means of evangelisation.

Conclusion
It is a striking fact that Vatican Council II stated that there were two universal calls which are interrelated, namely the calls to holiness and to evangelisation. In par 90 of *The Mission of the Redeemer*, Pope John Paul II stated, 'The universal call to holiness is closely linked to the universal call to mission.' Growth in holiness is often the result, in Paul's words of 'beholding the glory of the Lord'. In this chapter we have noted a number of ways in which we can contemplate the Lord in such a way that we are 'changed into his likeness from one degree of glory to another' (2 Cor 3:18). It is this kind of first hand religious experience that provides evangelisation with conviction, authority and pastoral effectiveness.

CHAPTER SIX

Sts Vincent Ferrer and Vincent de Paul: Extraordinary Evangelisers

Even before his birth at Valentia in Spain, it seemed that Vincent Ferrer was predestined by God to accomplish great things. A Dominican said prophetically to his father, 'I congratulate you William. In a few days you will have a son who will become a prodigy of learning and sanctity ... The world will resound with the fame of his wondrous deeds; he will fill heaven with joy and hell with terror. He will put on the habit which I wear, and will be received in the church with universal joy as one of its first apostles.' Vincent did join the Dominicans at the age of twenty two, became a doctor of theology, and began to teach and preach. During this time he wrote a *Treatise on the Spiritual Life* (hereafter *TOSL*) which mainly had the members of the Dominican Order in mind. It is a succinct, practical, and demanding summary of how to live a life of Christian perfection. In spite of his obvious holiness of life, Vincent was accused of heresy because he questioned the prevailing view when he taught that Judas may have gone to purgatory rather than hell. The charge was dismissed by his mentor, the antipope Benedict XIII, who burned the Inquisition's dossier and made Vincent his confessor.

Evangelist Extraordinaire
During a time of serious illness in 1399, Vincent had a vision of Christ standing between Sts Dominic and Francis, who told him to go forth and preach repentance and the immanence of the end times. That religious experience kick-started one of the most extraordinary missionary outreaches in the history of the church. For the next twenty years, Vincent travelled tirelessly the length and breadth of Europe preaching in places such as Marseilles, Geneva, Lausanne, Bologna and Freiburg. Although some books say that he visited Britain and Ireland, there is no

CHAPTER SIX

documentary evidence to verify that he did so. Popularly known as 'The angel of judgement,' Vincent was a crisis preacher who urged the people to turn back to the Lord before it was too late. He also preached on the immanent coming of the Antichrist. Nearly 600 years after his death, the judgement he preached has not come to pass. Perhaps it was averted as a result of his effective evangelisation.

Each day, Vincent celebrated Mass and preached at length to thousands of people. We know how he spoke because as many as 400 of his sermons are still extant. A selection of them have been published in English. He was evangelical in style. He knew all the scriptures by heart and often quoted them. He never referred to secular authors. As he explained, nowhere did Jesus say preach Ovid, Virgil or Homer. Clearly, Vincent's ministry was blessed by God. Everywhere he went, he was accompanied by up to fifty priests and sometimes thousands of people. Although he had no means of amplification, even those on the edge of vast crowds of 50,000 people or more, said that they could hear him clearly. Finally, not only was he instrumental in the conversion of countless thousands of nominally Christian people, he also won over tens of thousands of Jews and Moslems to the faith. Vincent also got involved in political matters. He had the special gift of reconciling enemies and was often called upon to act as judge and peacemaker. He counselled princes and settled disputes for families and those in high governmental positions.

Vincent had great admiration for his fellow Dominican, St Thomas Aquinas, and often referred to his writings. Thomas believed that the gifts of the Spirit which are listed in 1 Cor 12:8-10 were given in order to evangelise effectively. There are charisms of revelation, proclamation and demonstration. Vincent Ferrer was an outstanding example of what Thomas had in mind. He seemed to exercise most of the gifts mentioned by Paul. For instance, he regularly received revelation of a prophetic kind. Not only could he read hearts, he often foretold future events. For instance, in 1375, he said to starving crowds in Barcelona, 'Have courage, and be glad, for this very night two vessels will arrive in this port laden with wheat.' People were sceptical about this prediction because a storm was raging at sea. But everything happened as Vincent had foretold. He proclaimed the gospel with the aid of supernatural help. In the course of his canonisation process it was reported that although he always spoke in his own native dialect, people of other languages understood every word Vincent spoke without interpretation. As his canonisation process also attested, he demonstrated the truth of the merciful love he proclaimed by means of deeds of power. It is estimated that over a period of twenty years he performed more than 50,000 healings, exorcism and miracles, including more than thirty raisings from the dead.

Because St Vincent Ferrer's heart was moved to compassion by the economic plight of the people, he built hospitals, asylums, refuges and even bridges. The divisions and heresies in the church caused him great anguish of spirit. He believed that a revival of faith and morals depended upon the restoration of church unity and effective preaching. Although he supported the Avignon Popes, he came to see that his mentor Benedict XIII, was not the true successor of Peter. Eventually his prayers were answered when the Council of Constance (1414-17) reunited the church under Pope Martin V. Two years afterwards, worn out by his gargantuan efforts, Vincent died, as St Collette DeBoilet (1381-1447) had foretold, at Vannes in Brittany. As he himself had prophesised more than once during his lifetime, he was canonised by Pope Calixtus III in 1455.

Vincent de Paul influenced by Vincent Ferrer
When I read the life and works of Vincent Ferrer, I was surprised to find that some of his biographers mentioned that he had a significant influence on St Vincent de Paul, a great evangelist of the sixteenth century. In his book, *St Vincent Ferrer: The Angel of the Judgment,* Andrew Pradel OP claimed that the Spanish saint influenced 'blessed Nicholas Factor, a Franciscan and the great St Vincent de Paul ... St Vincent acknowledged St Vincent Ferrer as his own special patron. He made his life a daily study and had constantly in his hands the *Treatise on the Spiritual Life,* in order that he might conform thereto not only his own heart and actions, but also those of the priests of his institute.' In another book, entitled *St Vincent Ferrer, His Life, Spiritual Teaching, and Practical Devotion,* Pradel reiterated what he had

said in his other book and added, 'St Vincent de Paul gloried in St Vincent Ferrer as his patron; and we can well conceive that the examples of charity in the model would not be without its influence on the holy priest who essayed to walk in his footsteps.' Pradel says that a biographer named Antonio Teoli OP, who published a major biography of Vincent Ferrer in Rome in 1735, had mentioned that the Spanish saint had influenced St Vincent de Paul.

When I read these claims I wondered if any of the reputable biographies of St Vincent de Paul endorsed this point of view. Bishop Louis Abelly, who knew the founder of the Congregation of the Mission, says, 'He honoured Saint Vincent Ferrer, and it was noticed that on many of his retreats he read from the book written by this saint. He was so strongly influenced by what he had read about this saint's life and teachings that he often quoted them in the talks he gave to his community. He imitated this saint, particularly in his great zeal for the conversion of sinners and for the salvation of souls.' In the twentieth century, Pierre Coste said of St Vincent de Paul, 'His devotion extended to … St Vincent Ferrier, author of a *Treatise on the Spiritual Life*, which he loved to read.' These quotations raise two questions. Firstly, to what extent was Vincent de Paul influenced by the life and teachings of Vincent Ferrer? Secondly, did Vincent de Paul refer to Vincent Ferrer in his talks and writings?

Both Vincents lived during times of crisis
In a certain sense there were some parallels between the lives of the two men in so far as both of them lived at times when severe problems were evident in secular society and the church. Vincent Ferrer lived in the late middle ages when the continent of Europe was in deep trouble. Firstly, there was a little ice age in the 14th century when the weather got a good deal colder and had an adverse effect on agriculture. Secondly, the great famine of (1315-17) had a devastating effect and was marked by extreme levels of crime, disease, and death. Thirdly, the black death (1347-51) ravaged every country, including Spain, and resulted in the loss of between twenty and twenty-five million people, i.e. about a third of the population. There were six more waves of plague between 1350 and 1400. Fourthly, the hundred

years war (1337-1453) between England and France not only led to the martyrdom of St Joan of Arc (1412-1431), it had a widespread destructive and destabilising effect. Fifthly, because so many people had died as a result of bubonic plague and violence, the economy declined and poverty increased in some areas. Sixthly, the church was convulsed by the great schism which lasted from 1378 to 1417, and it was undermined by the heresies of people like John Wycliffe (1330-84) and John Huss (1372-1415). These scandalous situations compromised ecclesiastical authority, divided the faithful, and weakened spirituality.

Vincent de Paul lived at the beginning of the age of reason, when civil society and the church were once again in trouble. During his youth, France was devastated by the French Wars of Religion (1562-98) which were fought between Catholic and Huguenot factions. It is estimated that during this period between 2 and 4 million people died as a result of a combination of famine, disease and combat. Sometime later France was convulsed by a civil war known as the Fronde (1648-1653). As we know from the writings of St Vincent, it led to the dislocation of large numbers of people, hardship and famine. From a religious point of view, the Protestant Reformation had divided Christian Europe, including France. Although the Council of Trent had initiated a counter Reformation, by issuing many decrees which advocated reform and renewal, very few of them had been implemented in seventeenth-century France. As a result, there were obvious signs of decline in clerical and lay life. There was also the problem of Jansenism, a Catholic version of Calvinist Puritanism which stressed predestination. It was considered to be heretical by the church and duly condemned.

So it is not surprising that Vincent de Paul would have seen the response of Vincent Ferrer to the problems of his day, by means of evangelisation and church renewal, as a template which would have been relevant in the France of his time. Indeed, on one occasion Canon Richard Dognon of Verdun wrote to St Vincent de Paul and said, 'For the good of our century, God has passed on to you by a metempsychosis (a sort of reincarnation), which he alone can bring about, the spirit, affections, and design, together with the name of the great Patron of missionaries, Saint Vincent Ferrer. The apostolic missions he instituted in his time are manifestly more necessary than they ever were before.'

Vincent de Paul's interest in Vincent Ferrer
It is probable that Vincent had read one or more biographies of Vincent Ferrer. We know that shortly after Ferrer's death, the Bishop of Lucera, Peter Ranzano wrote the first official account of the Dominican's remarkable life (1455). It was followed by other biographies, such as one by Francis Castiglione (1470), and another, written in French, by Dominican Bernard Guyard (1634). It is quite possible that Vincent de Paul read this book. That said, it is unlikely that he had access to any of Vincent Ferrer's sermons. However, we are sure that he did read and re-read the *TOSL*. While we know that people such as Pierre Berulle, Francis de Sales and Benet of Canfield influenced Vincent's spirituality, the fact that Vincent Ferrer also influenced him is often overlooked.

Vincent de Paul used to refer to his namesake and quote his words, both in his letters and in the talks he gave to the Daughters of Charity and to the members of the Congregation of the Mission. There are no less than nine such quotations referred to in the general index of the French edition of the *Correspondence, Conferences and Documents*, edited by Pierre Coste. For example, Vincent de Paul wrote to Bernard Codoing about a business transaction which would require a knowledge of languages. He said, 'God will give you the grace, if he wishes, to make yourself understood by foreigners, just as he gave it to Vincent Ferrer.' In a conference Vincent gave to the priests of the Mission in May 1658, he spoke about the importance of deferring or condescending to the opinions of others in all things that are not sinful. He then referred to the following words in the *TOSL*: 'It is more advantageous to rule oneself by the will of another, provided it be good, although our own judgement may appear better and more perfect.' In the course of a talk to his priests about seminaries, St Vincent said, 'If St Vincent Ferrer strove for sanctification so that God would one day raise up good priests and apostolic workers for the reform of the ecclesiastical state, and for readying men for working for our perfection to co-operate in such a happy restoration when we see the ecclesiastical state now returning to what it should be.' On another occasion Vincent said, 'Let us work with a new love in the service of the poor, looking for the most destitute and abandoned among them. Let us recognise that before God they are our lords and masters, and we are unworthy to render them our small services.' The striking phrase, 'our lords and masters' seemed to have been borrowed from Vincent Ferrer who wrote, 'We should have a humble and sincere regard for our brethren, and cheerfully submit to them as our lords and masters.' In the light of references like these, it is surprising to find that some recent biographies, such as Jose Maria Roman's *St Vincent de Paul: A Biography*, and Bernard Pujo's, *Vincent de Paul the Trailblazer* seem to make no mention of St Vincent Ferrer.

The Two Vincents on Preaching
There is no doubt that St Vincent Ferrer was a remarkably effective evangelical preacher. He described his understanding of this ministry in a chapter in the *TOSL* entitled, 'On Preaching.' In it he advised: 'Use simple and familiar words in preaching and exhortation. To explain in detail what you mean; and so far as possible, illustrate what you say with some examples, in order that the sinner, finding his conscience guilty of the same sins which you reprehend, may feel as if you were speaking only to him. Do this, however, in such a way that your words, so to speak, may appear to come from the heart, without being mixed with any movement of indignation or pride, and to spring from the bowels of compassion, from the tender love of a father who is grieved at the faults of his children.' When one reads the sermons of Vincent Ferrer it is clear that he put these principles into practice. Furthermore, a number of points will probably strike anyone who reads the *TOSL*. Firstly, it contains virtually no quotations, either scriptural, patristic or contemporary. Secondly, the style is very simple and clear, and tends to speak briefly about the nature of the topic under discussion, e.g. Christian perfection, while going on to mention motives and means of practising it.

Authors such as Abbe Arnaud d'Angel, Jacques Delarue, and Jose Maria Roman include interesting sections on Vincent de Paul's views on preaching. They show how implicit in the

CHAPTER SIX

various things Vincent de Paul said about preaching over the years was the 'little method,' which he said was the method of Jesus Christ himself. He exclaimed on one occasion, 'Hurrah for simplicity, and for the "little method" which is in fact, the most excellent method and one that brings more glory because it moves hearts more than all this speechifying which only irritates the listener.' The method consists of three interrelated parts which need to be varied depending of the subject under consideration such as a virtue, the life of a saint, a parable etc. Firstly, it deals with the nature of the subject under discussion, e.g. salvation. Secondly, the preacher suggests motives for acting, such as, why a person should desire to experience salvation, e.g. sorrow for offending the Lord, and fear of losing heaven. Thirdly, the preacher deals with the means of doing something practical and specific, e.g. trusting in the free, unmerited gift of God's mercy, and making a good general confession.

Anyone who reads Vincent Ferrer's *TOSL* will notice that the little method comprising of nature, motives, and means, was implicit in the way he wrote. Furthermore, many things Vincent de Paul said about preaching seem to echo points which Vincent Ferrer had already made. We can look at a few examples. Firstly, as has already been noted, Vincent Ferrer did not quote secular authors. For his part, Vincent de Paul admonished preachers who tried 'to cause wonderment by filling their sermons with a great variety of things such as extracts from philosophy, mathematics, medicine, jurisprudence, quotations from Jewish Rabbis, Greek, Hebrew, Syriac, and Chaldaic words ... in a vain display of knowledge.' On one occasion, Vincent de Paul said, 'Do not use quotations from the profane authors, unless you use them as steppingstones to the holy scripture.' Secondly, Vincent Ferrer warned preachers not to speak in a spirit of pride. Vincent de Paul repeatedly warned against the same danger: 'We must remain faithful,' he said, 'to the simplicity and humility of our Saviour, Jesus Christ. He could have done startling things and spoken momentous words, but he did not do so.' Thirdly, Vincent Ferrer said that preaching aimed to help sinners to become aware of their sins in a way that would lead to repentance. Vincent de Paul said: 'Let us never desire to satisfy ourselves, but to satisfy God, to win souls, and to lead people to repentance, because all else is nothing but vanity and pride.' Fourthly, Vincent Ferrer stressed the importance of preaching the truth in a spirit of compassion like a loving father or mother. Vincent de Paul quoted his patron when he said, 'St Vincent Ferrer says that there is no means of profiting by preaching if one does not preach from the depths of compassion.' On another occasion he said something similar: 'We should use compassionate language to make our neighbours aware that we truly have their interests and sufferings at heart.' Fifthly, Vincent Ferrer recommended preachers to illustrate what they meant by everyday examples. Vincent de Paul said something similar: 'Notice how Jesus spoke in an understandable language, using the simple comparisons of a farmer, a field, a vine, a grain of mustard seed. This is how you must speak if you want to be understood by the people to whom you announce the word of God.'

Heroic Sanctity
While the two Vincents were remarkable evangelists, each in his own distinctive way, there were obvious differences between them. Vincent Ferrer was an eschatological prophet, who focused on the presence of the antichrist and the immanence of the end times and general judgement. Vincent de Paul did not focus on any of these topics. Vincent Ferrer was a remarkable wonder worker, whereas there is very little evidence that Vincent de Paul healed the sick or delivered them from evil spirits. Indeed there is an interesting discussion of the significance of deeds of power in the lives of the saints in Bishop Prospero Lambertini's (1675-1758) four volume, *De Servorum Dei Beatificatione, et Beatorum Canonizatione (On* the Beatification and Canonization of the Servants of God). The learned author, who later became Pope Benedict XIV, mentioned the charismatic activities of Vincent Ferrer, such as the fact that St Antonius (1389-1459), a Dominican Archbishop of Florence, testified during the canonisation process that although Vincent spoke in his Spanish dialect he was understood by people who spoke different languages.

Lambertini handled the canonisation process of Vincent de Paul. Speaking about the latter he said, 'Matthaeucci says that beside heroic virtues, the promoters of the faith are accustomed to require, for the sake of greater precaution, some grace *gratis data* [charismatic grace]. I confess that when I was promoter of the faith, I did not omit to make that observation. I did so in the cause of St Vincent de Paul and the prudent postulators replied, that graces *gratis datae* were not necessary in order to form a safe judgement on his virtues, some however, of them were not wanting in the servant of God. These are their words: "Although graces *gratis datae* are not necessary to prove heroic virtues, and therefore it is not necessary that St Vincent de Paul should have been endowed with them in order to perceive that he had attained to heroic virtue; but, however, we will bring forward many matters of moment, from which it may be inferred that the servant of God was possessed of those gifts which are now the subject of discussion".' Unfortunately Lambertini did not offer examples of Vincent's charismatic powers. One could hazard a guess that he thought that Vincent had the gifts of the utterance of wisdom and knowledge, as well as the gifts of the discernment of spirits and seeing visions, as was evidenced by the prophetic image he saw at the time of St Jane de Chantal's death.

Learning from the two Vincents
The findings of this chapter are intended to be indicative rather than conclusive. The subject of Vincent Ferrer's influence on St Vincent de Paul's spirituality deserves a more rigorous treatment from a methodological and textual point of view than I have been able to provide. Even so, it is my belief that, taken together, the example of the two Vincents teaches us at least five relevant lessons at this time of crisis in church and state. Firstly, our multiple problems, which are often the result of sinful forgetfulness of God are, paradoxically, a providential call to seek the Lord while he may still be found (cf Is 55:6). Secondly, while Christians are right to stress the primacy of the loving mercy of God, they also need to refer, not only to the divine justice which will be exercised on the last day, but also to the possibility of eternal separation from God. Thirdly, we can see from the lives of the two Vincents that effective evangelisation is rooted in personal holiness of life. Fourthly, when we share the gospel in different ways, we can expect God to demonstrate his saving power and presence by means of charitable works and action for justice. That was obvious in the life of St Vincent de Paul.

Fifthly, God can manifest the divine presence by means of charismatic deeds of power as was evident in the ministry of St Vincent Ferrer.

Commenting on charisms of power in an article entitled, 'The Charisms and the New Evangelisation,' Belgian Cardinal Godfried Danneels made an interesting point. 'In times of crisis like today,' he wrote, 'the Spirit multiplies his gifts. It is not surprising therefore that in our era, greater attention should be given to the charisms in a Catholic milieu … The more the life of the people of God is harsh, the more God grants his gifts. What would be the particular gifts today which the Lord gives us? Would it not be faith which moves mountains, which brings about miracles and which thus gives weight to the proclamation of the gospel?' If the Cardinal is right, the members of the Irish church can expect to receive some of the more extraordinary gifts of the Spirit. They will help to usher in the new springtime spoken about by Popes John Paul II and Benedict XVI.

Conclusion
There is a very moving example of how the new springtime might come about in Abelly's graphic account of a Vincentian mission which was conducted in 1641. It took place as a result of the repeated requests of the duchess of Aiguillon. She appealed to Vincent to evangelise the faubourg Saint Germain des Pres in Paris which was a very deprived, run down, crime ridden area. As a result of their grace-filled efforts, Abelly tells us that: 'Those who worked on this mission were astonished seeing the disproportion between the means used and the result attained. Besides the large crowds at their sermons and catechism instructions which they presented in the simple and familiar style suggested by Monsieur Vincent, they were filled with admiration at their results. They saw inveterate sinners, hardened usurers, fallen women, criminals who had spent their entire lives in crime, in a word, people without faith in God or anyone, throw themselves at their feet, their eyes bathed in tears, their hearts moved with sorrow for sins, begging mercy and forgiveness.' Let us pray that with the grace of God, modern Christians will be able to perform evangelistic deeds of mercy and power in our day which will rival those of the two Vincents in theirs.

SECTION TWO

Scripture

CHAPTER SEVEN

Scripture on Scripture

In everyday life language is used to describe pre-existing realities. For example, the word book refers to the object you are reading right now. In the Bible, however, instead of describing pre-existing objects, God's word is constitutive of reality. It contains the unique power to effect what it says. Scripture scholar, George Montague, points out in his book *Riding the Wind*: 'When the Hebrew speaks a word, he is not taking in the outside world and shaping it within himself. Rather he is thrusting something creative and powerful outward from himself into the external world and actually changing that world.' For example, in Gen 1:3 we read, 'God said, "Let there be light," and there was light.' As Is 55:10-11 testifies, 'As the rain and the snow come down from heaven, and do not return to it without watering the earth and making it bud and flourish, so that it yields seed for the sower and bread for the eater, so is my word that goes out from my mouth: It will not return to me empty, but will accomplish what I desire and achieve the purpose for which I sent it.'

The Word as a Noun and as a Verb
In the Old Testament the term for word is *Dabar*. It means 'to drive, to get behind, or push.' It can be used as a noun or as a verb. As a noun it is objective. It refers to the word of God which is true in itself. As a verb the word has a subjective aspect. It refers to the word of God which is true for a particular individual in a particular situation, to whom it is addressed. Johann Wolfgang von Goethe conveyed something of the dynamic power of the word of God as a verb in Samuel Taylor Coleridge's translation of *Faust*. Apparently Heinrich Faust was trying to translate the opening verses of John's gospel into his native German.

> In the beginning was *the Word*,' 'tis written;
> Here do I stumble: who can help me on?
> I cannot estimate 'the Word' so highly;
> I must translate it otherwise, if rightly
> I feel myself enlightened by its spirit.
> 'In the beginning was *the Mind*,' 'tis written:
> Repeat this line, and weigh its meaning well,
> Nor let thy pen decide too hastily:
> Is it the mind creates and fashions all?
> 'In the beginning was *the Power*,' it should be;
> Yet, even while I write the passage down,
> It warns me that I have not caught its meaning:
> Help me, then, Spirit! With deliberation,
> And perfect confidence, I will inscribe,
> At last, 'In the beginning was *the Deed*.'

The dynamic power of the word, referred to in Goethe's verses, is evident in the following scripture quotations: 'Call to me and I will answer you and tell you great and unsearchable things you do not know' (Jer 33:3). Again in Is 48:6-8 we read: 'From now on I will tell you of new things, of hidden things unknown to you. They are created now, and not long ago; you have not heard of them before today. So you cannot say, "Yes, I knew of them." You have neither heard nor understood; from of old your ear has not been open.' St Ignatius of Loyola reminds us in his *Spiritual Exercises*: 'It is not much knowledge that fills and satisfies the soul, but the intimate understanding and relish of the truth.' When people pay prayerful attention to the scriptures they do so in the hope that God's word will leap alive off the page into their hearts as an inspired and inspiring word of revelation.

The Old Testament points to Christ
All the books of the Old Testament point to Christ and find their fulfilment in him. Jesus himself made this clear to the two disciples on the road to Emmaus. Having poured out their sorrows to their companion, 'Jesus replied: "You foolish men! So slow to believe the full message of the prophets! Was it not ordained that the Christ should suffer and so enter his glory?" Then start-

ing with Moses and going through all the prophets he explained to them the passages throughout the scriptures that were about himself' (Lk 24:25-28). The gospels record the words and actions of Jesus. They are like so many panes in the stained glass window of his humanity. When they are illuminated by the Spirit and contemplated with the eyes of faith, they can become an unequalled source of revelation. Through them we begin to see what God is like. As Jesus said, 'To have seen me is to have seen the Father' (Jn 14:9). The remaining books of the New Testament record the impact and implications of Christ for the first Christians.

Jesus on the Word
If I am not mistaken the transfiguration of Jesus was the only occasion when God gave a direct instruction to humanity. Having declared that Jesus was his beloved Son he went on to say, 'Listen to him.' Mary echoed those prophetic words when she said to the servants at the marriage feast of Cana, 'Do whatever he tells you.' Surely these statements from God the Father and Mary the mother of Jesus are the foundation stone of all genuine Christian spirituality. We can begin to respond to them by listening to what Jesus said about his own words.
- 'Heaven and earth will pass away, but my words will never pass away ... (Mt 24:35)
- The words I have spoken to you are spirit and they are life ... (Jn 6:63)
- If you remain in me and my words remain in you, ask whatever you wish, and it will be given you ... (Jn 15:7)
- There is a judge for the one who rejects me and does not accept my words; that very word which I spoke will condemn him at the last day (Jn 12:48).

It is well worth mentioning that Jesus himself had a profound knowledge of the Old Testament and had deep insight into its spiritual meaning and how it related to himself. For example, when the Sadducees, who denied the resurrection of the dead, referred in a cynical way to the woman who was married to seven brothers, not only did Jesus say 'You are in error because you do not know the scriptures or the power of God' (Mt

22:29), he also referred with great insight to a text in Ex 3:6, and said, 'But as to the resurrection of the dead – have you never read what was said to you by God, I am the God of Abraham, and the God of Isaac, and the God of Jacob? He is not the God of the dead but of the living!' (Mt 22:31-32). We are also told that when Jesus met the two disciples on the road to Emmaus after his own resurrection, 'How foolish you are, and how slow of heart to believe all the prophets have spoken! Did not the Christ have to suffer these things and then enter his glory?' (Lk 24:27).

In his wonderful parable about the sower, in Mk 4:3-8, Mt 13:3-8, Lk 8:5-8, Jesus talked about the different ways in which people react to the seed which is God's word. In Mk 4:15-20 he referred to four possible responses to the utterances of the Lord. Firstly, there are three obstacles, Satan (4:15), persecutions (4:16-17), and worldly concerns (4:18-19). The parable ends by describing the characteristics of the true disciple as someone who, like Mary, hears the word, takes it to heart, and acts accordingly (4:20). It should be said that, besides making these spiritual points, the parable is also saying in a theological way that no matter what obstacles Jesus had to endure in his ministry, eventually he would be amazingly fruitful and effective. This eschatological interpretation has to do with the end times. As Lutheran scripture scholar Joachim Jeremias explained in *Rediscovering the Parables*, 'To human eyes much of the labour may seem futile and fruitless, resulting apparently in frequent failure; but Jesus is full of joyful confidence: God's hour is coming, and will bring with it a harvest of reward beyond all asking and understanding. In spite of every failure and opposition, God brings from hopeless beginnings the glorious end that he has promised.'

The New Testament authors often speak about the importance of God's word. In 2 Tim 3:15-17 we read: 'From infancy you have known the holy scriptures, which are able to make you wise for salvation through faith in Christ Jesus. All scripture is God-breathed and is useful for teaching, rebuking, correcting and training in righteousness, so that the man of God may be thoroughly equipped for every good work.' Paul says that Timothy has learnt the scriptures from youth i.e. the Old Testament, and what his grandmother and mother had taught him about Jesus. That point is well made in the story of Philip and the Ethiopian eunuch. Beginning with Is 53:7-8 he pointed to the Old Testament texts that indicated that Jesus was the promised Messiah, the Suffering Servant who died so that our sins might be forgiven (cf Acts 8:26-40).

All scripture is inspired
In 2 Tim 3:16 we read: 'All scripture is God-breathed,' in other words, all scripture is inspired by the Holy Spirit. There is a related text in 2 Pet 1:20-21 which states: 'You must understand that no prophecy of scripture came about by the prophet's own interpretation. For prophecy never had its origin in the will of man, but men spoke from God as they were carried along by the Holy Spirit.' Commenting on this notion of inspiration, the *Catechism of the Catholic Church* says in pars 105-107 that the church accepts that the Old and New Testaments were: 'Written under the inspiration of the Holy Spirit. They have God as their author. They have been handed on as such to the church herself. To compose the sacred books, God chose certain men who, all the while he employed them in this task, made full use of their own faculties and powers so that, though he acted in them and by them, it was as true authors that they consigned to writing whatever he wanted written, and no more. The inspired books teach the truth.' Then Paul says that the scriptures are useful for four reasons.
1. By reading the scriptures you can gain the wisdom that leads to salvation through faith in Christ Jesus. Speaking of faith in Christ, the *Amplified Bible* which tries to capture the nuances in the Greek text, says that faith in Christ is, 'through the leaning of the entire human personality on God in Christ Jesus in absolute trust and confidence in his power wisdom and goodness.'
2. Scripture is useful for teaching truth. The Word of God teaches the truth about who God is, what God is like, and what God wants. In the bible there is a gradual unveiling of that truth which came to its climax in the life and ministry of Jesus, who said of himself that he is the truth (cf Jn 14:6).
3. Scripture is good for rebuking error. Once a person knows the truth it shows up error and challenges it. The meaning here is more ethical than doctrinal, i.e. bringing sinners to their senses about their wrongdoing.

CHAPTER SEVEN

4. Scripture is good for correcting faults, and training people how to live in the right way. The Greek word, *paideia* ('training') comes from *pais*, ('child'). So it originally meant 'the rearing of a child.' Then it came to mean 'training, learning, instruction.' Christians need to be trained in 'righteousness,' and scripture provides that.

The Word of God as a two edged sword
The author of Heb 4:12-13 says: 'For the word of God is living and active. Sharper than any double-edged sword, it penetrates even to dividing soul and spirit, joints and marrow; it judges the thoughts and attitudes of the heart. Nothing in all creation is hidden from God's sight. Everything is uncovered and laid bare before the eyes of him to whom we must give account.' Apparently, this verse refers back to Ps 95:7, 'If only you would listen to his voice today!' It has in mind what I said about the word of God as a noun and a verb. Clearly, the author of Hebrews is referring to the fact that ideally, the word of God is a verb, a here-and-now word that accomplishes what it says. There are a number of examples of this dynamic power of the word. When the angel Gabriel made his momentous announcement that Mary was to become the mother of the Messiah, she replied, 'Be it done to me according to your word' (Lk 1:38). In other words, if that is what God says, even though it seems impossible from a human point of view, that word contains the power of its own fulfilment. It is interesting to note that Elizabeth declared in a prophetic way, 'Blessed is she who has believed that what the Lord has said to her will be accomplished!' (Lk 1:45).

The author of Hebrews also says that God's living word goes to the core of a person's being. When it does so, it reveals the truth to the person. This notion is mentioned on a number of occasions in the Old Testament. Here are two instances. In Jer 17:9-10 we read: 'The heart is deceitful above all things and beyond cure. Who can understand it? I the Lord search the heart and examine the mind, to reward a man according to his conduct, according to what his deeds deserve.' Again in Ps 139: 23-24, we read: 'Search me, O God, and know my heart; test me and know my anxious thoughts. See if there is any offensive way in me, and lead me in the way everlasting.'

The word of God evokes faith
In Rom 10:17 the apostle Paul tells us that, 'Faith comes from what is heard, and what is heard comes through the word of Christ.' This is the only place in the bible where we are told how faith is evoked. It comes from hearing the word of God as a verb, as the living alive, active word of God. Let's look at a biblical example. On one occasion Peter saw Jesus walking on water. Then we are told, 'Peter answered him, "Lord, if it is you, command me to come to you on the water." Jesus said, "Come".' Evidently Peter gave notional assent to the belief that with God all things are possible. But he seemed to know instinctively that unless his desire was in conformity with the will of God and his subsequent action was empowered by God, he would be unable to walk on water. Both were manifested when Jesus said 'come' in response to Peter's request. This one inspired and inspiring word, empowered Peter to defy gravity and to walk on water. With a heart brimming with confidence, Peter stepped out of the boat and began to walk toward Jesus. But as his attention was distracted by wind and waves, he lost the power of the word which he has just heard, and began to sink. He cried out to Jesus, asking him to save him from death by drowning. Jesus immediately reached out his hand and caught him, while saying to him, 'You of little faith, why did you doubt?' When they got into the boat, the wind ceased. And those in the boat worshipped him, saying, 'Truly you are the son of God.' When Peter saw Jesus, he addressed him as Lord, and asked permission to share in his miraculous power over nature.

Conclusion
Ps 119:105 says, 'Your word is a lamp to my feet and a light for my path.' In Prov 4:20-22 we read, 'My son, pay attention to what I say; listen closely to my words. Do not let them out of your sight, keep them within your heart; for they are life to those who find them and health to a man's whole body.' Finally, in Ezech 3:2 we are told that the Lord said to the prophet, 'Son of man, eat what is before you, eat this scroll; then go and speak to the house of Israel.' There is a similar text in Rev 10:9-10, 'I went to the angel and asked him to give me the little scroll. He said to me, "Take it and eat it ... in your mouth it will be as sweet as

honey".' This notion of eating, savouring and digesting God's word in a prayerful way, is probably one of the things that Jesus had in mind when he said, in his prayer, 'give us this day our daily bread' (Mt 6:11).

CHAPTER EIGHT

The Catholic Church on Reading and Praying the Scriptures

When I was growing up in the 1950s and 60s my parents were devout without being piotius. Every day they attended Mass and prayed together. Nevertheless, they didn't read the scriptures and discouraged us from doing so on the basis that we were not Protestants. They warned that there was always a danger we would misinterpret the scriptures. In any case the priests would tell us what we needed to know in their homilies. In spite of the oft repeated teaching of Vatican II to do with regular bible reading, Catholics are still reluctant to read and pray the scriptures. A few years ago I conducted two short retreats for the Legion of Mary. Although there were about 70 people attending each of them, only one person out of 140 had brought a bible! Archbishop Martin acknowledged this problem in 2010 when he spoke about the future of the Catholic Church in Ireland. He observed: 'This brings us to the deeper question about the level of understanding of the message of Jesus Christ which exists in our Catholic Church and in our society in Ireland today. What do we really know of the message of Jesus? The Irish Catholic tradition has greatly neglected the place of the scriptures. Catholics do not know the scriptures. They do not know how to use the scriptures. We do not take the time to encounter Jesus in the scriptures.'

The church's teaching
The church has firmly and consistently urged Catholics since the 60s to read and pray the scriptures. Here are just five representative examples of that teaching:

1) In the Constitution on Sacred Liturgy par 21 we read: 'The church has always venerated the divine scriptures just as she venerates the body of the Lord.' Not surprisingly, therefore, she encourages the faithful to develop a scripture-based spirituality.

2) In the *Catechism of the Catholic Church* par 133 we read, 'The church forcefully and specifically exhorts all the Christian faithful ... to learn the surpassing knowledge of Jesus Christ, by frequent reading of the scriptures.'

3) In *The Church in Europe,* par 65, John Paul urged, 'Enter the new millennium with the book of the gospels! May every member of the faithful hear the Council's plea to learn "the surpassing knowledge of Jesus Christ" (cf Phil 3:8) by frequent reading of the divine scriptures. "Ignorance of the scriptures is ignorance of Christ." May the holy bible continue to be a treasure for the church and for every Christian: in the careful study of God's word we will daily find nourishment and strength to carry out our mission ... Let us devour the bible (cf Rev 10:9), so that it can become our very life. Let us savour it deeply: it will make demands of us, but it will give us joy because it is sweet as honey (cf Rev 10:9-10). Filled with hope, we will be able to share it with every man and woman we encounter on our way.'

4) Pope Benedict said in par 86 of his apostolic declaration on *The Word of God*: 'The word of God is at the basis of all authentic Christian spirituality. The Synod Fathers thus took up the words of the Dogmatic Constitution *Dei Verbum*: "Let the faithful go gladly to the sacred text itself, whether in the sacred liturgy, which is full of the divine words, or in devout reading, or in such suitable exercises and various other helps which, with the approval and guidance of the pastors of the church, are happily spreading everywhere in our day. Let them remember, however, that prayer should accompany the reading of sacred scripture".'

5) Archbishop Martin of Dublin said, at the launch of the Irish Catechetical Directory, entitled , *Share the Good News* (5 January 2011): 'Where will our people, younger and older, come to their knowledge of Jesus and where will they find the nourishment needed to enable their relationship with Jesus to develop and mature as their lives evolve and encounter ever new challenges? A developed and mature Christian faith requires knowledge of the scriptures. This again is something revolutionary in Irish Catholicism where most families may not even possess a bible and probably not even a copy of the gospels, and where reading the scriptures is far from being the order of the day in the home or the classroom ... Each of us has to begin to

place the word of God at the centre of our own spirituality and of our Christian life. We have to know the scriptures, to love the scriptures, to understand the scriptures, to prayerfully read the scriptures. All of us have to learn to take up the scriptures *every day* [my italics].'

Lectio divina
For a long time the church has recommended the practice of *Lectio divina* (divine reading). For example, in his Letter to Gregory, Origen offered this advice: 'Devote yourself to the *lectio* of the divine scriptures; apply yourself to this with perseverance. Do your reading with the intent of believing in and pleasing God. If during the reading you encounter a closed door, knock and it will be opened to you by that guardian of whom Jesus said, "The gatekeeper will open it for him." By applying yourself in this way to *lectio divina*, search diligently and with unshakable trust in God for the meaning of the divine scriptures, which is hidden in great fullness within. You ought not, however, to be satisfied merely with knocking and seeking in order to understand the things of God, what is absolutely necessary is prayer. For this reason, the Saviour told us not only: "Seek and you will find", and "Knock and it shall be opened to you", but also added, "Ask and you shall receive."' In the 12th century Guigo the Carthusian described the overall purpose of *Lectio divina* when he wrote succinctly: 'Seek in reading and you will find in meditating; knock in prayer and it will be opened to you in contemplation.'

Lectio divina is a reading, on an individual or communal level, of a more or less lengthy passage of scripture, received as the word of God and leading, at the prompting of the Spirit, to meditation, prayer and contemplation. Pope John Paul II said in *As the Third Millennium Approaches*: 'It is especially necessary that listening to the word of God should become a life-giving encounter, in the ancient and ever valid tradition of *lectio divina*, which draws from the biblical text the living word which questions, directs and shapes our lives. In his apostolic declaration *The Word of God*, Pope Benedict XVI described this form of prayer in the following extended quotation: 'It opens with the reading (*lectio*) of a text, which leads to a desire to understand its true content: what does the biblical text say in itself? Without this, there is always a risk that the text will become a pretext for never moving beyond our own ideas. Next comes meditation (*meditatio*), which asks: what does the biblical text say to us? Here, each person, individually but also as a member of the community, must let himself or herself be moved and challenged. Following this comes prayer (*oratio*), which asks the question: what do we say to the Lord in response to his word? Prayer, as petition, intercession, thanksgiving and praise, is the primary way by which the word transforms us. Finally, *lectio divina* concludes with contemplation (*contemplatio*), during which we take up, as a gift from God, his own way of seeing and judging reality, and ask ourselves what conversion of mind, heart and life is the Lord asking of us?'

A Suggested Method of Scripture Prayer
Kiss the Bible as a sign of reverence for God's inspired word.

Before engaging in the *Lectio divina*, I ask the Lord to bless my prayer time. I usually say the following verse from The Divine Office.

> In the scriptures by the Spirit
> May we see the Saviour's face
> Hear his word and heed his calling
> Know his will and grow in grace.

or

Grant me, O Lord my God, a mind to know you, a heart to seek you, wisdom to find you, conduct pleasing to you, faithful perseverance in waiting for you, and a hope of finally embracing you. Amen. (St Thomas Aquinas)

or

Creator of all things, true source of light and wisdom, origin of all being, as I read the scriptures, graciously let a ray of your light penetrate the darkness of my understanding. Take from me the double darkness in which I have been born, an obscurity of sin and ignorance. Give me a keen understanding of your word, a retentive memory, and the ability to grasp things correctly and fundamentally. Grant me the talent of being exact in my explanations of your word and the ability to express myself to others with thoroughness and charm. Point out the beginning, direct the progress, and help in the completion of my scripture prayer. I ask this through Christ our Lord. Amen. (Prayer of St Thomas Aquinas adapted)

1. Choose the passage that you intend to read, e.g. one of the liturgical readings of that day or the following Sunday. Read the passage slowly two or three times. St Anselm wrote: 'The scriptures are not to be read in a noisy situation, but where things are quiet, not superficially and in a rush, but a little at a time.' It is a good idea to read the passage out loud, in a whisper at least, until a phrase, an image, or a word catches your attention in a special way.

2. Reflect on the meaning of these outstanding verses. As the Lord says: 'Pay attention to my words, listen carefully to my utterances. I say, do not let them out of your sight, keep them deep in your heart. They are life to those who grasp them, health for the entire body' (Prov 4:20-23). When reflecting on a passage of scripture keep two thoughts in mind. Firstly, what was the inspired author trying to say in this passage? Footnotes in some scholarly bibles, or a commentary can be helpful in this regard. Secondly, has the passage any relevance in my life and in the lives of the people around me? There are two ways of carrying out this advice:

- If you are reflecting on a doctrinal point, e.g. from the letters of St Paul, it can be helpful if you repeat a chosen word or sentence over and over again, while letting its meaning sink into the heart. It is rather like sucking a sweet. You let it dissolve in order to savour its taste and flavour.
- If you are reflecting on a scriptural story or parable, e.g. one from the gospels, it can be helpful to imagine the incident as if it were a video. See the scene and the characters who are involved; you may choose to be one of them, e.g. an onlooker in the crowd when Jesus is healing a blind man. Hear what is said. You may want to augment the dialogue in the text with some of your own additions. Notice what the characters do. Sense in an empathic way what the people in the incident feel. Try in a special way to sense in an understanding man-

ner what Jesus feels, and also try to become aware of your own emotional reaction to the story.

3. Pray from the heart, allowing rational reflection to express itself in the form of an affective conversation with the Lord. St Vincent de Paul once wrote: 'The soul is like a sailboat equipped with oars. The oars are not used unless the wind fails, and then progress isn't as rapid or as pleasant as when the ship is moving along under a fair breeze. Similarly, we have need of reflection in prayer when special assistance from the Holy Spirit is not forthcoming, but when the heavenly breeze blows upon the heart, we must yield ourselves to its influence.' We do this when we tell the Lord about our feelings such as love, joy, gratitude, sorrow, desire and the like, which were evoked by reflection on the text. In this regard, St Benedict said: 'Let the prayer be brief and pure.' Once distractions occur go back to reading and reflecting, in the way already described, until you can pray again.

4. Contemplate by being still and resting in the Lord. Reflection and prayerful self-disclosure can give way to a sense of the presence and attitudes of Christ. Speaking of this kind of contemplation, St Vincent de Paul remarked: 'It is not the result of human teaching. It is not attainable by human effort, and it is not bestowed on everyone ... In this state of quiet, the soul finds itself suddenly filled with spiritual illuminations and holy affections.' Writing about this kind of contemplation Pope Benedict has written, in *The Word of God*, 'Contemplation aims at creating within us a truly wise and discerning vision of reality, as God sees it, and at forming within us "the mind of Christ" (1 Cor 2:16).'

As a result of this kind of scripture prayer we begin to see Jesus more clearly and to love him more dearly. This leads to a desire to follow him more nearly in everyday life. It is good to make a resolution that flows from the scriptural reflection and prayer, e.g. by being for others what Jesus or God the Father was for you during your time of prayer. St Vincent de Paul says that such a resolution should be single, precise, definite and attainable. As Jesus observed: 'The seed on good soil stands for those with a noble and good heart, who hear the word, retain it, and by persevering produce a crop' (Lk 8:15).

Conclusion
Archbishop Diarmuid Martin of Dublin said in 2010: 'I see a role for Catholic movements, especially those which form the young in the true dimensions of personal and ecclesial faith, through the integration of prayer, of a personal knowledge of Jesus through the sacred scriptures, and of critical reflection on personal and professional life as a service to society. The challenge is great, but also urgent.' In January 2011, Archbishop Martin said that many parishes, 'have recognised the centrality of formation, prayer and knowledge of the scriptures in all their pastoral activity. But they know that there is a huge path still ahead. Pope Benedict stresses this need – which is more than urgent – for "provision to be made for the suitable preparation of priests and lay persons who can instruct the People of God in the genuine approach to scripture".' Speaking in October 2005, shortly after his election as Pope, Benedict XVI not only recommended *Lectio divina*, he said, 'If this practice is promoted with efficacy, I am convinced that it will produce a new spiritual springtime in the church.'

CHAPTER NINE

Interpreting Scripture

Recently, I watched the marvellous movie, *A Man for All Seasons* (1966), about the life and martyrdom of St Thomas More. At one point in Robert Bolt's outstanding screenplay, Sir Thomas was asked why he would not take an oath accepting the act of succession to do with the authority of the king over the church in England. At one point he responded, 'Some men think the earth is round, others think it flat. It is a matter capable of question. But if it is flat, will the King's command make it round? And if it is round, will the King's command flatten it?' In other words, no matter what we think subjectively, that does not change objective fact. That principle is important when it comes to reading the bible. Instead of trying to impose our own subjective ideas and prejudices on the sacred text we should seek, with God's help, to discover in an objective manner what it means in itself. Catholics do not interpret the bible in a literal, non-historical way. Rather, we study the circumstances in which it's different books were composed in order to discover the intentions and inspired teaching of its different authors. Speaking about this Pope John Paul II said: 'Attention must be given to the literary forms of the various biblical books in order to determine the intentions of the sacred writers. And it is most helpful, at times crucial, to be aware of the personal situation of the biblical writer, of the circumstances of culture, time, language, etc, which influenced the way the message was presented ... In this way, it is possible to avoid a narrow fundamentalism which distorts the whole truth.'

A fundamentalist approach
In 1993 the Pontifical Biblical Commission published a document on behalf of John Paul II, entitled, *Interpretation of the Bible in the Church*. In a section devoted to fundamentalism it says: 'Fundamentalist interpretation starts from the principle that the

bible, being the word of God, inspired and free from error, should be read and interpreted literally in all its details. But by "literal interpretation" it understands a naively literalist interpretation, one, that is to say, which excludes every effort at understanding the bible that takes account of its historical origins and development. It is opposed, therefore, to the use of the historical-critical method, as indeed to the use of any other scientific method for the interpretation of scripture.' In his book *Responses to 101 Questions on the Bible*, eminent Catholic scripture scholar, Ray Brown said, 'In my judgment, a literalist reading of the bible is intellectually indefensible and is quite unnecessary for the defence of the basic Christian doctrines.' Surely Brown is correct when he says that fundamentalism is intellectually indefensible.

Here is just one of many possible examples of statements in different gospels which cannot be reconciled if they are read in a literalist way. In Matthew's gospel we are told that, 'Jesus was born in Bethlehem in Judea, during the time of King Herod' (Mt 2:1). We know from history that at the age of seventy Herod the Great died in 4 BC. In Luke's gospel we are told that Jesus was born at the time when 'Caesar Augustus issued a decree that a census should be taken of the entire Roman world. This was the first census that took place while Quirinius was governor of Syria' (Lk 2:1-2). We know, from the writings of Jewish historian Josephus, that this census took place between 6 and 7 AD. In other words, there is a discrepancy of ten years in the accounts of the two evangelists as regards the date of Jesus' birth. The only way to understand this anomaly is to say that Matthew and Luke were writing about the nativity of Jesus from a theological rather than a strictly historical perspective. Happily in recent years a growing number of Catholics have begun to read the scriptures as a result of such things as having attended an Alpha Course or a Charismatic Prayer Meeting. Unfortunately, however, in spite of their good intentions, many men and women have tended towards a fundamentalist reading of the texts due to two factors, the influence of an ideological kind of Protestant fundamentalism, and the fact that they have been taught very little about a non literalist way of interpreting them.

Referring to the fundamentalism mentioned by his predecessor John Paul II, Pope Benedict XVI said in his apostolic declara-

CHAPTER NINE

tion on *The Word of God*, 'The "literalism" championed by the fundamentalist approach actually represents a betrayal of both the literal and the spiritual sense, and opens the way to various forms of manipulation as, for example, by disseminating anti-ecclesial interpretations of the scriptures. The basic problem with fundamentalist interpretation is that, refusing to take into account the historical character of biblical revelation, it makes itself incapable of accepting the full truth of the incarnation itself. As regards relationships with God, fundamentalism seeks to escape any closeness of the divine and the human ... for this reason, it tends to treat the biblical text as if it had been dictated word for word by the Spirit. It fails to recognise that the word of God has been formulated in language and expression conditioned by various periods.' Par 12 of the Dogmatic Constitution on *Divine Revelation* said that in order to avoid a simplistic and misleading fundamentalism, those who read the scriptures need to keep the following points in mind:

1. Attention must be paid to the literary forms of the scripture, e.g. historical, poetic, prophetic, apocalyptic etc.
2. The customary modes of expression at the time of writing.
3. The content and unity of the whole of scripture has to be taken into consideration.
4. Account too must be taken of the harmony between different elements of the faith.
5. All interpretations of scripture must ultimately be subject to the judgement of the church.

Clearly there is a need for Catholic parishes, not only to encourage a bible-centred spirituality, but also to provide teaching on how to interpret the scriptures according to the mind of the church. It is also important for the clergy to lead by example, e.g. in the way they expound the meaning of the liturgy of the word in their homilies.

The Historical Critical Method
Modern scripture scholarship relies a good deal on what is referred to as the historical critical approach to biblical texts. It consists of three main strands: attention to literary genres; study of their historical context; and an examination of their situation

in life, e.g. who the speaker of a passage was, his role in life, the nature of his audience, and so on. Many liberal scripture scholars are influenced by philosophical presuppositions when they use this method, e.g. if they are influenced by Immanuel Kant they may not accept the supernatural aspects of the texts and tend to ignore them or to explain them away as mythology. Many well educated Catholics and Protestants nowadays tend to interpret the bible in this way.

In the introduction to his *Jesus of Nazareth*, Pope Benedict says, 'The historical-critical method is an indispensable tool, given the structure of the Christian faith.' But he rejects the naturalistic approach and also says that the historical-critical method needs to be used within the wider context of the whole bible. He refers to this methodology, which was familiar to Fathers of the Church, such as Origin and Augustine, as 'canonical exegesis'. It is an holistic approach that sees individual passages not only in the context of their historical situation, but also in the context of the entire bible which has a christological dimension from beginning to end. It also takes account of church tradition, i.e. tried and tested interpretations such as those of the Fathers, which reflect the *sensus fidelium* (the faith of the people of God). Added to this is what is known as the analogy of faith. It refers to testing to see whether a particular interpretation of scripture corresponds to the overall teaching of the church.

Pope Benedict reiterated that point in the apostolic declaration on *The Word of God*, when he wrote: 'The Synod Fathers rightly stated that the positive fruit yielded by the use of modern historical-critical research is undeniable. While today's academic exegesis, including that of Catholic scholars, is highly competent in the field of historical-critical methodology and its latest developments, it must be said that comparable attention needs to be paid to the theological dimension of the biblical texts.'

For example, I have heard Gene Robinson, a homosexual bishop in the Episcopal Church of America, argue that when St Paul wrote Rom 1:22-27 he was actually talking about heterosexuals who engage in same-sex acts and not homosexuals. He said, 'We have to understand that the notion of a homosexual sexual orientation is a notion that's only about 125 years old.'

Others say that the New Testament is not condemning homosexual acts as such, but rather it is condemning a permissive and lewd approach to them. While I'm sure that a narrow understanding of the historical critical method may offer some kind of textual justification for such interpretations, they would fail on a number of counts as far as Catholic exegesis is concerned. They neither accord with tradition, current teaching, or with other moral teachings of the church to do with intrinsically disordered acts, such as adultery and fornication.

The four traditional senses of scripture
With the Spirit's help, Christians have to learn to interpret the authentic meaning of the scriptures in a non-fundamentalist way. The saints had a good deal of valuable guidance to offer in this regard. St Bede wrote in the 8th century: 'The sacred scriptures are interpreted in a fourfold way.' Speaking about this, pars 115-118 of the *Catechism of the Catholic Church* have this to say: 'According to an ancient tradition, one can distinguish between two senses of scripture: the literal and the spiritual, the latter being subdivided into the allegorical, moral and anagogical senses. The profound concordance of the four senses guarantees all its richness to the living reading of scripture in the church.'

1) The literal sense is the meaning conveyed by the words of scripture and discovered by the historical-critical method which follows rules of sound interpretation: 'All other senses of sacred scripture are based on the literal.' Commenting on the literal sense, *Interpretation of the Bible in Church* says that , 'One arrives at this sense by means of a careful analysis of the text, within its literary and historical context. The principal task of exegesis is to carry out this analysis, making use of all the resources of literary and historical research, with a view to defining the literal sense of the biblical texts with the greatest possible accuracy.' Not many of us are trained scripture scholars. But all of us can make use of reliable scripture books such as *The New Jerome Scripture Commentary*, in order to discover the literal meaning of the text which was intended by the author.

2) The spiritual sense. Thanks to the unity of God's plan, not only the text of scripture but also the realities and events about which it speaks can be signs.

a) The allegorical sense. We can acquire a more profound understanding of events by recognising their significance in Christ; thus the crossing of the Red Sea is a sign or type of Christ's victory and also of Christian Baptism.

b) The moral sense. The events reported in scripture ought to lead us to act justly. As St Paul says, they were written 'for our instruction'.

c) The anagogical sense (Greek: *anagoge*, 'leading'). We can view realities and events in terms of their eternal significance, leading us toward our true homeland: thus the church on earth is a sign of the heavenly Jerusalem.

A medieval couplet summarises the significance of the four senses: 'The Letter speaks of deeds; Allegory to faith; The Moral how to act; Anagogy our destiny.' Let us take an example of what the church teaches, to do with the temple in Jerusalem:

1) The Literal Sense

Firstly, there is the literal or historical meaning. It is discovered by painstaking research which seeks to find out such things as the historical background and meanings intended by the authors of the different biblical books which may be historical, poetic, sapiential, prophetic etc. For example, over the centuries there were three temples. Archaeology has discovered a lot about the one which was built by ten thousand men during the reign of King Herod the Great just before Jesus was born. We know that some of the perfectly cut stones in its massive walls were approximately 567 to 628 tons in weight. It's adornment, including gold decorations, was completed in 64 AD. At 35 acres in area, it was the largest religious building in the world. It is estimated that the temple courts could hold up to 300,000 people. Is it any wonder that in Mk 13:1 we read, 'As he was leaving the temple, one of his disciples said to him, "Look, Teacher! What massive stones! What magnificent buildings!"'

The dimensions of the temple's four sides were, north 351 yards, south 309, east 518, and west 536. There were porticos on the north, east and west sides which were 45 feet wide. They had ornate carved roofs which were supported by 30 feet high pillars. The Royal Portico on the southern side was the most impressive with 162 fifty feet high pillars which were surmounted

CHAPTER NINE

by Corinthian capitals. The inner temple building which contained the Holy of Holies stood in the centre of the court of the gentiles. It was surrounded by a high wall which enclosed courts for Jewish men, women and priests, together with the altar of sacrifice. Speaking about the Holy of Holies, Heb 9:7 says, 'But only the high priest entered the inner room, and that only once a year, and never without blood, which he offered for himself and for the sins the people had committed in ignorance.' Jesus was circumcised in the temple as a baby, found there at the age of twelve, and ministered within its precincts during his public ministry. He forecast the destruction of the temple in Mt 24:1-2 and his words were fulfilled in 70 AD by the Roman army.

2) The allegorical sense
Secondly, there is the allegorical or metaphorical meaning of scripture texts. Frequently an object or event represents everlasting truths which are indirectly intimated in the text. For example, Jesus mentioned his body when he referred in a metaphorical way to the temple. He said, 'Destroy this temple, and I will raise it again in three days' (Jn 2:19). In other texts mention of the temple in Jerusalem could be interpreted in a symbolic way as a reference to the body of a Christian. In 1 Cor 6:19 we read, 'Do you not know that your body is a temple of the Holy Spirit, who is in you, whom you have received from God?' The people of God are also referred to as a temple. For instance, when he addressed the Christian community Paul said: 'Don't you know that you yourselves are God's temple and that God's Spirit lives in you? If anyone destroys God's temple, God will destroy him; for God's temple is sacred, and you are that temple' (1 Cor 3:16-17).

3) The moral sense
Thirdly, the church refers to the moral sense of the scriptures. They are intended to lead us to act appropriately as Christians. St Paul had this in mind when he said that the scriptures were written 'for our instruction' (cf 2 Tim 3:16). If the temple in Jerusalem was to be interpreted in this moral sense, it could be seen as a symbol of the human body and its various experiences. Speaking about this, St Paul says: 'Flee from sexual immorality.

All other sins a man commits are outside his body, but he who sins sexually sins against his own body. Do you not know that your body is a temple of the Holy Spirit?' (1 Cor 6:18-19).

4) The anagogical sense
Fourthly, the church refers to the anagogical sense of scripture texts which are about future events and heavenly things. When Christians appreciate the deeper spiritual meaning of a text, it can contain intimations of transcendental and eternal realities. For instance when Jesus predicted the destruction of the temple in Jerusalem (Mt 24:1-2), it was also a symbolic image of the end times. In Rev 11:19 the temple becomes a symbol of God's eternal dwelling: 'Then God's temple in heaven was opened, and within his temple was seen the ark of his covenant.'

The full sense of scripture
Some contemporary scholars have added a new category, the deeper or fuller sense of scripture. Biblical scholar Ray Brown said in his book *The Sensus Plenior of Sacred Scripture* (1955) that it refers to, 'That additional, deeper meaning, intended by God but not clearly intended by the human author, which is seen to exist in the words of a biblical text (or group of texts, or even a whole book) when they are studied in the light of further revelation or development in the understanding of revelation.' For example, we are told in Ex 17:6 that Moses struck a rock in the wilderness, and water flowed out to nourish the people. This passage describes a very real historical event. However, in the light of later events this event was also seen as a symbol of how the waters of saving grace flowed from the wounded side of Christ, the Rock of salvation, as he hung upon the cross. That theme is also related to Christ as the living temple in Rev 21:22. Then in Rev 22:1-2, we are told that: 'The angel showed me the river of the water of life, as clear as crystal, flowing from the throne of God and of the Lamb [in the midst of the temple] down the middle of the great street of the city. On each side of the river stood the tree of life, bearing twelve crops of fruit, yielding its fruit every month. And the leaves of the tree are for the healing of the nations.' Brown would argue that while the author of Exodus did not know about the rock being a symbol of

Christ the living temple, that meaning, though not consciously intended, was implicit in what he wrote.

Problematic passages in the bible
Anyone who reads the bible, especially the Old Testament, is well aware that it contains very off putting material to do with wanton violence and immorality. Here is just one shocking example. The Jews had been captives in Babylon. Finally they were freed. In Ps 137:9 we read these vengeful and merciless words: 'O Babylon, you will be destroyed. Happy is the one who pays you back for what you have done to us. Happy is the one who takes your babies and smashes them against the rocks!' How should we interpret off-putting passages like these? In the apostolic declaration, *The Word of God,* Pope Benedict says: 'It must be remembered first and foremost that biblical revelation is *deeply rooted in history* (my italics). God's plan is manifested progressively and it is accomplished slowly, in successive stages and despite human resistance. God chose a people and patiently worked to guide and educate them. Revelation is suited to the cultural and moral level of distant times and thus describes facts and customs, such as cheating and trickery, and acts of violence and massacre, without explicitly denouncing the immorality of such things.' In other words, there is an evolution of moral and religious consciousness evident in the Old Testament. Whereas in the earliest passages there is a tendency to project human characteristics on to God, such as anger, retribution, and jealousy, in the later writings anthropomorphic tendencies are less in evidence. For example, whereas King David was a violent man, his descendent Jesus was opposed to violence.

French-American cultural critic, René Girard, argues in his influential books, such as *Violence and the Sacred, Things* and *Scapegoat,* that Jesus exposed the folly of violence. He argues that violence is the result of scapegoating, i.e. projecting all that is vile and negative on to one's enemies who are mistreated, abused and even killed. Ironically, when people band together to attack the enemy they experience a quasi religious sense of belonging. He also talks about the phenomenon of 'sacred violence' such as rebellions, uprisings and civil wars that often become the foundation stones of political systems. Ironically, although a state may have been founded on a sacralised act of violence, such as the rebellion of 1916 in Ireland, the threat of subsequent violence to gain one's political aims is anathema and opposed by the state.

Girard shows that paradoxically, in the New Testament, the all-powerful Lord of history was the innocent victim of merciless violence, not its perpetrator. The story of the crucifixion invites those who contemplate it, to see scapegoating violence as unjustifiable, and to recognise their own complicity in it. By acclaiming the victim as Lord, the gospels slowly begin to awaken an empathy for victims and oppressed minorities everywhere. As soon as people sense the sufferings of victims instead of objectifying and demonising them in an impersonal way, violence becomes problematic and harder and harder to justify. So according to Girard the teaching of the New Testament transcends the justification of violence which is evident in the Old Testament. As Jesus said, 'Love your enemies, do good to those who hate you, bless those who curse you, pray for those who mistreat you. If someone strikes you on one cheek, turn to him the other also' (Lk 6:27-29).

Conclusion

I do not think there will be any in-depth renewal of a genuine kind unless there is a return to reading and praying the scriptures. As par 21 of the Dogmatic Constitution on Divine Revelation reminds us, besides being useful for devotional reading and meditation, the scriptures are meant to become the very source of our strength and hope: 'For in the sacred books, the Father who is in heaven meets his children with great love and speaks with them; and the force and power in the word of God is so great that it stands as the support and energy of the church, the strength of faith for her sons, the food of the soul, the pure and everlasting source of spiritual life. Consequently these words are perfectly applicable to sacred scripture: "For the word of God is living and active" (Heb. 4:12) and "it has power to build you up and give you your heritage among all those who are sanctified" (Acts 20:32; 1 Thess. 2:13).'

Two extremes have to be avoided when reading and praying the scriptures. On the one hand, we have to avoid doing so in an un-nuanced, literal way. On the other hand, we have to avoid a mistake that well-informed, but under evangelised Christians are inclined to make, by putting too much emphasis on a rationalistic, un-supernatural approach to the biblical texts. It could be said that piety without scholarship can lead to naïve forms of subjectivism, while scholarship without piety can lead to lifeless head knowledge; but scholarship informed by heartfelt piety leads to a transformation of one's Christian understanding and way of acting.

CHAPTER TEN

Claiming the Promises of Scripture

Most believers ask God for graces and favours. Some do so with great intensity and sincerity. Yet despite Christ's many promises to answer prayer, they often experience disappointment. The ailing child eventually dies. The unemployed relative fails to get a job. The woman enduring arthritic pain continues to suffer. The terrible war continues year after year. Not surprisingly the question is asked: 'Why doesn't God respond to our requests?' Ultimately only the Lord knows (cf Rom 11:34). That said, Jesus repeatedly promises in the gospels that our petitions will be answered.

To come to terms with this problem we need, firstly to look at what the bible has to say about the promises of God in general, and those to do with petitionary prayer in particular. According to the *Shorter Oxford Dictionary* a promise is a: 'declaration made to another person with respect to the future, stating that one will do, or refrain from doing some specified act, or that one will give some specified thing'. Promises are usually associated with specified conditions, eg: 'If you make a down payment of 20,000 euro by Friday next, and a further payment of 300,000 euro by 10 May next year, then I promise to sell you my house even if I get a better offer in the meantime.' There are two main reasons why promises like this are not kept. On the one hand, either the person who made the promise had no intention of carrying it out, or as things worked out he or she was unable to do so. On the other hand, the person to whom the promise was made may have been either unwilling or unable to meet the stated conditions.

When God makes a promise, God is both willing and able to fulfil it. As Heb 10:23 reminds us: 'He who has promised is faithful.' The author of 2 Tim 2:13 adds: 'God remains faithful for he cannot deny himself.' In Heb 6:16-17 we read: 'When a man takes an oath, he is calling upon someone greater than himself to force him to do what he has promised or to punish him if he later refuses to do it; the oath ends all argument about it. God also bound himself with an oath, so that those he promised to

CHAPTER TEN

help would be perfectly sure and never need to wonder whether he might change his plans.' In other words, Christians are sure of the promises of God because they are sure of the God of the promises, who swears by his own self that what has been promised will be fulfiled. Understood in that sense, sure hope for the future is the offspring of a certain faith in the present (cf Heb 11:2).

Like, human promises, those God makes are usually associated with conditions. For example, we often pray for peace. In 2 Chron 7:14 we read this reassuring promise: 'If my people who bear my name humble themselves and pray and seek my presence and turn from their wicked way, then I will listen from heaven and forgive their sins and restore their country.' In this verse the Lord undertakes to fulfill three promises if and when the people fulfill four designated conditions. It is no different in the gospels. In Mt 11:28-30 Jesus promises: 'Come to me, all that are weary and are carrying heavy burdens, and I will give you rest.' Understandably, many hassled people stop short at this point by focusing on the promise. But in the next verse the Lord mentions two conditions: 'Take my yoke upon you, ie the great commandment of love, and learn from me; for I am gentle and humble of heart, then you will find rest for your souls.' It is my firm belief that one of the principal reasons why we experience disappointment in petitionary prayer is the fact that while we hear what God promises to do in response to petitionary prayer, we often fail to either notice or to fulfil the associated conditions.

The Example of Abraham and Mary

Abraham was outstanding for his unwavering trust in God. Although he and his wife were senior citizens the Lord promised that they would have a child who would become the father of a great nation. Abraham believed what God had told him without 'leaning on his understanding' (Prov 3:5). In due course Isaac was born. Speaking about the faith of Abraham, St Paul commented: 'Without weakening in his faith, he faced the fact that his body was as good as dead – since he was about a hundred years old – and that Sarah's womb was also dead. Yet he did not waver through unbelief regarding the promise of God, but was strengthened in his faith and gave glory to God, being fully persuaded that God had power to do what he had promised' (Rom 4:19-21). No wonder the fourth Eucharist Prayer refers to Abraham as our 'Father in faith'.

Surely, the Virgin Mary is our mother in faith. When Gabriel appeared to her he promised her that she would become the mother of the Messiah, by the overshadowing of the Holy Spirit, to whom nothing is impossible. In response, Mary said: 'May it be to me as you have said' (Lk 1:38). Instead of relying on her limited, rational understanding, she trusted in God with all her heart. She knew how the Lord had said that his divine word would not return to him without achieving the purpose for which it was sent (cf Is 55:10-11). If we were to ask those who have devotion to Mary why she is blessed, I think we would get a great variety of answers. While their responses would probably be true in a general sense, it is interesting to note what God says through the prophetic lips of Elizabeth: 'Blessed is she who has believed that what the Lord has promised will be accomplished.' (Lk 1:45). In other words, Mary like Abraham is blessed, principally because of her trust in the God of the promises and in the promises of God. If, like Abraham and Mary, we want to live by faith, we need to take shelter under the umbrella of God's promises in all the events of our lives.

A remarkable promise
The bible contains numerous promises which God made to his people. However, St Paul pointed to their Christocentric focus when he observed in 2 Cor 1:20: 'For no matter how many promises God has made, they are "Yes" in Christ. And so through him the "Amen" is spoken by us to the glory of God.' While the promises in the Old Testament came to fulfilment in Christ, Jesus himself made many wonderful promises himself. In this chapter I want to focus on one in particular. Among other things, I believe that it has great implications for the new evangelisation called for by Popes John Paul II and Benedict XVI. In the RSV translation we read: 'Truly, truly, I say to you, he who believes in me will also do the works that I do; and greater works than these will he do, because I go to the Father. Whatever you ask in my name, I will do it, that the Father may be glorified in the Son; if you ask anything in my name, I will do

CHAPTER TEN

it' (Jn 14:12-14). This promise can evoke the very faith that it presupposes for its fulfilment. As St Paul says in Rom 10:17: 'Faith comes from hearing the message, and the message is heard through the word of Christ.' The word of Christ is 'living and active' (Heb 4:12), 'spirit and life' (Jn 6:63), and will not return to God without achieving the purpose for which it was sent (cf Is 55:11).

Jesus was so united with his Father that he could say in Jn 10:30: 'I and the Father are one.' As far as his sinless human nature was concerned the Holy Spirit enabled him to constantly receive revelation from God. As he said himself: 'For I did not speak of my own accord, but the Father who sent me *commanded me what to say and how to say it* [my italics]' (Jn 12:49-50). On another occasion he said: 'I tell you the truth, the Son can do nothing by himself; he can do only what he sees his Father doing, because whatever the Father does the Son also does' (Jn 5:19-20). In the Greek of John's gospel, Jesus introduced his promise in 14:12-14 with the words: 'Amen, amen.' They are derived from the Hebrew word *'mn*, meaning 'to show oneself firm and stable.' In other words Jesus is saying: 'Just as my Father is reliable, dependable and faithful you can rely on me when I say that the person who believes in me will do the works that I do, and even greater works.' What did Jesus do? It could be argued that he did three main things.

The deeds of Jesus
Firstly, he related to people in a merciful and loving way and acted accordingly. He testified: 'As the Father has loved me, so have I loved you' (Jn 15:9). In 1 Cor 13:4-7 St Paul described the qualities of that love. We could slightly rephrase his words to read: 'Jesus is patient, Jesus is kind. He does not envy, he does not boast, he is not proud. He is not rude, he is not self-seeking, he is not easily angered, he keeps no record of wrongs. Jesus does not delight in evil but rejoices with the truth. Jesus always protects, always trusts, always hopes, always perseveres.' All of Jesus' dealings with people were informed by these and other qualities of love. It could be argued that the love of Jesus was epitomised by his compassion. St Thomas Aquinas says that 'compassion is heartfelt identification with another's distress,

driving us to do what we can to help ... As far as outward activity is concerned, compassion is a Christian's whole rule of life,' and we can add, just as it was in the life of Jesus.

Secondly, in his preaching and teaching Jesus proclaimed the good news of the coming of the kingdom of God by means of the free gift of his Father's unconditional mercy and love. In Lk 4:22 we are told that: 'All spoke well of him and were amazed at the gracious words that came from his lips.' Again in Mt 7:28-29 we are told that: 'The crowds were amazed at his teaching, because he taught as one who had authority.' In Jn 7:46 we are informed that the temple guards could not bring themselves to arrest Jesus, as the Pharisees had instructed them to do, because 'No one ever spoke the way this man does.'

Thirdly, Jesus demonstrated the coming of the kingdom by performing deeds of power. As John Paul II said, in par 14 of *Redemptoris Missio*, 'Jesus' many healings clearly show his great compassion in the face of human distress, but they also signify that in the kingdom there will no longer be sickness or suffering, and that his mission, from the very beginning, is meant to free people from these evils. In Jesus' eyes, healings are also a sign of spiritual salvation, namely liberation from sin. By performing acts of healing, he invites people to faith, conversion and the desire for forgiveness (cf. Lk 5:24). 'When John the Baptist was facing execution in prison we are told that he sent messengers to Jesus. They asked him, "Are you the one who was to come, or should we expect someone else?"' (Lk 7:20). Jesus responded: 'Go back and report to John what you have seen and heard: The blind receive sight, the lame walk, those who have leprosy are cured, the deaf hear, the dead are raised, and the good news is preached to the poor' (Lk 7:22-23). On another occasion when Jesus encountered unbelief and antagonism he said: 'Why then do you accuse me of blasphemy because I said, I am God's Son"? Do not believe me unless I do what my Father does. But if I do it, even though you do not believe me, believe the miracles, that you may know and understand that the Father is in me, and I in the Father' (Jn 10:37-39). In the post resurrection period Peter was able to say: 'You know what has happened throughout Judea, beginning in Galilee after the baptism that John preached – how God anointed Jesus of Nazareth with the Holy

CHAPTER TEN

Spirit and power, and how he went around doing good and healing all who were under the power of the devil, because God was with him' (Acts 10:37-38).

During his public ministry it is clear that Jesus commissioned the apostles to do what he had being doing. For instance, in Mt 10:5-8 we are told: 'These twelve Jesus sent out with the following instructions: "Do not go among the Gentiles or enter any town of the Samaritans. Go rather to the lost sheep of Israel. As you go, preach this message: 'The kingdom of heaven is near.' Heal the sick, raise the dead, cleanse those who have leprosy, drive out demons."' Before he ascended to his Father in heaven Jesus reiterated that commission when he said: 'Go into all the world and preach the good news to all creation ... And these signs will accompany those who believe: In my name they will drive out demons ... they will place their hands on sick people, and they will get well' (Mk 16:15-18).

Deeds of power in the early church

It is clear in the Acts of the Apostles that, besides acting and speaking in a loving and compassionate way, the first believers did perform deeds of power. For instance, we are told that: 'The apostles performed many miraculous signs and wonders among the people' (Acts 5:12). St Paul also performed many deeds of power. He acknowledged that they were an integral part of his evangelisation. For instance he testified: 'My message and my preaching were not with wise and persuasive words, but with a demonstration of the Spirit's power, so that your faith might not rest on men's wisdom, but on God's power} (1 Cor 2:4-5). For instance, Paul raised Eutychus from the dead (Acts 20:9-10) and when he was in Malta, apparently he healed every sick person who was brought to him (Acts 26:9). It is not surprising therefore that in 1 Cor 14:1 he said that the believers should make love their aim and 'eagerly desire spiritual gifts', including the ability to perform deeds of power. In 1 Cor 12:9-10 he referred specifically to those gifts in these words: 'To each is given the manifestation of the Spirit for the common good. To one is given through the Spirit ... faith by the same Spirit, to another gifts of healing by the one Spirit, to another the working of miracles.'

We know that in the early Christian centuries the evangelisation of the believers was often accompanied by deeds of power. For instance, St Irenaeus (2nd century), who was a disciple of John the evangelist, wrote: 'Those who are in truth his disciples, receiving grace from him, do in his name perform miracles, so as to promote the welfare of other men, according to the gift which each one has received from him. For some do certainly and truly drive out devils, so that those who have thus been cleansed from evil spirits frequently both believe in Christ, and join themselves to the church. Others have foreknowledge of things to come: they see visions, and utter prophetic expressions. Others still, heal the sick by laying their hands upon them, and they are made whole. Yea, moreover, as I have said, the dead even have been raised up, and remained among us for many years ... The name of our Lord Jesus Christ even now confers benefits [upon people], and cures thoroughly and effectively all who anywhere believe on him.' Can modern believers expect to do the kinds of deeds described by the apostles and St Iranaeus?

Reasons for contemporary doubts
It would seem that the way in which people understand the promise of Jesus in Jn 14:12-14 is influenced by the environment in which we live. A number of factors effect the way in which people interpret it.

Firstly, although we do witness extraordinarily loving lives, and occasionally hear anointed preaching and teaching, there has not been much evidence of deeds of power in recent centuries. In spite of offering many prayers of intercession for others, most parishioners would rarely if ever hear of people being healed as a result of sacramental or non sacramental ministry. As a result it is not surprising that they tend to rationalise the promise of Jesus by interpreting it in a metaphorical way. For example, John Marsh says in his commentary *St John*, that rather than focusing on Jesus' deeds of power such as healings and exorcisms, we should focus on their purpose, namely, to enlighten the eyes of the heart in such a way that people are lead to conversion. He maintains that modern believers can do what Jesus did, and even greater things, by bringing more people to faith than the Lord ever did, by relying on the witness of a compassionate life and inspiring preaching, rather than healings or

CHAPTER TEN

miracles. Some Christians would support this point of view with what is known as the cessationist theory. They argue that the gifts were given to the early believers in order to get the church established. Afterwards they were withdrawn. For example, although St Augustine changed his mind on this point, he once said: 'For those that are baptised do not now receive the Spirit on the imposition of hands, so as to speak in the tongues of all the peoples; neither are the sick healed by the shadow of the preachers of Christ falling on them as they pass; and other such things as were then done, are now manifestly ceased.'

Secondly, since the rise of science in the post-Enlightenment period there has been a growing tendency to exclude the supernatural realm. Many liberal scripture scholars, such as Rudolf Bultmann, are influenced by rationalist presuppositions which reject miraculous occurrences as mere mythology. For example, in his interesting and informative book *The Historical Figure of Jesus*, well-known scripture scholar, E. P. Sanders, says that he agrees with the following quotation from Cicero (106-43 AD): 'For nothing can happen without cause; nothing happens that cannot happen, and when what was capable of happening has happened, it may not be interpreted as a miracle. Consequently there are no miracles ... We therefore draw this conclusion: what was incapable of happening never happened, and what was capable of happening is not a miracle' (*De Divinatione* 2.28). He explains away the healings of Jesus as psychosomatic in nature, and the exorcisms as a primitive form of magic or suggestion. He explains the miracles of Jesus in purely natural terms, eg the stilling of the storm was a coincidence, when Jesus appeared to be walking on water he was in fact walking on land, and he has recourse to group psychology in order to explain the feeding of the multitude. When Jesus and the disciples started sharing their food, everyone in the crowd, who had brought food with them, was encouraged to do the same. Nowadays, an increasing number of well-educated Catholics and Protestants tend to interpret the Bible in the same reductionist way.

To establish both the meaning and practical implication of the two extraordinary verses in Jn 14:12-13, I will firstly examine what St Thomas Aquinas had to say about them; that will be followed by a look at the way in which some contemporary scripture scholars interpret the same verses; and finally, I will reflect on the theological meaning and some of the practical implications which these verses imply for the contemporary church.

St Thomas Aquinas on Jn 14:12-13

Pars 48-49 of *Verbum Domini*, the Post-synodal Declaration of Benedict XVI observe: 'The interpretation of sacred scripture would remain incomplete were it not to include listening to those who have truly lived the word of God: namely, the saints. ... The most profound interpretation of scripture comes precisely from those who let themselves be shaped by the word of God through listening, reading and assiduous meditation.' St Thomas Aquinas is referred to as the Angelic Doctor because of his supernatural gifts of wisdom and knowledge. His views on Jn 14:12-14 can be found in two main places. Firstly, at the request of Pope Urban IV, he compiled a continuous commentary on all four gospels, entitled the *Catena Aurea*, or 'Golden Chain'. It consisted of relevant comments from Latin and Greek fathers of the church on every verse in the four gospels. Bl Cardinal Newman translated this formidable work into English in the nineteenth century. Secondly, Thomas wrote a large commentary of his own on the fourth gospel. Although Jn 14:12-13 consists of about 50 words, he devoted no less than 2,071 words commenting on the short passage. It is obvious from his many references to the fathers of the church that his exegesis was deeply influenced by them.

Before looking at what St Thomas said about the verses in question, it needs to be pointed out that his approach to the scriptures differed from that of modern scripture scholars who use such things as archeology, philology and the historical critical method in order to get at the meaning of texts. All that Thomas had at his disposal was his personal copy of the bible, the teaching of all the Latin and Greek fathers, and his own prayerful reflection on the text which was informed by his encyclopaedic knowledge of logic, philosophy and theology. It is quite possible that he had committed the whole of the bible to memory when he was imprisoned by his family, which later enabled him to quote it at will. Thomas had four main aims when he wrote his commentary on St John.

CHAPTER TEN

1. He wanted to establish the literal, or historical, sense of the narrative.
2. He wanted to explain the spiritual sense in four interrelated ways. There was a medieval couplet which succinctly said: 'The letter speaks of deeds; allegory about the faith; The moral about our actions; anagogy about our destiny.'
3. He wanted to refute doctrinal error by referring to the inspired Word of God.
4. He wanted to confirm people in the Catholic faith given by God through his church, the Body of Christ.

Having quoted our Lord's words: 'Truly, truly, I say to you, he who believes in me will also do the works that I do', he went on to say: 'For just as the Son acts because the Father dwells in him by a unity of nature, so also those who believe act because Christ dwells in them by faith: that Christ may dwell in your hearts through faith' (Eph 3:17). 'Now the works which Christ accomplished and the disciples do by the power of Christ are miracles.' It is clear from this statement that St Thomas interpreted our Lord's words in a literal way. Then he went on to quote Jesus' promise that believers would do greater deeds than the ones he himself had performed. He explained how this could be possible by offering two examples which he borrowed from St Augustine. Firstly, while the woman with the issue of blood was healed when she touched the garment of Jesus, people were healed by the mere shadow of Peter falling upon them. Secondly, he said that when Jesus encouraged the rich young man to sell his possessions he failed to respond, whereas when Peter preached after Pentecost people sold their possessions and brought the money to lay it at the feet of the apostles (Acts 4:34). While those examples are relevant up to a point, it is a little surprising that he did not advert to the fact that Jesus raised dead people like Lazarus to life. In that instance it is hard to see how believers equal what he did, still less do greater things. However, even in this instance he could have adverted to the fact that from St Paul onward saints such as St Francis of Assisi have raised people from the dead. Finally, Thomas made the important observation that the promises of Jesus were not restricted to the apostles but extended to all those, including the present generation, who believe in him. Implicit in this point is a rejection of the cessationist theory of the charisms, namely that they died out as soon as the church was well established.

Thomas went on to say that the mighty promises of Jesus were related to the fact that he was going to his Father. He said that this truth has three possible implications. Firstly, although Jesus worked as long as he was in the world, the believers took his place after his ascension. Secondly, although the Jews thought that faith in Jesus would be eradicated if Jesus was killed, this did not happen. In fact it grew stronger, thereby enabling the believers to do greater things than Jesus as a result of their union with their risen Lord. Thirdly, since Jesus has received even greater glory in heaven than he had on earth it is understandable that he promised to manifest that glory by giving believers the power to do greater things than he himself had performed.

Thomas went on to state that what he had said by way of comment on the words of Jesus is underpinned by the promise of the Lord to answer prayer: 'Whatever you ask in my name, I will do it.' This is a powerful undertaking to respond to petitionary and intercessory prayers which are made in the name of Jesus, even to the point of healings and miracles. Thomas said that sometimes God postpones doing what we ask so that our desire for it will increase and so that he can grant it at the right time. We all know that sometimes it appears as if God fails to answer our prayers. Firstly, Thomas explains that this may be due to the fact that it is a worldly prayer which does not pertain to salvation. He wrote: 'The reason being that our Lord does not just look at one's desire, but rather the helpfulness of what is desired.' Secondly: 'We may ask for something which does not pertain to our salvation in our ignorance. We sometimes ask for what we think is helpful, but really is not. But God takes care of us, and does not do what we ask. Thus Paul, who laboured more than all others, asked our Lord three times to take away a thorn in his flesh, but he did not receive what he asked because it was not useful for him' (2 Cor 12:8).

Thomas then goes on to comment on the words: 'Whatever you ask in my name, I will do it, that the Father may be glorified in the Son.' He says that Augustine punctuates this passage in

CHAPTER TEN

the following way: 'Whatever you ask the Father in my name, I will do it.' Then he begins a new sentence which reads: 'That the Father may be glorified in the Son, if you ask me anything in my name, I will do it.' This is like saying: 'I will do what you ask in my name so that the Father may be glorified in the Son, and everything that the Son does is directed to the glory of the Father.' 'I do not seek my own glory' (Jn 8:50). We also should direct all our works to the glory of God: 'Do all to the glory of God' (1 Cor 10:31). Not only is Jesus the glory of the Father for us, the sign of the Father's presence to us, the revelation of his love, power, and wisdom; he is also God's glory in us who accept him in living faith and who acts in us and through us in response to prayers offered in the name of Jesus with expectant faith. This notion had a central role to play in the spirituality of St Ignatius of Loyola.

It is worth mentioning the fact that St Thomas discussed the charisms of power in 1 Cor 12:8-10 in his *Commentary on First Corinthians*. He returned to that same subject in a thirty-thousand word section of his *Summa Theologica*, and again briefly in his *Summa Contra Gentiles*. He divided the charisms into three groups, those of revelation, proclamation and demonstration. The latter include healings and miracle working. In 1979, Francis McNutt gave memorable expression to the Thomistic understanding of the role of deeds of power in effective evangelisation in an article entitled 'What God has joined together.' It was about the complementary relationship between the charismatic and the institutional elements in the church. He wrote: 'A gift of preaching is strengthened by other manifestations of the power of the Holy Spirit. St Paul states that in his sermons he did not depend on arguments that belonged to philosophy but on a "demonstration of the Spirit and power"' (1 Cor 2:4). St Thomas Aquinas, in his commentary on this passage, states that the preacher of the gospel should preach as Jesus did, confirming the message either through healings and miracles or by living such a holy life that can only be explained by the power of the Spirit. If I preach the power of Jesus Christ to save and redeem the whole person, people want to see that power made real. They want to see the saving, freeing power of Jesus when we pray that the spiritually sick be given the power to repent, and that the emotionally and physically sick be healed, and may be made better as a sign that the message of salvation and healing are true.'

Some contemporary interpretation of Jn 14:12-14
In the foreword of his book *Jesus of Nazareth*, Pope Benedict XVI wrote in an illuminating way about modern scripture scholarship in general, and about the benefits and limitations of the historical critical method in particular. He warned on the one hand about the dangers of a secularised and reductionist interpretation of texts, and on the other against a naïve fundamentalism that interprets them in an uncritical, and literal way. In his post-synodal declaration, *Verbum Domini*, Benedict wrote: 'The Dogmatic Constitution indicates three fundamental criteria for an appreciation of the divine dimension of the bible:

1) The text must be interpreted with attention to the unity of the whole of scripture: nowadays this is called canonical exegesis;
2) Account is be taken of the living tradition of the whole church; and, finally,
3) Respect must be shown for the analogy of faith, ie interpreting particular scripture truths in the light of the whole of Christian dogma. 'Only where both methodological levels, the historical-critical and the theological, are respected, can one speak of a theological exegesis.'

In this section I propose to look at what some exegetes have said about Jn 14:12-14.

The late Raymond Brown (1928-1998) was probably the premier Johannine scripture scholar writing in English in the last generation. In 1970 he published vol 2 of his commentary, *The Gospel According to John, XIII-XXI*. He began his exegesis of Jn 14:12-14 by stating, as was already noted above, that in the Greek text, Jesus begins by saying: 'Amen, Amen I say to you.' Brown summarises its meaning as follows: 'Jesus has heard from the Father all he says (Jn 7:26, 28) and the "amen" with which he introduces what he says assures that God guarantees the truth of his statements.' Brown understands the Lord's promise that the believers will do the works he did, in a literal way. According to him, the idea that Jesus' disciples were and

CHAPTER TEN

would be given power to perform marvellous works is found in many New Testament writings. He points out that while the word 'works' could certainly apply to healings and miracles – in this regard he refers to Mt 21:21; Mk 16:17-18; Acts 3:6; 9:34;40 – it would also be true to say that in John there is less emphasis on the marvellous character of the greater works, than in the other gospels.

Brown suggests that Christ's reference to the 'greater works' may refer to Jn 5:20-22 which reads: 'For the Father loves the Son and shows him all he does. Yes, to your amazement he will show him even greater things than these. For just as the Father raises the dead and gives them life, even so the Son gives life to whom he is pleased to give it. Moreover, the Father judges no one, but has entrusted all judgement to the Son.' These verses are about giving supernatural life and judging. The disciples will bring Jesus' life to others by 'bearing fruit' (Jn 15:16), and will share in judging by the power they receive over sin (Jn 20:21-23) and by the gift of the Paraclete 'who will prove the world wrong about judgement' (Jn 16:8,11). Brown says that the promise of 'greater works' is possible because of the changed situation after Jesus' resurrection. It would probably true to say that while Brown does believe that Jesus refers, among other things, to the believer's ability to perform deeds of power in the name of Jesus, he sees them as a means to an end. As a result, he says, that the focus should shift from the deeds themselves to their purpose. Implicit in that point is the fact that God's purposes can often be achieved without deeds of power. There have been many saints, among them Vincent de Paul, who were very successful evangelists who did not perform deeds of power.

Eminent German scripture scholar, Rudolf Schnackenburg (1914-2002), wrote a massive commentary on John's gospel. In volume three he considered both the promise that Jesus' disciples would do his works, and that God would answer their prayers, as a version of a tradition already referred to in the synoptics. He said: 'A traditional and historical consideration of Mk 11:23-25 will help us here to understand the two promises of Jn 14:12-14. Two of Jesus' sayings are merged together in this synoptic text: faith that is free from all doubt has the strength to move mountains; and prayer in faith is always heard. The early church was very preoccupied with the promise of miraculous power ... The fourth evangelist was also familiar with this tradition ... and included it in his theology.' Schnackenburg saw Jesus as the one who makes this possible: 'The works that Jesus promises every believer will do are consciously placed alongside Jesus' own works in the text and this juxtaposition suggests a possible interpretation, namely that the one who is really acting in these works is Jesus himself, even after his departure to the Father (see v 13).' The works of Jesus which are performed by those who believe in him need to be understood in light of their goal: 'They have to be seen ... in the same light as Jesus' works on earth ... [as] not simply miracles, but 'signs', with the special intention of pointing either to Jesus as the giver of life or to his gift of life. They are not simply external works, but rather spiritual works which help man to achieve salvation.'

Peter Williamson, a professor of scripture at Sacred Heart Seminary in Detroit says that Jn 14:13 'affirms that believers in Jesus will do miracles like Jesus did, which, like Jesus' own works, point beyond themselves to reveal who Jesus is and the salvation he brings.' Having done so he goes on to nuance and contextualise that statement: 'This writer is inclined to agree with Brown and Schnackenburg. The "greater works" which believers in Jesus will perform are their participation in the Father's work through Jesus of salvation, of giving life and judging. If one word were to be chosen to sum up the "greater works" believers in Jesus will perform, one could perhaps choose "evangelisation".' Jesus' disciples accomplish these "greater works" through their testimony (Jn 19:35; 21:24) in word and deed (Jn 13:35; 17:23) to the truth about Jesus with the help of the Paraclete, which produces the extraordinary result of begetting children of God (Jn 1:12), bringing judgement on the world and sin (Jn 16:8-11; 20:22-23), and becoming themselves the chosen instruments (Jn 15:16) through whom the Father fulfills his intention to save the human race (Jn 3:16-17) by means of the past and present activity of his eternal Son. These works are greater than the miracles which Jesus performed, since they embody the reality to which Jesus' signs pointed, which could not be fulfilled until Jesus was glorified and the Spirit had been given (Jn 7:38-39).'

CHAPTER TEN

A more recent commentary on the fourth gospel has been written by Australian scholar, Francis J. Maloney entitled, *The Gospel of John*. It is clear from what this exegete says about Jn 14:12, that he disagrees with Rudolf Bultmann's view that just as the words and works of Jesus revealed the Father, so the disciples will reveal his presence and purposes as effectively as Jesus by means of effective preaching. Maloney agrees with Raymond Brown when he says that one cannot try to obscure the importance of works, by talking only of kerygmatic preaching. He says: 'The absence of Jesus created by his departure will not lead to the cessation of the works of the Father by which Jesus has made him known but the disciples will not automatically do these greater works. They are exhorted to ask in the name of Jesus so that the works will continue to be done.' Talking about the notion of greater works, Maloney says that many have tried to explain this phrase by saying that Christian missionaries would make many more conversions than Jesus did. However, he says that this point of view does not do theological justice to the words of Jesus. He states: 'The departure of Jesus sets up a privileged in-between-time [ie in between the ascension of Jesus and his coming again at the end of the world]. A feature of that interim time are the greater works, done by Jesus even in his absence.'

Although Maloney implies that Jesus' mention of works and greater works refers to deeds of power, such as healings and miracles, he doesn't say so explicitly. That caution or ambiguity of attitude is also evident in Pheme Perkins's commentary on the same verses in *The New Jerome Biblical Commentary*. Referring to the disciple's ability to do greater things than Jesus she says: 'This saying may have originally referred to the possibility of the disciples doing miracles in the name of Jesus.' This sentence seems to express a two-sided doubt. Firstly, Perkins's use of the word 'originally', implies that while the first disciples may have believed they could do deeds of power, nowadays we could argue that their accounts of healings and miracles are mythological in nature. Secondly, Perkins's use of the word 'originally' implies that nowadays enlightened disciples would not expect to perform deeds of power either because of the cessationist argument, or a naturalist *a priori* assumption that they cannot occur.

Implications for evangelisation

a. *Cesessationism v continuationism*
The church does not accept the cessationist argument which was adverted to a little earlier, and favours what can be referred to as continuationism. This has been obvious in statements made by recent popes. John Paul II said: 'At the beginning of the Christian era extraordinary things were accomplished under the influence of charisms ... This has always been the case in the church and is so in our own day as well.' Pope Benedict echoed those sentiments when he wrote: 'In the heart of a world adversely affected by rationalistic scepticism, a new experience of the Holy Spirit has come about, amounting to a worldwide renewal movement. What the New Testament describes with reference to the charisms as visible signs of the coming of the Spirit is no longer merely ancient, past history: this history is becoming a burning reality today.' It is a significant fact while he was still Cardinal Prefect of the Congregation for the Doctrine of the Faith, Benedict issued an Instruction on Prayers for Healing, which in par 5 gave qualified approval of the exercise of the charism of healing by lay people. It is clear that the two pontiffs assert continuationism as far as deeds of power are concerned. This is largely due to the fact that they have been exercised by faithful people in the past and present, especially since the advent of the Charismatic Movement which was anticipated by the teaching of par 12 of the Dogmatic Constitution, *Lumen Gentium* of the Second Vatican Council. Speaking of the charisms listed in 1 Cor 12:8-10 it says: "These charisms, whether they be the more outstanding or the more simple and widely diffused, are to be received with thanksgiving and consolation for they are perfectly suited to and useful for the needs of the church.'

b. *Filled by the Spirit*
In my experience it usually takes an adult religious awakening, what is sometimes referred to as an infilling, effusion or baptism of the Spirit (cf Eph 3:18), before most Christians become fully aware of the inner presence, guidance, and empowerment of the Lord. A number of bishop's conferences have written about this Christian phenomenon. For instance, in 1994 the Irish Bishops said: 'The outpouring of the Spirit is a conversion gift through

which one receives a new and significant commitment to the Lordship of Jesus, and an openness to the power and gifts of the Holy Spirit.' In 1997 an American Bishops Committee said: 'The grace of baptism in the Holy Spirit is two-fold: it is first and foremost a coming to a living awareness of the true reality of Jesus Christ, as the Son of God who loved us and gave himself up for us, who is the risen Lord and Head of his Body. Secondly, as a result of this grace, there is an increased docility to the Holy Spirit and his power and gifts.' It is clear in charismatic literature that some writers link baptism in the Spirit with the sacraments of baptism and confirmation. In their view this phenomenon is a release or effusion of a grace that is already present. It is a manifestation in consciousness of a potential received in the sacraments of initiation. Other writers stress the fact that baptism in the Spirit not only brings people into a new relationship with Jesus as Lord, this new infilling is often associated with the giving of gifts of the Spirit.

I suspect that the two views of the in-filling of the Spirit are complementary rather than contradictory. This religious experience is rooted in the graces received in the sacraments of initiation, but besides releasing their potential, there is no reason to think that something new, such as the charisms mentioned in 1 Cor 12:8-10, are not added. It has always struck me that when Jesus was baptised in the Spirit in the Jordan, and the apostles and the disciples were inundated by the Holy Spirit in the upper room at Pentecost, not only did they experience an unprecedented manifestation of the length and breadth, the height and depth of the incomprehensible love of God, (cf Eph 3:18) they were also empowered and gifted to witness in an effective way to that love. Whereas Jesus does not seem to have preached or performed any deeds of power before his baptism, there was no stopping him afterwards. It was the same with the first Christians. Following Pentecost they began to proclaim the reign of God's liberating merciful love and to demonstrate its presence by means of healings, exorcisms and miracles. People who are filled (cf Eph 5:18) and transformed by the Spirit (cf 2 Cor 3:18) become living witnesses able to speak of Christ from personal experience and from a deeper understanding of the word of

God. There is usually a new desire to spread the gospel and a new clarity about its content.

c. A Trinitarian understanding

What Jesus promised the apostles and us can only be properly understood within a Trinitarian context. As we have already noted, Jesus repeatedly said that he was fully united with his Father who not only revealed to him what he wanted him to do and say, he also empowered him to do it. That was why Jesus could say to Philip: 'Anyone who has seen me has seen the Father' (Jn 14:9). When we are born again in baptism by water and the Spirit, Jesus lives within us by the Spirit. As Paul put it: 'I no longer live, but Christ lives in me. The life I live in the body, I live by faith in the Son of God, who loved me and gave himself for me' (Gal 2:20-21).

That same point is reiterated in par 521 of the *Catechism of the Catholic Church*. It reads: 'Christ enables us to live in him all that he himself lived, and he lives it in us.' This notion is borrowed from *The Kingdom of Christ in the Souls of Christians* which was written by St John Eudes (1601-1680). In it he said: 'We can say that any true Christian, who is a member of Jesus Christ, and who is united to him by his grace, *continues and completes*, [my italics] through all the actions that he carries out in the spirit of Christ, the actions that Jesus Christ accomplished during the time of his temporary life on earth.' Because of his or her intimate union with Christ and his evangelistic mission, a Christian can be enabled by the Spirit to do in Christ's name, all that he himself did and even greater things. As Paul says in Phil 2:13: 'It is God who works in you to will and to act according to his good purpose.' Notice that Paul asserts three points here:

1) God, by the Spirit of Jesus, lives in the person, as Paul asks rhetorically in 2 Cor 13:5: 'Do you not realise that Christ Jesus is in you?'
2) Christ enables the believer to embrace the Father's holy will which he reveals in ordinary and charismatic ways (cf Gal 5:18) to anyone who is obedient to the law of love (cf Acts 5:32; 2 Jn 6:6).
3) God also empowers the person by the same Spirit that raised Jesus from the dead (cf Eph 1:19), to carry out the

divine will, if necessary even to the point of healings and miracles.

When Christians act lovingly, speak about the kingdom of God, or perform deeds of power through the indwelling of Jesus by the power of the Spirit, God the Father is glorified because his power and presence are manifested in and through them.

d. The Body of Christ

We live in individualistic times. That fact sometimes blinds Christians to the realisation that the gifts of the Spirit are given to individuals as members of Christ's mystical body on earth. It is clear in Paul's references to the gifts in Rom 12:4-6; 1 Cor 12:27-30; Eph 4:11-13 that he sees them as endowments of Christ, in his body the church. There is an important implication of this. Not everyone can expect to have the charism of faith and the ability to perform healings and miracles, but the body or community can. That is why Paul uses phrases such as, 'to some is given ... to another ...' in 1 Cor 12:8-10. The gifts that Christ exercised, are distributed among different members of the church. I think it is because of this awareness that par 12 of the dogmatic Constitution *Lumen Gentium* says: 'Extraordinary gifts are not to be rashly sought after, nor are the fruits of apostolic labour to be presumptuously expected from them.' This cautionary word is addressed to individuals, and to communities. But as was noted above, Paul says in 1 Cor 14:1: 'Make love your aim, and earnestly desire the spiritual gifts.' Is it any wonder that Pope Paul VI said at the launch of Cardinal Suenen's influential book *A New Pentecost?*: 'How wonderful it would be if the Lord would again pour out the charisms in increased abundance, in order to make the church fruitful, beautiful and marvellous, and to enable it to win the attention and astonishment of the profane and secularised world.' Remembering Christ's words: 'I will grant whatever you ask in my name' (Jn 14:14), we need to pray that the Lord will pour out the Spirit and a full spectrum of ordinary and extraordinary gifts upon the contemporary church.

e. The pivotal role of the charism of expectant faith

The gifts of power, which Jesus exercised in the course of his public ministry, are released by the gift of expectant as opposed to hesitant faith. Paul refers to it in 1 Cor 12:9 and 1 Cor 13:2. It could be argued that when Jesus talked about faith, he usually had the unhesitating kind in mind. As he said in Mk 11:24: 'Whatever you ask for in prayer, believe that you have received it, [in the present] and it will be yours [in the future].' It would seem that when Jesus commended a person for having faith, eg the Centurion who asked Jesus to heal his servant (Mt 8:10), or admonished a person for his lack of faith, eg Peter when he was sinking in the lake (Mt 14:31), he had expectant faith in mind. In my experience, and that of many other people, the gift of faith is evoked by an inspired knowledge of God's will which can be revealed by a relevant word of scripture which jumps alive off the page into the heart. It can also be prompted by an inspired word of knowledge which reveals facts about a person or situation, which is not learned through the efforts of the natural mind, but by an intuition freely given by God. It discloses the truth which the Spirit wishes to be known concerning a particular person or situation.

The late Kathryn Kuhlman (1907-1976), one of the best known women evangelists in the twentieth century, was notable for her gift of charismatic faith. Paraphrasing Heb 11:2, she said on one occasion: 'Faith is that quality or power by which the things desired become the things possessed.' Implicit in this definition is the interplay between past and future which has already been adverted to. It is mentioned in texts such as Mk 11:23-24 and 1 Jn 5:14-16. If a person is convinced as a result of an inspiration of the Spirit in the present, that a scripture promise is being fulfilled (in the present), it will be (in the future). In another place Kathryn said: 'Faith is more than belief. It is more than confidence. It is more than trust. It is more than the sum total of these things ... Faith, as God himself imparts it to the heart, is spiritual. It's warm. It's vital. It lives. It throbs. Its power is absolutely irresistible when it is imparted to the heart by the Lord ... Heart belief is faith. Mind belief is nothing more than deep desire combined with mental assent.' Kathryn asserted that the faith she spoke about is a grace, a free gift of the Lord. It is not acquired by good works, acts of service or heroic self-sacrifice. She remarked with disarming simplicity, but great insight: 'You do not pray for faith; you seek the Lord, and faith will come.' Kathryn also said that charismatic faith is not the result of effort of a subjective and self-absorbed kind. Paradoxically, it is when, we forget about ourselves and concentrate on the Lord, by means of contemplative attention, that faith is evoked in the heart. 'Look up', said Kathryn, 'and see Jesus! He is your faith, He is our faith. It is not faith that you must seek, but Jesus.' She said that faith is often compromised, as it was for the apostles during the storm on the lake, by looking at God in the light of the problem, rather than looking at the problem in the light of heartfelt relationship with God.

Conclusion
In the light of all that has been said in this chapter, members of the contemporary church would do well to claim the mighty promises of Christ especially the ones in Jn 14:12-14. I am convinced that in our society where secularism is banishing God to the margins of life, we need to exercise deeds of power in order to call into question the anti supernatural prejudice of many people. In a talk about Dame Julian of Norwich, Pope Benedict said in 2010: 'God's promises are always greater that our expectations. If we commend the purest and deepest desires of our heart to God and to his immense love, we will never be disappointed, and 'all manner of thing shall be well".'

CHAPTER ELEVEN

Careless Words

There is a memorable scene in *The Miracle Worker*, a film about Helen Keller who was deaf, blind and mute. One fateful day she was in the garden of her home with her nurse Annie Sullivan. Annie grabbed her hand, put it into water flowing from a pump, and repeatedly spelt out the word water in her palm. Then there was a wonderful eureka moment when it dawned on Helen that the word water represented the reality which was flowing over her fingers. With that insight she was able to acquire language and to communicate. Eventually she even got a university degree. Recently I recalled that incident when I read the following words of St Thomas Aquinas: 'The object of faith is not the statement but the reality.'

It struck me that religious people who wish to evangelise either by preaching or bearing verbal witness to Jesus in one-to-one situations, face an ongoing danger of taking refuge in lots of words about God, while losing touch with the reality that they represent. In a way Jesus adverted to that split when he said, 'These people honour me with their lips, but their hearts are far from me' (Mt 15:8). I think that he also had this kind of divided attitude in mind when he said, 'I tell you, on the day of judgement men will render account for every careless word they utter; for by your words you will be justified, and by your words you will be condemned' (Mt 12:36-37).

Ineffective words
What did Jesus mean by the phrase, 'every careless word'? In Greek, *argon*, the term for 'careless,' means idle, unproductive, useless, unprofitable or barren. To put it another way, although they may be true in themselves, careless words are uninspiring utterances that merely come from our own minds, memories and book learning. They fail to follow the advice of St Peter who wrote, 'If anyone speaks, he should do it as one speaking the

very words of God' (1 Pet 4:11). As St Augustine said in one of his sermons, ' He is undoubtedly barren who preaches outwardly the word of God without hearing it inwardly.' Writing about careless words, Raniero Cantalamessa says: 'They are the empty, fruitless, purely human words spoken by those whose duty it is to proclaim the living, life-changing words of God ... They are the idle words of false prophets, that is, the words of those who want us to believe that they speak to us in God's name, but in fact are simply putting forward their own ideas. They do not draw what they say from the heart of God, but merely think it up themselves.' The wonderful promises of scripture to do with the efficacy of God's word do not apply where careless, sterile, unproductive words are concerned.

There are other texts in the New Testament which throw light on the possible meaning of our Lord's words. For example, in Col 4:3 we read, 'Pray for us, too, that God may open a door for our message, so that we may proclaim the mystery of Christ ... Pray that I may proclaim it clearly, as I should.' That little phrase, 'that I may proclaim it clearly, as I should,' is illumined by a verse in Col 3:16, 'Let the word of Christ dwell in you richly as you teach and admonish one another with all wisdom.' It is probable that St Vincent de Paul had sentiments like these in mind when he said to a young priest: 'It is therefore, Father, essential for you to be empty of self in order to put on Jesus Christ. You know that like produces like, a sheep begets a sheep and a human being another human being. So too, if he who guides others, who forms them, who speaks to them, is only animated by a human spirit, those who will see, hear and study to imitate him will become utterly human. No matter what he may say or do, he will inspire them only with the appearance but not the reality. He will communicate to them the spirit with which he himself is animated, as we see in the case of teachers who imprint their maxims and methods of work on their disciples.'

There is another way to understand the notion of careless words. In the New Jerusalem Bible translation, Mt 12:36 talks about 'every unfounded word,' while saying in a footnote that it refers to calumny. I'm not sure if that is an accurate account of what Matthew was intending to say in the Greek. If it is, it is referred to in Jas 3:8 which says, 'no human being can tame the tongue. It is always ready to pour out its deadly poison.' Talking about everyday conversation the author of Eph 5:4 says, 'Nor should there be obscenity, foolish talk or coarse joking, which are out of place.' Again in Col 3:8 we are told, 'you must rid yourselves of all such things as these: anger, rage, malice, slander, and filthy language from your lips. Do not lie to each other.' Instead in Col 4:6 we read, 'Let your conversation be always full of grace, seasoned with salt, so that you may know how to answer everyone.' In 1 Cor 14:26 Paul gives an example of what he means, 'When you come together, everyone has a hymn, or a word of instruction, a revelation, a tongue or an interpretation. All of these must be done for the strengthening of the church.' Finally, in Col 3:16 we read, 'Speak to one another with psalms, hymns and spiritual songs.'

Surely one of the reasons why the church is in decline is because so many careless words, understood in either way, are being spoken in everyday conversation and in pulpits, classrooms and lecture halls. On 29 January 1966, Charles Davis, a well known British theologian, wrote perceptively about effective preaching and teaching in *America* magazine: 'Much speaking in different places on themes of renewal has brought me into contact with many people seeking to revivify their faith. I have found a sense of emptiness, but together with it a deep yearning for God. There is an emptiness at the core of people's lives, an emptiness waiting to be filled. They are troubled about their faith; they find it slipping ... The more perceptive know they are looking for God ... Who will speak to them quite simply of God as of a person he intimately knows, and make the reality and presence of God come alive for them once more?' Some years later Karl Rahner spoke the following words on the occasion of an ordination. Although they were specifically addressed to priests, surely they also have a relevance for lay people: 'There is so much chatter in the world and there are many clever, shallow words in the world. But I ask you, my brothers and sisters, have we not a crying need for someone to speak to us of God, of eternal life, and of grace, of sin, of judgement and of God's mercy? Is that not still the most important message today? What more do people want? What greater and holier mission can the priest have than speaking God's word to his brothers and sisters?'

CHAPTER ELEVEN

Contemplation and the reinvigoration of Christian language

All of us need to go beyond head knowledge to heart awareness, from words about God to the realities they signify. As St Ignatius of Loyola once pointed out in his *Spiritual Exercises*, 'It is not knowing much, but realising and relishing things interiorly, that contents and satisfies the soul.' Scripture promises the kind of experiential knowledge which Ignatius spoke about and it is fulfilled by means of contemplative prayer. In Jer 33:3-4 we are assured, 'Call to me and I will answer you and tell you great and unsearchable things you do not know,' and in Is 48:6-7 we are told, 'From now on I will tell you of new things, of hidden things unknown to you.' On one occasion Jesus echoed these Old Testament promises when he said that when 'the Spirit of truth, comes, he will guide you into all truth … He will bring glory to me by taking from what is mine and making it known to you' (Jn 16:13-15). We Christians need to imitate Jesus who testified, 'I did not speak of my own accord, but the Father who sent me commanded me what to say and how to say it' (Jn 12:49). We know that, like Moses of old, the Father used to speak to Jesus face to face, during his many hours of prayer. Referring to this type of conversation with the Lord, St Vincent de Paul advised: 'When in doubt, have recourse to God and say to him, "O Lord, you are the Father of light, teach me what to say in these circumstances" … so that you may learn directly from God what you shall have to say following the example of Moses who proclaimed to the people of Israel only that which God had revealed to him.'

Happily all of us who have been filled with the Holy Spirit have known precious moments when the word of God has leapt off the pages of scripture, alive with meaning and relevance, into our hearts, as a word which is addressed to us in the here-and-now circumstances of life. It is this type of inspired word that 'judges the thoughts and attitudes of the heart' (Heb 4:12-13), and as Paul assures us in Rom 10:17, brings ourselves and others to faith in Christ. Thanks be to God, it is also the anointed word that leads to effective ministry, even to the point of healings and miracles. 'If you abide in me,' says Jesus, 'and my words abide in you, ask whatever you will, and it shall be done for you' (Jn 15:7-8).

Christians have to be careful when they utter prophecies or words of knowledge. They have to discern, if necessary with the help of others, whether they are from God or not. As scripture says, 'Do not believe every spirit, but test the spirits to see whether they are from God, because many false prophets have gone out into the world' (1 Jn 4:1). This note of caution also applies to the many contemporary visionaries and seers who are claiming to receive on-going private revelation from God. We need to rely on the discernment of the bishops, where their utterances are concerned, lest we be led astray by careless words. For more on this topic see chapter twenty six on different types of private revelation.

Conclusion

In Lk 6:45, Jesus said: 'The good man brings good things out of the good stored up in his heart, and the evil man brings evil things out of the evil stored up in his heart. For out of the overflow of his heart his mouth speaks.' So we have to be careful by pondering God's word in our hearts, and speaking that word to others. During World War II there were many posters which read, 'careless talk costs lives.' Whereas scripture does not say that such talk kills the body, it certainly suggests that it can fail to give life to the soul, one's own or that of others. There is a prayer in *The Divine Office* which says, 'As we proclaim your saving power to others, let us not ourselves lose hold of your salvation.'

SECTION THREE

Community

CHAPTER TWELVE

Christ's Presence in the Eucharistic Community

According to tradition, St Luke the Evangelist was born in Antioch, in the Roman province of Syria. It is believed that he wrote the third gospel and the *Acts of the Apostles* somewhere between 70 and 100 AD. He died before 150, at the age of 84. He was buried in Thebes in Greece. St Jerome says that in the second year of the reign of the emperor Constantius in 338, Luke's bones were brought to Constantinople, to the Basilica of the Holy Apostles. Sometime before 1177, the relics were brought to Padua in Italy where they have remained ever since. However, in 1980, a review of Prague's metropolitan archive confirmed that in 1364, Luke's skull had been sent to St Vitus's Cathedral at the request of Emperor Charles IV. Two hundred and one years later, in 1565, the remaining Paduan bones were housed in the Basilica of St Justina. Recent DNA tests on Luke's bones indicate that before his death he was suffering from a grave disease of the joints and spinal cord, as well as emphysema of the lungs. Although he wrote a gospel and the *Acts of the Apostles*, Luke had never met the Lord in person. So he had to answer a question which is still relevant today, 'How do those of us who have faith in the Risen Lord encounter him in person?' Luke's account of the meeting of Jesus with the disciples on the road to Emmaus is his sophisticated answer.

This story, which does not appear in the other gospels, is probably based on an historical incident. However, Luke tells it as if it were a parable. What he is saying is that believers can meet the Risen Jesus in and through the eucharistic community. As Pope John Paul II observed in par 6 of his letter *Church of the Eucharist* (2003): 'To contemplate Christ involves being able to recognise him wherever he manifests himself, in his many forms of presence, but above all in the living sacrament of his body and his blood ... Whenever the church celebrates the Eucharist, the faithful can in some way relive the experience of the two disciples on the road to Emmaus: "their eyes were opened and they recognised him" (Lk 24:31).'

When one examines the text in Lk 24:13-35 it becomes apparent that it refers to four presences of Christ which are mentioned in par 7 of the Constitution of the Sacred Liturgy of the Second Vatican Council.
1. Christ is present in the gathering of the people.
2. Christ is present in the priest who presides.
3. Christ is present in the readings from scripture and in the homily.
4. Christ is sacramentally present in the consecrated bread and wine.

Let's look in a little more detail at each of these four forms of presence in Luke's story.

Christ is present in the Christian community
In Mt 18:20 Jesus assured believers that, 'where two or three come together in my name, there am I with them.' Surprisingly, a contemporary psychotherapist, Irene de Castillejo echoed that point when she observed, 'For there to be a meeting, it seems as though a third, a something else, is always present. You may call it Love or the Holy Spirit.' In the road to Emmaus story Luke tells us that two followers of Jesus were travelling the seven miles from Jerusalem to Emmaus. What Luke was suggesting by this observation is the fact that the disciples were distancing themselves from the place where their dreams had been broken. A stranger joined them, who unbeknown to them was Jesus. They were downhearted and disillusioned because they had pinned their hopes of deliverance from Roman oppression, upon Jesus. But now those hopes had been shattered because Jesus had been crucified and had died ignominiously on the cross. In spite of hearing a rumour that he had appeared to some women, they were inconsolable.

It seems to me that Luke is saying that if Christians meet together to share their joys or sorrows, the Lord is secretly in their midst, whether they sense his presence or not. In recent times many Irish Catholics have resembled the two men on the road to

Emmaus as they discussed the upsetting conclusions of the Ferns, Ryan, Murphy and Cloyne Reports on child sex abuse by clergy and religious. Many people who trusted in bishops, priests and members of religious orders feel a terrible sense of disillusionment and let down. As a result, many men and women have lost heart and feel like distancing themselves from the church. What Luke is saying is that when believers share their sorrows and heartaches, Christ is present in their midst, albeit in an anonymous way.

Christ is present in the Word
We are told by Luke that, having listened to his companions, the stranger began to quote scripture texts beginning with Moses and going through the prophets. They were all about the messiah to come who would have to suffer and die for the people. I have often wondered what texts he cited. In 150 AD St Justin Martyr, one of the post-apostolic Fathers of the church, listed the verses he thought that Jesus might have referred to, in pars 30-53 of his *First Apology*. We are told by Luke that Jesus not only quoted the Old Testament texts, he then went on to explain their meaning and relevance. In other words he gave a homily on the readings.

Speaking about the biblical readings at Mass, par 7 of the *Constitution on the Liturgy* says that Christ himself 'is present in his word, since it is he who speaks when scripture is read in church' That point was reiterated in par 9 of the *General Instruction of the Roman Missal*, where it says that when the scriptures are read in church, 'God himself is speaking to his people, and Christ, present in his word, is proclaiming the gospel.' It is Christ, too, who speaks through the priest when he gives a homily based on the readings. It should have at least three characteristics. Firstly, it ought to explain what it is the inspired author was trying to express within the particular circumstances of his time. Secondly, the priest should relate the key spiritual insights in the readings to modern day circumstances. The great Protestant theologian Karl Barth once said that a Christian should always have the newspaper in one hand, so to speak, and the bible in the other. What he meant by that remark was that believers should try to understand and evaluate the issues of the day in the light of God's word. Thirdly, the homilist should prepare to

CHAPTER TWELVE

preach to the congregation by means of prayerful, Spirit-filled reflection on the readings, e.g. by engaging in *Lectio Divina*. In par 59 of Pope Benedict's declaration on *The Word of God* we read: 'The homily is part of the liturgical action and is meant to foster a deeper understanding of the word of God, so that it can bear fruit in the lives of the faithful ... For this reason preachers need to be in close and constant contact with the sacred text; they should prepare for the homily by meditation and prayer, so as to preach with conviction and passion.'

No wonder John Paul II said in par 40 of his letter *The Coming Third Millennium*, that all Catholics, lay and clerical, 'In order to recognise who Christ truly is, Christians should turn with renewed interest to the Bible, whether it be through the liturgy, rich in the divine word, or through devotional reading.' One way of responding to the Holy Father's advice would be to prayerfully reflect on the readings from the Mass of the coming Sunday. During the past year we have begun to have 'A word on the Word' meetings in our parish every week. They last for one hour and consist of two sections.

Having explained what the theme of the first and third reading is, we begin with a period of bible sharing. It consists of the following steps: 1) A prayer for inspiration. 2) One of the readings for the following Sunday's Mass is read by a participant. 3) We recall what is in the reading for one minute. 4) The same text is read by another person. 5) We prayerfully reflect on the text for between five and seven minutes. We encourage the participants to address two questions, what was the inspired writer intending to say? How does his message relate to life today? 6) The participants share in twos for between five and seven minutes by telling one another what came to them during the time of quiet. 7) We widen the discussion so that anyone can share with the group. That can go on for up to fifteen minutes. It is fascinating to see how many complementary insights the participants can contribute.

When the bible sharing is complete, the person who is animating the session offers an exegetical and spiritual analysis of one or more of the readings. This part of the meeting offers insights which might not be readily be available to those who have not had an opportunity of studying the bible. We are finding that these meetings draw a regular and appreciative clientele each week. They comment on the fact that not only are the meetings useful and edifying, they are a great preparation for the liturgy of the word on the following Sunday.

Christ is present in the priest
In so far as the two disciples welcomed the unknown stranger they welcomed the Lord. In a sense he was their angel. As Heb 13:2-3 says, 'Do not forget to entertain strangers, for by so doing some people have entertained angels without knowing it.' The word angel means messenger in Greek. Jesus, the Stranger, is in fact God's messenger, the one who brings the good news of the saving merits of his death and resurrection to the two men. While it is true that all baptised Christians are members of the Body of Christ, priests are graced in a special way to act in the person of Christ the head. So, although all priests are flawed human beings, nevertheless Christ the head of the Church acts in and through them in a special way. As Pope John Paul II said in par 29 of his encyclical *On The Eucharist*, the phrase *in persona Christi* 'means more than offering "in the name of" or "in the place of" Christ. *In persona* means in specific sacramental terms identification with the eternal High Priest who is the author and principal subject of this sacrifice of his, a sacrifice in which, in truth, nobody can take his place.' It should be explained that while all Christians can act in the person of Christ in virtue of their baptism, in certain circumstances only ordained priests can act in the person of Christ the head. During a general audience on 14 April 2010, Pope Benedict explained, 'the priest who acts *in persona Christi Capitis* (in the person of Christ the head) and in representation of the Lord, never acts in the name of someone who is absent, but in the very Person of the Risen Christ, who makes himself present with his truly effective action. He really acts and does what the priest could not do: the consecration of the wine and the bread so that they will really be the presence of the Lord, and the absolution of sins.'

There is an Irish folk tale that gets this point across. 'A man has a disagreement with a priest and resolves not to go to Mass in future. One Sunday he meets a stranger who asks him to accompany him on a walk. He leads him to a stream. The man drinks from the stream and pronounces it to be the purest water he ever drank. The stranger walks with him to the source of the stream and finds that it springs from the mouth of a dead dog. The stranger then explains that the Mass can benefit him even if the priest is unworthy because the pure water of Christ's grace flows from him.'

Christ is present in the consecrated bread and wine
The Emmaus story reaches its climax when the two disciples reach their destination. They invite their travelling companion to join them. The evangelist tells us what happened: 'When he was at the table with them, he took bread, gave thanks, broke it and began to give it to them' (Lk 24:30-31). This is clearly a eucharistic text because it contains the four verbs which we associated with the celebration of the Eucharist, to take, to bless, to break and to give. Luke tells us that the eyes of the two men were finally opened and they recognised that the stranger was actually the Risen Lord, and then he disappeared from their sight. What Luke is telling us is that Christ is really and truly present in the eucharistic community where the other forms of presence converge in holy communion.

I know a priest who a few years ago conducted a retreat in London for a large number of nuns. At one point he got a prophetic word for the congregation. Part of it went something like this. 'My people, if you want to discern my presence in the consecrated bread and wine, you must first discern my presence in other people, especially the poor, and in my word.' Later in that Mass, apparently the same priest got a word of knowledge in the form of a prophetic utterance. It said that one of the sisters had been seriously injured in a car accident some years before and was still suffering painful problems in her spine and hip. When the priest asked if there was anyone present who matched that description, one of the sisters put up her hand. The priest prayed for her and she received a permanent healing. It was as if the Lord was confirming the word of prophesy about recognising the interrelated presences of the Lord in people and in the word as a prelude to recognising him in the consecrated bread and wine.

In his apostolic declaration on *The Word of God,* Pope Benedict added support to this interpretation when he said in this extended quotation: 'Luke's account of the disciples on the way to Emmaus enables us to reflect further on this link between the hearing of the word and the breaking of the bread (cf Lk 24:13-35). Jesus approached the disciples on the day after the Sabbath, listened as they spoke of their dashed hopes and, joining them on their journey, "interpreted to them in all the scriptures the things concerning himself" (24:27). The two disciples began to look at the scriptures in a new way in the company of this traveller who seemed so surprisingly familiar with their lives. What had taken place in those days no longer appeared to them as failure, but as fulfilment and a new beginning. And yet, apparently not even these words were enough for the two disciples. The gospel of Luke relates that "their eyes were opened and they recognised him" (24:31) only when Jesus took the bread, said the blessing, broke it and gave it to them, whereas earlier "their eyes were kept from recognising him" (24:16). The presence of Jesus, first with his words and then with the act of breaking bread, made it possible for the disciples to recognise him. Now they were able to appreciate in a new way all that they had previously experienced with him: "Did not our hearts burn within us while he talked to us on the road, while he opened to us the scriptures?" (24:32).'

Go, the Mass is ended
Luke tells us that as soon as the two disciples recognised the presence of their risen Lord they rushed back to Jerusalem to tell the good news to the other disciples. So it is not surprising that at the end of each Eucharist, the priest may say, 'Go and announce the Gospel of The Lord.' Pope John Paul II spoke about this in the Phoenix Park in 1979. He said that implicit in the words of dismissal at the end of the Eucharist is the commission not only to witness to the good news of God's merciful love by the way we live, but also to verbally share the good news with those we meet. By these means we come, not only to share in people's experiences, both happy and sad, we can also illumine those experiences in the light of our own experience of the four interrelated forms of Christ's presence in the eucharistic community. We conclude with a conflation of two lovely prayers of Pope Benedict XVI:

CHAPTER TWELVE

Lord Jesus Christ, pilgrim of Emmaus,
you make yourself close to us for love,
even if, at times, discouragement and sadness
prevent us from discovering your presence.
You are the flame that revives our faith.
You are the light that purifies our hope.
You are the force that stirs our charity.
Teach us to recognise you in the word,
in the house and on the Table where the Bread of Life is shared,
in generous service of our suffering neighbour.

… And when the evening falls, Lord, help us to say, 'Stay with us.'
Stay with us, Lord, because all around us the shadows are deepening, and you are the Light.
Stay with us, Lord, when mists of doubt rise up around our Catholic faith for you are Truth itself.
Stay with our families that they may be nests where life is respected from conception to natural death for you are Life itself.
Stay, Lord, with our most vulnerable, our poor, our lonely, our elderly, and our sick. You are our Hope. Amen.

CHAPTER THIRTEEN

St Ignatius of Antioch on Unity in the Community

When I studied for a postgraduate degree a few years ago, I attended a course on the post-apostolic Fathers. These were the Christian writers who were the immediate successors of the first generation of Christians. I became particularly interested in the seven letters of St Ignatius of Antioch to different churches. He was martyred for his faith sometime between 98 and 117 AD. As someone who is passionate about the need for ecumenism, I was fascinated by his emphasis on the primary importance of ecclesial unity. Although some readers may find that this chapter is a bit dry and academic, I'd like to encapsulate the bishop's important ideas. Not only do they afford us a valuable insight into the initial evolution of Christian doctrine, they are still relevant today. Writing about Ignatius Pope Benedict XVI has observed:

> No church Father has expressed the longing for union with Christ and for life in him with the intensity of Ignatius ... Ignatius' irresistible longing for union with Christ was the foundation of a real 'mysticism of unity.' Speaking of himself Ignatius said: 'I therefore did what befitted me as a man devoted to unity' (*Philadelphians* 8).

Pope Benedict referred to Ignatius as the Doctor of four interrelated unities. Firstly, the unity of God. Secondly, the unity of the human and the divine natures in Christ. Thirdly, the unity of the church. Fourthly, the unity of the faithful.

Unity in God
Although Ignatius was writing in the apostolic era, it is surprising to see how he already had a nascent theology of the Trinity. Speaking of the Christian community, he said in *Ephesians* 9 that their unity had its origin in the unity of God:

> You are stones of a temple, prepared beforehand for the

building of God the Father, hoisted up to the heights by the crane of Jesus Christ, which is the cross, using the rope of the Holy Spirit.

In *Magnesians* 13 Ignatius expressed the hope that the community 'may prosper, physically and spiritually, in faith and love, in the Son, and the Father and in the Holy Spirit.' Finally, in the introduction to *Philadelphians*, Ignatius referred to the fact that the bishop of a diocese is an icon of the Trinity, and in virtue of that fact a centre of unity:

> Ignatius the image-bearer to the church of the Father and of Jesus Christ ... appointed by the mind of Jesus Christ, whom in accordance with his own will, securely established by his Holy Spirit.

As was noted in chapter two, because of the principle of the communication of attributes, not only can the attributes of the eternal Word be predicated of the humanity of Christ, by extension, what can be predicated of one person of the Trinity can be predicated of another. If the Father and the Son are divine, so is the Holy Spirit. This is worth mentioning, because Ignatius maintained that the Holy Spirit is the rope which binds the community together, thereby implying that the Spirit was divine.

The Unity of the divine and human natures in Christ
We know that in the post-apostolic era, Docetism was a threat to Christian orthodoxy. This heresy maintained that Jesus' physical body and crucifixion were illusions. Jesus only seemed to have a physical body and to physically die, but in reality he was incorporeal, a pure spirit. Needless to say, Ignatius asserted the unity of the humanity and divinity of Jesus Christ. There are three places in his letters where he made creed-like statements that asserted this point. For instance, in *Trallians* 9 we have a concise statement of Ignatius's position:

> Be deaf, therefore, whenever anyone speaks to you apart from Jesus Christ, who was of the family of David, who was the son of Mary; who really was born, who both ate and drank; who really was persecuted under Pontius Pilate, who really was crucified and died while those in heaven and on

earth and under the earth looked on; who, moreover, really was raised from the dead when his Father raised him up, who – his Father, that is – in the same way will likewise also raise up in Christ Jesus all who believe in him, apart from whom we have no true life.

It is worth noting that Ignatius used the word 'really' four times in this passage. He clearly intended to counteract the Docetist belief that Jesus only seemed to do the things he did. Later in *Trallians* 10, we have the same contrast between the words 'truly' and 'appearance.' Ignatius stated:

> For he suffered all these things for our sakes, in order that we might be saved, and he truly suffered just as he truly raised himself – not, as certain unbelievers say, that he suffered in appearance only. Indeed, their fate will be determined by what they think: they will become disembodied and demonic.

Unity of the Church
Ignatius talked repeatedly about the unity of the church. He said that this unity centred on the bishop together with his priests and deacons, and on the sacrament of the Eucharist. Referring to the bishop and his clergy in *Magnesians* 6 he wrote:

> Be eager to do everything in godly harmony, the bishop presiding in the place of God and the presbyters in the places of the council of the apostles and the deacons, who are especially dear to me, since they are entrusted with the ministry of Jesus Christ, who before all ages was with the Father and appeared at the end of time.

When Ignatius said that the bishop presides in the place of God, i.e. the Trinity, he was saying that the unity of the church is rooted in the unity of the triune God, in and through the bishop and his clergy. In *Magnesians* 7 Ignatius developed his thinking when he said to the laity:

> Therefore as the Lord is nothing without the Father, either by himself or through the apostles, (for he was united to him) so you must not do anything without the bishops and the presbyters (i.e. priests).

Ignatius hammered home this point in a number of places. In *Trallians* 2 he said to the faithful: 'You are subject to the bishop as to Jesus Christ.' A little later he added: 'Do nothing without the bishop, but be subject also to the council of presbyters as to the apostles of Jesus Christ.' In *Trallians* 3 he added: 'Let everyone respect the deacons as Jesus Christ, just as they should respect the bishop, who is the model of the Father, and the presbyters as God's council and as the band of the apostles.' He reiterated the same point, in almost exactly the same words, in *Smyrnaeans* 8.

Ignatius referred to the Eucharist as a focus of unity in *Smyrnaeans* 6, 8; *Romans* 7; and *Philadelphians* 4. For instance, in *Smyrnaenans* 6 he defended the sacrament from heretical interpretations:

> Take note of those who hold heterodox opinions on the grace of Jesus Christ which has come to us, and see how contrary their opinions are to the mind of God ... They abstain from the Eucharist and from prayer because they do not confess that the Eucharist is the flesh of our Saviour Jesus Christ, flesh which suffered for our sins and which the Father, in his goodness, raised up again. They who deny the gift of God are perishing in their disputes.'

In *Philadelphians* 4 he stressed the fact that the Eucharist was a focal point of ecclesial unity. Notice that the word 'one' is mentioned no less than five times:

> Take care therefore to participate in one Eucharist (for there is one flesh of our Lord Jesus Christ, and one cup that leads to unity through his blood; there is one altar, just as there is one bishop, together with the council of presbyters and the deacons my fellow-servants), that in order that whatever you do, you may do in accordance with God.

The Unity of the Faithful
The letters of Ignatius contain many passionate appeals that the laity be united with one another and with God in and through the bishop together with his clergy, who are God's representatives. In *Polycarp* 1 he said: 'Focus on unity, for there is nothing

better.' In *Smyrnaenans* 8 he warned: 'Flee from divisions as the beginning of evils.' In *Ephesians* 5 he spoke about the connection between unity in the community and the Trinity: 'I congratulate you who are united with him, as the church is with Jesus Christ and as Jesus Christ is with the Father, so that all things may be harmonious in unity.' Ignatius repeatedly exhorted the recipients of his letters to be united. A number of representative texts will be quoted here. Perhaps the most moving of them all is in *Philadelphians* 7. Ignatius said that it came to him as a prophetic word from God by the power of the Holy Spirit:

> Do nothing without the bishop. Guard your bodies as temples of God. Love unity. Flee from divisions. Become imitators of Jesus Christ, just as he is of his Father.

In *Philadelphians* 2 he again warned against divisions while stressing that unity is founded on the Christian truths he had expounded: 'Therefore, as children of the light of truth, flee from division and false teaching.' In *Magnesians* 7 he added in a passage where the word 'one' occurs no less than eleven times:

> Gathering together let there be one prayer, one petition, one mind, one hope, with love and blameless joy, which is Jesus Christ, than whom nothing is better. Let all of you run together as to one temple of God, as to one altar, to one Jesus Christ, who came forth from one Father and remained with the One and returned to the One.'

Ignatius used an attractive musical analogy in *Ephesians* 4 to describe the unity of the community:

> You must join in the chorus every one of you, so that being harmonious in unanimity and taking your pitch from God, you may sing in unison with one voice through Jesus Christ to the Father, in order that he may both hear you and, on the basis of what you do well, acknowledge that you are members of his Son. It is, therefore, advantageous for you to be in perfect unity, in order that you may always have a share in God.

In *Ephesians* 10 Ignatius contrasted the attitudes of the Christians to those of the rest of mankind in an instructive way, because in doing so he was describing the behaviours that either build or break Christian unity:

> In response to their anger, be gentle; in response to their boasts, be humble; in response to their slander, offer prayers; in response to their errors, be steadfast in faith; in response to their cruelty, be civilised; do not be eager to imitate them.

Apart from this verse, Ignatius does not say a great deal about the attitudes and actions that are alien to unity. In *Ephesians* 5 he talks about 'arrogance;' in *Ephesians* 16; *Trallians* 6; *Philadelphians* 2 and elsewhere, he refers to the corrupting power of 'evil teaching;' and in *Romans* 7 he talks about the evil of 'envy.'

Conclusion

Surely Ignatius's beliefs, e.g. that Christ is present in the consecrated bread and wine, poses a theological challenge to those Protestants who do not believe in the real as opposed to a symbolic presence in the Eucharist. Those who watch Marcus Grodi's *The Journey Home* on EWTN will know that many former Protestants who appear on that programme say that their reading of the post-apostolic Fathers influenced their decision to become Catholic.

Surely the teaching of Ignatius about the importance of unity is very relevant to the contemporary church in Ireland convulsed as it is by the fallout and implications of the SAVI, Ferns, Ryan, Murphy and Cloyne reports. We lay people, religious, priests and bishops need to avoid seeing the speck in the eye of a brother or sister while failing to acknowledge the plank in our own (cf Mt 7:4). If we do not abide by the words, 'in humility consider others better than yourselves' (Phil 2:3) inevitably there will be disunity. Jesus has warned us that, 'If a house is divided against itself, that house cannot stand' (Mk 3:24-25). Is it any surprise therefore, that Benedict XVI has stated that church unity is the *sine qua non* of effective ministry and evangelisation:

> The realism of Ignatius invites the faithful of yesterday and today to a progressive synthesis between configuration to Christ (union with him, life in him) and dedication to his

church (union with the bishop, generous service to the community and the world). In other words, one must achieve a synthesis between communion of the church within itself and the mission of proclamation of the gospel to others, until one dimension speaks through the other, and believers are evermore 'in possession of that indivisible spirit that is Jesus Christ himself' (*Magnesians* 15).

CHAPTER FOURTEEN

Proclamation of the Gospel and Community

Sociologist David Putman, author of *Bowling Alone: The Collapse and Revival of American Community*, has noted the fact that in Western capitalist democracies, like Ireland and Britain, there has been an erosion of community bonds and an increasing emphasis on individualism. For example, we have moved from large, extended families of a stable kind, to smaller, more atomic ones which are often unstable, e.g. because of the incidence of divorce. Families seem to engage in fewer activities together, such as sharing meals. T. S. Eliot described this state of affairs when he observed in *Choruses on the Rock*, 'And now you live dispersed on ribbon roads, and no man knows or cares who is his neighbour unless his neighbour makes too much disturbance, but all dash to and fro in motor cars, familiar with the roads and settled nowhere. Nor does the family even move about together, but every son would have his motor cycle, and daughters ride away on casual pillions.' Because of these and similar trends, it is harder to run voluntary organisations because many people haven't the time to spare due to work and recreational commitments. As a result, what is referred to as social capital, such as good-will, trust, and mutual solidarity, is decreased. This means that needy individuals have fewer people and groups they can rely on. So one of the most urgent needs in contemporary society is to provide for, and foster a sense of unconditional belonging. That is something which many Christian communities can and do offer.

The primacy of unconditional belonging
A number of years ago I visited a vibrant Protestant church in Belfast. I was very impressed by the fact that there were so many young adults in attendance. I asked Paul Reid, the pastor, what was the secret. He said that from a Christian point of view it would seem that three B's are involved in the lives of Christians.

Traditionally there was the B of right belief. That was followed by the B of right behaviour. Finally, there was the B of belonging. He said that in modern society, where individualism is rampant and social alienation is common, people have an overriding need for a feeling of unconditional belonging.

In his *The Elementary Forms of Religious Life*, sociologist Emile Durkheim stated that, 'A religion is a unified system of beliefs and practices relative to sacred things, that is to say, things set apart and forbidden – beliefs and practices which unite into one single moral community called a church, *all those who adhere to them* [my italics].' Notice that this definition of religion, understands it mainly in terms of its function rather than transcendence, namely its ability to bind its adherents. Although the word religion usually refers to beliefs, rituals and morals, it is worth noting that etymologically, it is derived from a Latin word which means 'to tie up,' ' to tie fast'. Understood in this sense, religion is about relationships, about those things which bind the members together in the joy of ultimate belonging. It establishes a connection between people, between people and God, and between people and their own deepest selves.

Sociologists argue that religious rituals are important. They can help in creating a firm sense of group identity. Humans have always used them to create social bonds. Families develop rituals of their own such as meeting to celebrate anniversaries, having singsongs, eating spiced beef at Christmas, going to church on Sundays etc. Ritual activity seems pretty obvious in football clubs like Liverpool and Manchester United with their use of chants, scarves, banners, flags, and club colours. The same is true in religion where things like sacraments, customs and traditions, play a symbolic role in binding their members together. The word symbol is interesting in this regard. It comes from the Greek word *symbolon* and means 'thrown together'. Symbols have an ability to overcome multiplicity and division by bringing disparate things together in unity. The word symbolical is the opposite to the English word 'diabolical' which is derived from a Greek word *diaballo*, meaning to separate or alienate. In other words, symbolical activities of a ritualistic kind have a unique integrative power which overcomes alienation and unites people.

Sadly, in modern individualistic society the role of recognised rituals has declined. Anthropologist Mary Douglas has warned in her influential book *Natural Symbols*, that the church can weaken its own cohesion by abandoning some of its rituals, such as abstaining from meat on Fridays, fasting during Lent, being silent in church and the like. It has to be said of course that Carl Jung was probably correct when he said that if rituals and symbols are disconnected from the genuine religious experiences that inspired them in the first place, they can ossify. Then, instead of being an expression of a sense of togetherness and meaning, they can militate against it. Clearly, there is an ongoing need for replacement rituals and symbols of a meaningful and enlivening kind. Happily, the churches continue to act as focal points for a sense of belonging which they express in ritual signs and behaviours. What is good about them is that they act at a pre-rational level of awareness. This is the case for all participants whether they are clever and well educated or not.

The challenge posed by civil religion
In 2010 Archbishop Martin of Dublin gave a very interesting talk in Rimini, in Italy. At one point the archbishop said, 'As Ireland becomes secularised, a culture still steeped in formal religious values inevitably degenerates into a form of civil religion.' Civil religion is a set of quasi-religious attitudes, beliefs, rituals, and symbols that tie members of a political community together. In the eighteenth century Jean-Jacques Rousseau was probably the first person to introduce the idea in his book, *The Social Contract*. The term was first used in modern times by American Robert Bellah in 1967. Commenting on this phenomenon within an Irish context Dr Martin's said: 'The church provides a unique space in which people, even though secularised, can share the events of their lives and find a ritual to express the more profound human experiences of joy, sorrow or fear. However, if the church becomes just a place where lay persons gather to celebrate human experiences without a deep reference to God, then this civil religion ends up by being empty and does not respond to the search for God who is missing in the lives of many. When people turn to a church from which they are in reality alienated, they tend to desire that the church becomes

'their' church, rather than the place where Christ addresses them and invites them to meet him and be challenged by his love. I have the impression that when many people say "We are the Church" they actually want to say "I am the Church", meaning "I am creating a church according to my needs and my lifestyle." There is a danger that when some say that the church is the 'People of God', they really want to say that it is up to the people to determine who God is and how God is useful. But, whoever encounters only their own God does not encounter the God revealed in Jesus Christ.'

Let me give just one of many possible examples of what the Archbishop had in mind. When some people who have died are brought to the church, instead of focusing in faith on the next life and the need to pray for their souls, relatives, friends and neighbours are inclined to focus solely on the achievements of the departed in this life. These tendencies pose a real challenge for the clergy. Great pressure can be placed upon them to strip religious rituals of their specifically Christian content in the name of a secularised form of civil religion. For instance, in his homily the priest should avoid talking about things like sin, purgatory, the need to pray for the dead and the like. Briefly put, there are at least two implications of this trend. Firstly, not only should the church resist the tendency to secularise its sacraments and rituals, it needs to work for renewal, e.g. by means of greater fidelity to reading and praying the scriptures. Secondly, instead of civil religion been located in the church, it needs to be developed and situated in secular society. In this connection I was interested to see that in 2010 Frank Field MP, a practising Anglican, suggested to the Conservative and Liberal coalition government in Britain that it should develop a secular, non-church ritual which could be used to celebrate the birth of babies, and to highlight the duties of their carers.

Arguably, providing a sense of belonging for the spiritual pilgrims of our day is the essence of effective pre-evangelisation. Religious people are, literally, those who are bound together by a common experience of a love that simultaneously connects them to one another, to their deepest identities and ultimately to God whose presence is mediated by those relationships. If the spiritual pilgrims of our day, especially young people, experience a sense of belonging within a caring Christian community, they will be more likely to discover who they are and what they want. Then they may be more open to accept the Christian beliefs that inform that community. It is only within this loving context that the issue of right behaviour can be tackled. Ideally, right action should be an expression of a sense of Christian belonging and belief, rather than a dutiful substitute for both, as was sometimes the case in the past. The Alpha course, which engages in basic evangelisation, understands this principle very well. Ideally, each session of the course begins with a meal, in the belief that by fostering friendships Alpha fosters a sense of belonging which mediates the unconditional mercy and love of God to those who seek for meaning in life.

The parish as a community of communities
Let's admit it, many Catholic parishes are rather anonymous. If a person stops coming to church, it is quite possible that no one will notice. If that same person subsequently has a conversion experience and returns to weekly Mass there may be no one to welcome him or her back. So it is not surprising that there is an increasing recognition that, ideally, a parish should be a community of communities, a federation of smaller groups whose members enjoy a sense of belonging and mutual nurturance. Pope John Paul II said in par 26 of his apostolic declaration, *The Lay Members of Christ's Faithful People*: 'So that all parishes may be truly communities of Christians, local ecclesial authorities ought to foster ... small basic or so-called 'living' communities, where the faithful can communicate the word of God and express it in service and love to one another; these communities are true expressions of ecclesial communion and centres of evangelisation, in communion with their pastors.'

A number of bishops have also acknowledged this point. For example, Archbishop Martin of Dublin said in an address entitled 'The Priest Evangeliser and Witness': 'I believe that the transmission of the faith in the years to come will have to be more and more linked with the creation of faith communities, like the basic ecclesial communities that we speak about in the context of Africa or Latin America. These communities will help people, young and old, to be formed in their faith and to live out their faith concretely in a cultural context which is less and less supportive of faith. These communities must then, however, find their nourishment through their insertion into the broader communion of the church in the common celebration of the Eucharist. Our parishes must become communions of communities, finding their unity again in the liturgy.' I witnessed what Archbishop Martin might have had in mind when I visited St Estorgio, a large parish in central Milan. Fr Pigi Perini, the parish priest, has fostered the growth of as many as 125 parish cell groups, each of which has about eight to ten members who are devoted to evangelisation, e.g. by putting on Alpha courses.

Effective proclamation and the experience of community
In *Basic Evangelisation: Guidelines for Catholics* (2010), I have included a chapter entitled, 'An Evangelising Diocese and Parish,' which suggests what structural and spiritual changes will have to be made in order to link the experience of belonging to effective evangelisation. When people come to commit themselves to the Lord in a personal way as a result of such things as attending an RCIA, Alpha course, or Cursillo weekend, the question arises, what happens next? Do they merely join the other parishioners for weekly Mass, or is something more required? It is becoming increasingly obvious that parishes need a network of smaller groups of a supportive kind which not only provide recently turned-on Catholics with a sense of belonging but also the possibility of on-going faith formation. People who have come to have personal faith in Christ should be given a list of all the different groups in the parish, with a brief description of what they do, when and where they meet, together with contact phone numbers and email addresses. They can be invited to join one or more of them.

Conclusion
In Acts 2:44-5 we read, 'All who believed were together and had all things in common; and they sold their possessions and goods and distributed them to all, as any had need.' In these words, Saint Luke provides a kind of definition of the church, where communion (i.e. *koinonia*) becomes the springboard to effective evangelisation (i.e. *kerygma*). As Luke tells us: 'All the believers

were one in heart and mind. No one claimed that any of his possessions was his own, but they shared everything they had. With great power the apostles continued to testify to the resurrection of the Lord Jesus, and much grace was upon them all' (Acts 4:32-33).

CHAPTER FIFTEEN

Catholics and Protestants Witnessing Together

In the 1970s, when the troubles were at their worst in Northern Ireland, the Rev Cecil Kerr of the Church of Ireland told me that there was a museum in Moscow which promoted atheism. Apparently, it had one section devoted to Ulster. The general gist of the display was this, 'Have nothing to do with Christianity, it is a sickness that mistakes itself for a cure. See how these Irish Christians hate, maim and kill one another.' For many years, the scandal of the division between the Christian churches, both in Ireland and elsewhere in the world, has had an adverse effect on the credibility of Christian evangelisation.

The Catholic commitment to ecumenism
Ever since the Second Vatican Council in the 1960s the Catholic Church has advocated the importance of fostering Christian unity. What the church has in mind is unity in charity, prayer and working together whenever possible. That kind of co-operation creates a suitable context in which divisive doctrinal matters can be discussed. As many people involved in ecumenism know from personal experience, convergence of views is possible within such an environment. When he spoke to ecumenical leaders in Dublin in 1979, Pope John Paul II said: 'Dear brothers: with a conviction linked to our faith, we realise that the destiny of the world is at stake, because the credibility of the gospel has been challenged. Only in perfect unity can we Christians adequately give witness to the truth.' Shortly before he died in 2005, John Paul reiterated that point in par 54 of a document entitled *The Church in Europe*: 'The task of evangelisation involves moving toward one another and moving forward together as Christians, and it must begin from within; evangelisation and unity, evangelisation and ecumenism are indissolubly linked.'

During my years of contact with the Christian Renewal

Centre in Rostrevor, Co Down, which had been founded in 1974 by Rev Cecil Kerr, I had a number of memorable experiences which convinced me how correct John Paul was about the importance of unity. I'd like to recall three of them.

The cross higher than our flags
On an occasion in the 1980s a number of us, Protestant, Anglican and Catholic, were engaged in intercessory prayer. At one point a vivid image spontaneously came into my mind. I could see a number of tall flagpoles with their respective flags flapping in the wind. At the base of each flagpole were groups of people. They were shouting and gesticulating angrily at the people gathered around the other flagpoles. Then in the middle I saw the cross. At first the people didn't even notice it. Then, one by one, the protesters began to pay attention to the crucified One. As they acknowledged his presence, their anger turned to shame. Each group began to lower its flag, some slowly, others more rapidly. Soon the cross stood higher than all the flags. Then people began to drift away from their flagpoles and to gather around the foot of the cross. It seemed as if the Lord were saying: 'At the moment the flags of your denominational and nationalistic pride are raised higher than the cross. But when you look to him who was lifted up from the earth to draw all peoples to himself, you will lower the flags of your pride. Then, and only then, will you find peace, for in the power of the cross the dividing wall of your divisions will crumble.'

That prayer experience taught me that humility in particular can help us to overcome our divisions. I have seen many Catholics and Protestants display an attitude of superiority, conceit and even arrogance with regard to one another. Catholics sometimes feel in a superior sort of way that they belong to the one true church and have the fullness of truth, while many Protestants for their part believe they alone know the truth, as for Catholics they are not saved and probably not Christian at all. One thing is for sure, those condescending attitudes are not those of Jesus who 'made himself nothing, taking the very nature of a servant' (Phil 2:7). Over the years I have found that the following texts are a great help when attending inter-church meetings. 'Do nothing out of selfish ambition or vain conceit, but *in humility consider others better than yourselves* [my italics]' (Phil 2:3). Paul said something similar in Rom 12:3, 10: 'Do not think of yourself more highly than you ought ... *Honour one another above yourselves* [my italics].' The phrases 'in humility consider others better than yourselves' and 'honour one another above yourselves,' are really striking and challenging. They are not about the truths we believe in, but rather about our attitudes to one another. Paul was clearly talking in an implicit way about the need to treat members of other Christian denominations with reverence and respect. Like our Lord, we should have a metaphorical towel of humility around our waists as we serve one another in a spirit of reverence. I have found that when I have tried to act in this way, I have been overwhelmed by the generosity of the response. For example, Presbyterians have asked me to conduct a retreat for them. I have been invited to speak in Church of Ireland, Presbyterian and Lutheran parishes, and have given talks to Lutheran and Church of England clergy. On one memorable occasion I was even asked, with the consent of the local Anglican and Catholic bishops, to celebrate the first Roman Catholic Mass since the Reformation in an Anglican cathedral in Wales.

Unity commands a blessing
On another occasion in the 1980s, Cecil Kerr arranged that a number of people connected with the Christian Renewal Centre would lead a day of renewal in Larne. If my memory serves me correctly, Rev Harry Woodhead of the Church of Ireland, Rev David McKee, a Presbyterian minister, Mr Larry Kelly a Catholic layman, and myself were part of the team. David was assigned to give the talks. I can recall him talking in rather vivid terms about the saving power of the blood of the lamb (cf Rev 7:14). Afterwards, he invited anyone who wished to come forward for ministry to do so. As a result there were long queues of Catholics and Protestants. As David prayed for them, many men and women from different denominations began to fall back on the floor under the power of the Spirit. Although I was unfamiliar at the time with that strange phenomenon, I moved quickly to stand behind people in order to catch them as they fell backwards. It was an awesome experience. When our time

of ministry was over, David came to me and said, 'Pat, that is the first time I have seen anything like this in my ministry. The power of God was really manifested today. Why do you think it happened?' 'Well David, ' I said, 'for one thing, you preached in the power of the Spirit. But more than that, you did so in the context of inter-church unity. I feel that the Lord was revealing his approval of our united witness. Remember what Ps 133:1,3 says, "How good and pleasant it is when brothers and sisters live together in unity! ... For *there the Lord bestows his blessing*" [my italics].' David's response was brief, but solemn. 'Pat, I'm sure you are right!'

Unity and mission
My third memory dates from the late 1990s. Cecil Kerr and others had got an inter-church group together to write a document entitled, *Evangelicals and Catholics Together in Ireland*. A similar document had already been produced in the United States. Over a period of months we had many theological discussions. I can recall that, predictably, the issue that evoked the greatest passion was that of justification. Eventually there was a meeting of minds and an agreed statement. Part of it read: 'The New Testament makes it clear that the gift of justification is received through faith. "By grace you have been saved through faith; and this is not your own doing, it is the gift of God" (Eph 2:8) ... In affirming that "we are justified by faith alone" we also affirm that "the faith that justifies is not alone," or it is dead and unable to save. Genuine saving faith is always expressed by works of loving obedience, bearing fruits worthy of grace and proving our repentance, just as "fruit ever comes from the living root of a good tree".' Shortly afterwards, our statement was superseded by par 15 of the *Joint Declaration On The Doctrine Of Justification* by the Lutheran World Federation and the Catholic Church. It reads: 'Together we confess: By grace alone, in faith in Christ's saving work and not because of any merit on our part, we are accepted by God and receive the Holy Spirit, who renews our hearts while equipping and calling us to good works.'

During those theological discussions we also wrote a section entitled, 'We Witness Together.' I want to quote an extract from that part of the document: 'As believers, we commit ourselves, in obedience to the Great Commission of our Lord, to evangelise everyone. We must share the fullness of God's saving truth with all, including members of our several communities. Evangelicals must speak the gospel to Catholics and Catholics to Evangelicals, always speaking the truth in love, so that "working hard to maintain the unity of the Spirit in the bond of peace … the body of Christ may be built up until we all reach unity in the faith and in the knowledge of the Son of God" (Eph 4:3, 12-13).' The teaching of our Lord is unmistakable. The credibility of his mission in the world (and in Ireland in particular) is dependent upon the unity and love of his disciples as expressed in Jesus' prayer in John 17:21: 'May they all be one; as you Father are in Me, and I in you, so also may they be in us, that the world may believe that you sent me.'

Conclusion
Statistics confirm the fact that secularisation and secularism are having a corrosive effect on all our churches. By and large, practice rates have been falling for years in all our denominations. Clearly, we need to commit ourselves to a new evangelisation. Our efforts to spread the good news of salvation in Jesus Christ will be credible and effective to the extent that it is done in a spirit of unity. As was mentioned in a preceding chapter, *koinonia* (i.e. communion) and *kerygma* (i.e. basic proclamation of the gospel) are inextricably linked. As Pope John Paul II said to the ecumenical gathering in Dublin in 1979: 'Dear brothers: with a conviction linked to our faith, we realise that the destiny of the world is at stake, because the credibility of the gospel has been challenged. Only in perfect unity can we Christians adequately give witness to the truth. And so our fidelity to Jesus Christ urges us to do more, to pray more, to love more.'

(In 2010 the community in the Christian Renewal Centre in Rostrevor ceased its activities. The board of trustees transferred the house to Youth With a Mission. I am confident that it will continue to foster reconciliation between the churches as it engages in its evangelistic training and activities. Shortly after the changeover had taken place my friend Cecil Kerr, founder of the Renewal Centre, passed to the Lord following a long illness. May this wonderful man of faith, rest in peace).

CHAPTER SIXTEEN

Sharing During Times of Economic Need

During the great depression in the nineteen thirties there was a song, 'Brother can you spare a dime?' One verse read, 'Once I built a railroad, I made it run, made it race against time. Once I built a railroad; now it's done. Brother, can you spare a dime? Once I built a tower, up to the sun, brick, and rivet, and lime; Once I built a tower, now it's done. Brother, can you spare a dime?' Whenever worldwide recession kicks in, more and more people lose their jobs and incomes. As well as having to continue to pay mortgages and debts they struggle to buy the basic necessities of life. Faced by an uncertain future it is not surprising that many of them become depressed, anxious and even suicidal. How should Christians react to those who are experiencing such hardships?

What does the bible say?
Let's look at what the bible has to say. In Deut 15:10-11 we read: 'Give liberally and be ungrudging when you do so, for on this account the Lord your God will bless you in all your work and in all that you undertake. Since there will never cease to be some in need on the earth, I therefore command you, "Open your hand to the poor and needy neighbour in your land".' Later in the Old Testament we read about the friendship between David and Jonathan, recounted in 1 Sam 18-20. We are told: 'Jonathan became one spirit with David and loved him as himself ... He swore eternal friendship with David because of his deep affection for him. He took off the robe he was wearing and gave it to David, together with his armour and also his sword, bow and belt.' This ideal of shared love being expressed in a sharing of goods was to come to fruition in the life of the early church. When St Luke described the first Christian community, he saw it as the fulfilment of the Old Testament ideal. United by their

faith in Jesus, the first believers 'were one in heart and soul, and no one said that any of the things he possessed was his own, but they had everything in common' (Acts 4:32).

St Paul linked generosity to those in need with the celebration of the Eucharist. In 1 Cor 11:20-22 he said: 'When you come together, it is not the Lord's Supper you eat, for as you eat, each of you goes ahead without waiting for anybody else. One remains hungry, another gets drunk. Don't you have homes to eat and drink in? Or do you despise the church of God and humiliate those who have nothing? What shall I say to you? Shall I praise you for this? Certainly not!' In the early church Christians from all walks of life were welcome to attend the Eucharist when it was celebrated in the house of a well off person. Usually he or she had a room large enough to contain all those who wanted to attend. There were prosperous people as well as those who were poor or slaves. However, the better off members of the community used to have a meal together either before or after the Eucharist at which the poor and the slaves were not always welcome. Paul was angered by this. He felt that the non-inclusion of the poor and the slaves offended the sense of *koinonia* or fellowship which was such a key feature of the Eucharist. He argued that if the Eucharist was to be treated with respect, the well off members of the community were bound in charity to invite the less well off members to their meals. Commenting on Paul's words St John Chrysostom wrote: 'You have tasted the Blood of the Lord, yet you do not recognise your brother ... You dishonour this table when you do not judge worthy of sharing your food someone judged worthy to take part in this meal ... God freed you from all your sins and invited you here, but you have not become more merciful.' Surely, that point is relevant in times of recession when so many people who belong to the family of faith have fallen on hard times.

Elsewhere in the letters of St Paul it is evident that he encouraged the better off members of the gentile church to be generous to fellow Christians who were in need, especially those in Jerusalem. The Pauline author of 1 Tim 6:17-18 was well aware that the love of riches was the root of many evils. In order to overcome the temptation of greed he said: 'As for those who in the present age are rich, command them not to be haughty, or to set their hopes on the uncertainty of riches, but rather on God who richly provides us with everything for our enjoyment. They are to do good, to be rich in good works, generous, and ready to share.' Paul promised those who were generous: 'You will be enriched in every way for your great generosity, which will produce thanksgiving to God through us; for the rendering of this ministry not only supplies the needs of the saints but also overflows with many thanksgivings to God' (2 Cor 9:11-12). Quoting words of Jesus, which are not recorded in the gospels, St Paul testified: 'It is more blessed to give than to receive' (Acts 20:35).

The earth is the common possession of all
In the post-apostolic era, the Fathers of the church added another dimension to Christian thinking when they wrote about the tension between the right to the necessities of life and the right to private property. For instance, in sec 19 of *The Letter of Barnabas* (100 AD), members of the Christian community are told: 'You shall share everything with your neighbour, and not claim that anything is your own ... You shall not hesitate to give, nor shall you grumble when giving, but you will know who is the good paymaster of the reward.' In the *Didache* 4:8 (150 AD) we read: 'You shall not turn away from someone in need, but shall share everything with your brother or sister, and do not claim that anything is your own. For you are sharers in what is imperishable, how much more so in perishable things.' St Ambrose stated in *Duties of the Clergy*, 1. 132 (391 AD): 'God has ordered all things to be produced so that there should be food in common for all, and that the earth should be the common possession of all. Nature, therefore, has produced a common right for all, but greed has made it a right for a few.'

The implications of these teachings were outlined by Pope John Paul II in par 14 of his encyclical *Human Work* where he said that the church has always understood the right to private property, 'within the broader context of the right common to all to use the goods of the whole of creation: the right to private property is subordinated to the right to common use, to the fact that goods are meant for everyone.' Some years later that point was reiterated in par 2403 of the *Catechism of the Catholic Church*: 'The right to private property, acquired by work or received from others by inheritance or gift, does not do away with the original gift of the earth to the whole of mankind. The universal destination of goods remains primordial, even if the promotion of the common good requires respect for the right to private property and its exercise.' In other words, the right of everyone to the fruits of the earth is prior to anyone's right to private property

Examples of generosity to those in need
Many years ago I was a member of a Charismatic community group that tried to live like the believers described in Acts 4:32-36. At one point, a member, whose wife was also in our community group, lost his job. Although he was entitled to unemployment benefit and child allowances, he and his six children really did not have enough to live on. As a result, the members of the group decided to make weekly financial contributions to supplement his income. To do so required sacrifice and belt tightening by all of us. As far as I can remember the weekly payments were required for nearly a year. The couple who were being helped were amazed and edified by the generosity of the prayer group. When the man eventually got another job, he didn't forget the kindness that he and his family had experienced. In thanksgiving, he founded a charity called Christian Sharing which collected thousands of pounds for people in need in other countries.

Some time after that episode I was invited to conduct a retreat for priests in the town of Ambo in Ethiopia. While I was there, I happened to see a number of lepers who were begging outside a baths which was supplied with water from hot springs. When I made enquiries about them a local priest told me that he and a number of lay people had conducted a survey which discovered that there were about 170 lepers living in appalling conditions outside the town. They eked out their existence by begging. They had no government support, no education for their children, no health care, and no jobs. He told me that he and his lay colleagues had plans to help the lepers but they couldn't implement them due to a lack of financial resources. I promised the priest that, when he and his lay collaborators tried to implement their plans on behalf of the lepers, I would try to raise some money to help them.

CHAPTER SIXTEEN

When I came back to Ireland I merely told a lay friend what I had seen. Without being asked, she started to collect money from people she knew. This was the outcome of an inspired dream she had, in which the Lord told my friend that he wanted her to help the lepers. In the meantime the priest in Ambo employed a local man to spearhead some improvements. Many of the lepers homes were refurbished, they were given blankets, and equipment was bought which enabled them to earn a living for themselves. Having seen these developments the Ethiopian government also began to contribute some money to the project. Over the years a relatively small number of Irish people in the North of Ireland have contributed tens of thousands of pounds to the lepers of the Ambo project. In more recent years young members of the Vincentian Lay Missionaries (VLM) in Ireland have visited the lepers in Ambo.

Early in 2011 I spent five weeks in Detroit. The state of Michigan, and especially Detroit itself, are experiencing a lot of economic hardship due to the recession, and the decline of the automobile industry. As a result many people have lost their jobs and are struggling to pay their bills and to hang on to their homes. In the parish where I was living, the local conference of the St Vincent de Paul was doing great work. Besides helping people to pay electricity and water bills and many other good works, they had a food pantry. In reality it was an area in the pastor's house where donated foodstuffs were stored. Each weekend there was a collection of non-perishable food items that parishioners brought to the church in order to help the needy members of the community who were struggling to make ends meet. If any particular foodstuff was running low a request was placed in the parish newsletter. So much food came in each weekend, it overflowed on to a corridor. Then people, such as unemployed parents of large families, could call to the priest's house and discreetly request supplies. I must say that I found the whole enterprise most edifying. It was a good example of Christian faith expressed through love (cf Gal 5:6).

Sacrificial giving will bring Blessing
I'm convinced that more and more of our fellow Christians will experience economic hardship as the downturn worsens. If we

wish to live in accord with the urgings of God's love within, we should be prepared to share what we can with those in need. This kind of generosity requires sacrifice by digging in to savings and cutting back on non-essential spending, while trusting in him who looks after the lilies of the field and the birds of the air (cf Mt 6:26). At a political level, Christians should be prepared to accept legislation which asks them to make reasonable sacrifices in the name of the common good and needs of the less well off members of society.

I can remember reading many years ago how John Wesley, the founder of Methodism, used to give a tenth of his income to his church. When he grew wealthier as a result of book royalties and donations, instead of giving a tenth of his larger income, he continued to live on what he got as a young priest and gave all the rest to the church. It may be that Christian groups and parishes should begin to ask their members to give such things as money, food, clothing and furniture to a contingency fund which could be administered by the Vincent de Paul Society and used for the foreseeable future to help those in need, firstly, in their own midst, and if possible outside the community. As Pope Benedict XVI said in par 25 of his encyclical *God is Love*: 'The church also has a specific responsibility: within the ecclesial family, no member should suffer through being in need. The teaching of the Letter to the Galatians is emphatic: "So then, as we have opportunity, let us do good to all, and especially to those who are of the household of faith" (6:10).'

Conclusion
I am convinced that this kind of sacrificial giving will have many beneficial effects. Firstly, it will help those in need. Secondly, it will bear witness to the providential love of God in a practical and credible way. Thirdly, it will build and strengthen the bonds of unity. Fourthly, it will call down a spiritual blessing on those who give generously. St Paul rightly linked the related notions of Christian generosity and thanksgiving when he said: 'You will be enriched in every way for your great generosity, which will produce thanksgiving to God through us; for the rendering of this ministry not only supplies the needs of the saints but also overflows with many thanksgivings to God' (2 Cor 9:11-12).

SECTION FOUR

Prayer

CHAPTER SEVENTEEN

The Teaching of Jesus on Prayer in Mark's Gospel

There are many well-known descriptions of prayer. For example, par 2559 of *The Catechism of the Catholic Church* quotes an oft quoted saying of St John Damascene: 'Prayer is a matter of raising one's mind and heart to God, or the requesting of good things from God.' It could be argued that this saying is unsatisfactory in so far as it emphasises what the person praying does, while neglecting to mention what it is that the Lord does. In the Instruction, *Some Aspects of Christian Meditation* there is a more balanced description in par 3: 'Prayer is defined, properly speaking, as a personal, intimate and profound dialogue between man and God.' The best definitions of prayer tend to see it in relational terms as a conversation, discussion, dialogue, conference or colloquy. It is true that we raise our minds and hearts to God, but the Lord responds by revealing the divine presence, mind and heart to us. In her autobiography St Teresa of Avila provided a classic description when she said: 'Prayer is nothing other than an intimate friendship, a frequent, but private, heart to heart conversation with him by whom we know ourselves to be loved.' It could be argued that Moses epitomised Teresa's description of prayer. In Ex 33:11 we are told that when he entered the Tent of Meeting, he would pour out his concerns to God and 'the Lord used to speak to Moses face to face, as one speaks to a friend.'

Jesus the man of prayer, *par excellence,* was the new Moses. There is something mysterious and ultimately inaccessible about his inner life. This is not surprising because we are contemplating the infinite depths of the divine Son of God. However, we have reason to believe that we can gain some insight into his prayer life. Firstly, as Mark was well aware, although the prayer of Jesus transcended that of the saintly men and women of Old Testament times, it had an affinity with their experience of God, e.g. Mk 6:46 is reminiscent of the theophany

CHAPTER SEVENTEEN

experienced by Moses on Mount Sinai (cf Exod 19:3; 16, 24). Secondly, the gospel of Mark not only gives us some information about the ways in which Jesus prayed, it also recounts one of his spontaneous prayers (cf Mk 15:34). Thirdly, in Mark's gospel we have Jesus' teaching on prayer. Brief though it is, we can presume that it was based on the Lord's personal experience and example. Fourthly, through baptism and the outpouring of the Spirit, Jesus truly lives in believers and they live in him (cf par 251 of *The Catechism of the Catholic Church*). As adopted sons and daughters of God they 'have the mind of Christ' (1 Cor 2:16). This means that their prayer lives can enable them to have a certain affinity with the inner life of Jesus, thereby providing them with an interpretative key that can be used, with caution, to unlock some of the secrets of his intimate relationship with the Father.

Although, as God, Jesus was filled with the Spirit from the moment of his conception, as far as his human nature was concerned he grew in age, wisdom and grace (cf Lk 2:40). From early childhood onwards, Joseph and Mary would have instructed him on how to pray. He first heard the psalms at home and then in the local synagogue. In one place St Augustine referred to Mary as 'the woman of the tambourine' and it was she, who more than anyone else, taught her Son to be 'the royal singer of the psalms!' Enlightened by the Spirit, the varied sentiments of these scriptural prayers expressed the nascent religious stirrings of his own heart. When he got a bit older, he participated in the fixed order of prayer observed by the Jewish people. He would have attended the weekly Sabbath worship, said grace before and after meals, and paused three times daily to pray, i.e. at 9 am, at 12 noon and at 3 pm (cf Ps 55:17; Dan 6:10). As a devout Jew, he would have recited well-known prayers such as the *Shema*, *Berakah* and *Kaddish*.

It would probably be true to say that, of all the gospels, that of Mark contains the smallest number of verses to do with the teaching of Jesus on prayer. That said, they are precious because, not only do they give us an inspired insight into the nature of Christian prayer, they are still highly relevant today. Before examining two key texts in Mk 11:22-25 and Mk 14:36 in later chapters, we will look at the other texts in Mark's gospel which are about prayer.

The Exorcism of the Epileptic Boy
In Mk 9:14-29 there is an account of how a father brought his possessed boy to the disciples. According to Malachy Marrion, who wrote a doctoral thesis on subject of Prayer in Mark and in the Q Material, this passage could be the product of the joining of two distinct stories, or two accounts of the same event. In spite of their best efforts, the disciples could not exorcise the disturbed boy. Then the father brought him to Jesus who exorcised him quickly and effectively. When the disciples asked him why they had failed to drive out the evil spirit, Jesus replied in verse 29, 'This kind can come out only through prayer.' Presumably, the disciples had prayed. But we have reason to believe that Jesus was talking about the prayer of expectant rather than hesitant faith. He rebuked the disciples and the other bystanders calling them a 'faithless generation'. Then he said to the distraught father in verse 23, 'All things can be done for the one who believes.'

A number of observation can be made about this text. Firstly, it stresses the all-important role of faith in prayer. The evangelist had stressed this point in Mk 1:15; 5:36. Although none of the commentaries consulted mention this fact, Jesus seems to be referring to the charism of expectant faith which was mentioned by St Paul in 1 Cor 12:9; 13:2. It could be described as a gratuitous as opposed to a sanctifying grace, which is granted to some disciples of Jesus by the Holy Spirit. Rooted in the gifts of wisdom and knowledge, it enables them in particular situations of need, to discern with trusting conviction, of a heartfelt and expectant kind, that in answer to a prayer of either petition, intercession or command, the unconditional mercy and love of God will be manifested, if necessary, through a deed of power such as an exorcism, healing or miracle. Such edifying epiphanies of salvation are anticipations, in the present, of the future transformation of all things in the end times.

Secondly, it is evident that Jesus expected this kind of faith from the boy's father, the disciples and the bystanders. Thirdly, implicit in Jesus' words was an intimation that he was talking about the kind of unquestioning trust that enabled him to perform deeds of power. This is a controversial point of view. In his *Summa Theologica*, St. Thomas stated emphatically that Jesus hadn't faith: 'From the very moment of his conception' he wrote, 'Christ had the full vision of the very being of God, as we will hold later on. Therefore he *could not have had faith* [my italics].' When Thomas spoke of faith, he was referring, presumably, to faith in God's existence and justifying faith. However, he also asserted in the *Summa* that Jesus had all the charisms, which includes the charism of faith.

Scripture scholar Ian Wallis has pointed out in *The Faith of Jesus Christ in Early Christian Traditions*, that there are numerous New Testament texts, of an ambiguous nature, where the faith of Jesus seems to be implicit. For example, having said that 'all things are possible to the one who believes,' it could be asked, who does the word 'one' refer to, the father, the disciples, or to Jesus himself? It certainly referred to the people gathered there, but could it be argued that it applied to Jesus also? After all, it was he who had exorcised the boy with a word. That charismatic deed of power implied that he was the only one who unhesitatingly trusted that all things, including exorcism, were possible to the God who was active in and through him. As Christopher Marshall commented in his book, *Faith as a Theme in Mark's Gospel*: 'The father is being implicitly called to emulate the faith of Jesus. And it is the faith of both parties that permits success.' Fourthly, Malachy Marrion points out in an interesting distinction, that while the father's request for help was an intercessory prayer, Jesus' words of exorcism were not a form of prayer. He says this because they are addressed to the evil spirit and not directly to God. As such they are neither petitionary or intercessory. It is a debatable point. Surely, if a Christian acts in the name of Jesus, e.g. by commanding an evil spirit to leave a person, implicit in that act of faith, is a raising of the mind and heart to the God who is active in the situation in and through the person who is ministering in the name of the Lord.

Cleansing of the Temple
In Mk 11:15-17 we have Mark's brief description of the cleansing of the Temple, during which Jesus said: 'Is it not written, "My house shall be called a house of prayer for all the nations"? But you have made it a den of robbers.' The text Jesus had in mind when he said this was probably Is 56:7 which reads: 'These I will

bring to my holy mountain, and make them joyful in my house of prayer; their burnt offerings and their sacrifices will be accepted on my altar; for my house shall be called a house of prayer for all peoples.' Jesus was angered by the fact that the Temple was being desecrated by commercialism. Besides having to pay an annual temple tax, the poor were being ripped off because of strict rules about presenting animals without blemish. If they bought them at a reasonable price in Jerusalem, the temple authorities would find fault with them, so poor people had to buy their sacrifices within the Temple where they were charged exorbitant prices. By the way, they had to change their currency for temple coinage. Once again they were ripped off by the money changers. Furthermore, gentiles who entered the court of the Gentiles found it hard to pray because of the commercial activity and noise. All this caused moral outrage in Jesus. The temple was supposed to be a place of welcome and prayer for all, including gentiles, but in actual fact it was nothing of the kind. He referred to it 'a den of thieves' (Mk 11:17).

Polemic against the Religious Authorities
In Mk 12:40 we have another polemic against the religious authorities: 'They devour widows' houses,' declared Jesus, 'and for the sake of appearance say long prayers.' Once again Jesus was protesting against dishonest, hypocritical religious practices. In their commentary on *The Gospel of Mark,* authors John Donahue and Daniel Harrington explain that lawyers with a reputation for piety could be appointed as trustees over the property of widows and as a result might get a share of their estates. Jesus was opposed to them because, like the Scribes and Pharisees, they deliberately set out to earn a good reputation by long and ostentatious prayers, thereby putting themselves in a position to make money from vulnerable members of Jewish society.

Pray about the Testing in the End Times
In his doctoral thesis, Malachy Marrion devoted a surprising amount of space to this incident. He makes the observation that Mk 13:14-20 is more an example of apocalyptic exhortation than

apocalyptic prophecy. It is possible that the imagery Jesus used was drawn from accounts of the destruction of Jerusalem. If so, this would have indicated that Mark's gospel was written after 70 AD. People would have had to flee the destruction. Speaking compassionately about pregnant women and those nursing infants, Jesus said in verse 18: 'Pray that it may not be in winter.' In that season the weather was cold and harsh. Jesus seems to have asked the disciples to pray, not that the end would not come, but that it would not come during the Winter.

Keep awake and pray
There is a more important word of teaching which was spoken during the agony in the garden of Gethsemane: 'Keep awake and pray,' said Jesus, 'that you may not come into the time of trial; the spirit indeed is willing, but the flesh is weak' (Mk 14:38). This injunction to engage in on-going prayer carries echoes from psalms 42:8, 63:6; and 77:2, all of which talk about praying during the night. Mention of the time of trial, is not only about the present crisis in the garden, but also an anticipatory reference to the greater crisis of the end times, already referred to in Mk 13:14-20. This notion finds a similar resonance in the petition in the Lord's prayer which says: 'Lead us not into temptation' (Mt 6:13). One is reminded here of Paul's well known admission: 'I do not understand my own actions. For I do not do what I want, but I do the very thing I hate ... For I do not do the good I want, but the evil I do not want is what I do' (Rom 7:15:19). In Gal 5:17 he explained: 'What the flesh desires is opposed to the Spirit, and what the Spirit desires is opposed to the flesh.' However, in 1 Cor 10:13 Paul assures us that, 'No temptation has seized you except what is common to man. And God is faithful; he will not let you be tempted beyond what you can bear. But when you are tempted, he will also provide a way out so that you can stand up under it.'

Conclusion
Although the references to prayer and praying may be fewer in Mark than in the other gospels, they reward our attention and reflection. They emphasise the importance of such things as integrity, single-mindedness, awareness, sincerity and expectant

faith. Speaking about the phrase, 'stay awake' Andre Louf says in his excellent book, *Teach Us to Pray*, 'Each and every method of prayer has but one objective: to find the heart and alert it.' The heart is the central point in our being, where mind and body meet. Only profound concentration of a quiet kind can enable us to get in touch with our heart and the prayer within it.

CHAPTER EIGHTEEN

The Power of Prayer in Mark's Gospel

In the preceding chapter we looked at a number of things that Jesus said about prayer. However, there is a major teaching about its power in Mk 11:1-33. It is an important text which has a lot to teach those who engage in Christian ministry of any kind. Mark situates the verses to do with moving mountains, on the road from Bethany to Jerusalem, during the last week of Christ's life. On the way, Jesus cursed a fig tree for not bearing fruit, and the next day, Peter noticed that it had withered and dried up from the roots. Mark's saying is situated within a complex context which contains five interconnected episodes. While they tend to go in twos, it is not always clear how the episodes should be twinned. They are to be found in:

1. Mk 11: 1-11, the entry into Jerusalem
2. Mk 11:12-14, the cursing of the fig tree
3. Mk 11:15-19, the cleansing of the temple
4. Mk 11:20-25, the discovery that the fig tree has withered, and Jesus' teaching on faith, prayer and mutual forgiveness
5. Mk 11:27-33, the challenge to Jesus' authority

There is reason to think that nos 2 and 3 interpret one another, and 3 and 4 interpret one another.

In his book *A Marginal Jew*, John Meier looks at this chapter within its literary and theological context. He suggests that originally, the pre-Markan source included three elements: Jesus' entry into Jerusalem; his cleansing of the temple; and the challenge to his authority. As this tradition developed, the pre-Markan author, upon whom the evangelist relied, emphasised that the cleansing of the temple was not an act of purification and reform, but rather a prophetic judgement on the temple, and its unrepentant devotees. He suggests that he did this by inventing the story of the cursing of the fig tree. There is general agreement that it is a difficult action to interpret. C. S. Mann says in the *Anchor Bible* commentary on Mark: 'Either Jesus thought that in him the New Age was dawning and that, therefore, the fig tree should already be showing signs of that age, or the fig tree was itself a demonstration of the fact that the New Age was not yet ready to be ushered in ... The notion of the tree withering to its roots is reminiscent of a similar account in Jonah 4:7. It shows that the word Jesus spoke had the power to accomplish what it said, i.e. the death of the tree.' In *A Marginal Jew*, John Meier adds in similar vein: 'Mk 11:22-24 apparently makes Jesus' powerful curse of the fig tree a paradigm of the *power of faith filled prayer* [my italics], despite the fact that this cursing miracle, like most of the miracle stories in Mark, says nothing about Jesus praying or believing.' Just as the fruitless tree was cursed, so the temple and its cult would die only to be replaced by the new community of faith. Mark, who probably adopted this pre-existing material, added a theological dimension by tacking on what seem to be pre-existing sayings about faith, prayer and forgiveness. They now take centre stage.

Have firm faith in God
Jesus responded to Peter's cry of amazement on seeing the withered, fig tree by saying, 'Have faith in God' (*RSV*). This is a much debated phrase. Apparently the Greek version is awkward, and is hardly defensible from a grammatical point of view. It has been translated in a number of ways. Some later manuscripts, render the phrase as, 'if you have faith in God.' Other translations opt for, 'whoever believes,' or 'do you have faith in God?' Another scholar, W. S. Lane has suggested the following translation in his book *The Gospel According to Mark*: 'You have the faithfulness of God' It would seem that this version is based on theological assumptions rather than grammar. He says: 'On this understanding the solemnly introduced assurances of verses 23-24 are grounded explicitly on God's faithfulness and not on the ability of man to banish from his heart the presumption of doubt.'

Christopher Marshall discusses the issue of complete reliance on God and observes: 'The disciples are beckoned to trust actively in God, for although the existing temple has been disqualified, they are the beginning of God's new house of prayer for all nations ... Mark conceives of faith then not simply as the basis of entry to the new community, but as its continuing way of operating.' Derek Prince and George Montague maintain that what Jesus actually said in its most literal form, was, 'have God's faith,' in others words, through the gift of the Spirit, share in God's own disposition, presumably that of Jesus. However one translates the Greek phrase, it seems clear that it does not refer either to justifying faith or to the fruit of the Spirit. This would imply that Jesus was referring to trusting faith and probably the charism of faith which has already been referred to in the foregoing chapter in connection with the exorcism of the boy. It is an unwavering trust in the Lord and firm confidence in the disciple's ability to share in God's powerful activity. The injunction has an eschatological dimension in so far as words and deeds of power are intimations of the New Age to come.

The prayer of command
The verse in Mk 11:23, about commanding a mountain to move into the sea, is a key one, because it is similar to 1 Cor 13:2, where the moving of mountains requires the exercise of the charism of faith. Mk 11:23 says that the disciples who have faith in God will be able to tell a mountain to move, into the sea. It is unlikely that Jesus intended this phrase to be understood in a literal way. In a parallel passage in Lk 17:6, there is mention of a mulberry tree. As hyperbole, the phrase refers to everyday obstacles which stand in the path of the coming of the kingdom of God, such as the lack of faith and receptivity which was so evident in the Temple. The second observation to be made about this verse is the surprising fact that Jesus doesn't encourage those who have faith in God to ask the Father to move the mountain. Instead he encouraged them to have such faith in God that they can receive and dispose of the power of the Lord by means of a word of authority. Like all biblical promises this one was associated with 'if' clauses. Jesus stated clearly that the ability to participate in the purposes of God, even to the point of exorcisms, healings and miracles, depended upon the ability of the believers to speak the word of power without any doubt in their hearts.

The word 'heart' in Greek is *kardia*. It referred in a metaphorical way to the origin of a person's feelings, desires, thoughts and will (cf Eph 3:16; Rom 8:27; 1 Pet 3:4). It is there that one discerns with certainty that God is about to act. This kind of inner certainty depends on three things. Firstly, an intimate relationship between God and the believer. Secondly, an experiential, rather than a notional knowledge of God's will. Writing about this important point Christopher Marshall observed: 'The exertion of God's transcendent power, which faith seeks, is always subject to the constraint of God's will. The certainty of faith, in other words, *presupposes revelatory insight* [my italics] into the divine intention, though this must be actualised by the believer's volitional commitment to refuse doubt and seek undivided faith (cf 5:36; 9:22-24).' Writing about the kind of faith Jesus expected, Edward O' Connor observed in his book *Faith in the Synoptic Gospels: A Problem in the Correlation of Scripture*: 'Evidently, the faith which he is speaking of is not belief in the strict sense of assent to a truth, but the confident expectation, based on trust in God, which should animate our prayer. Future events, without *a special revelation about them* [my italics], can only be the object of hope and not belief.' Thirdly, one needs a commission to exercise such delegated authority (cf Mk 3:14; 6:7; 12). Therefore, expectant faith is not the result of wishful thinking, psyching oneself up, or mere mental assent to the promises of God. If the person has such an awareness and firm confidence, God will move the mountain. It is not the believer who performs the deed of power, it is God's power working in and through him or her.

Asking with expectant faith
Mark then includes a second saying, this one about expectant faith as expressed in and through petitionary prayer. Jesus promises: 'Therefore I tell you, whatever you ask for in prayer, believe that you have received it, and it will be yours' (Mk 11:24-25). Sharyn Echols Dowd, author of *Prayer, Power and The Problem of Suffering* suggests that this verse could be more accurately translated as 'Keep on believing that you have received everything that you are praying and asking for, and it will be done for you.' In many ways this is a vitally important condition. Verse 24 can only be properly understood in the light of verses 20-23. Christopher Marshall points out that for Mark the

degree of expectancy referred to in this verse is not the unvarying prerequisite for all answered prayer. 'Rather he affirms that when prayer is made with such certitude, it is always answered.' The conviction of the person praying goes beyond wishful thinking or notional certainty. Such unhesitating faith is firm evidence that the petition is being offered in accord with God's revealed will.

There are two forms of trust, hesitant and expectant. A person with hesitant trust accepts God's promises at a notional level, believing them to be true. However, when faced by a particular problem such as an illness, he or she may not be quite sure whether God is going to act, right now, in these particular circumstances. Typically the person prays a prayer of petition in the hope that God may do something in the future, if what is asked is in accordance with God's will. A person with expectant faith accepts that the promises of God are true at a notional level. However, as a result of a divine inspiration in a particular situation of need, he or she has no inner doubt about them, and confidently believes that God is acting, in the here and now. The seed of God's grace has been planted. Having taken invisible root in the present it will go on to bear visible fruit in the future. Instead of having to see evidence in order to believe, this kind of confident faith believes in order to see. One is reminded in this context of the well known description of faith in Heb 11:1: 'Now faith is the assurance of things hoped for (in the future), the conviction of things not seen (in the present).' That same emphasis on the assurance of faith in the present is also evident in 1 Jn 5:14 where we read: 'This is the confidence which we have in him, that if we ask anything according to his will he hears us. And if we know that he hears us in whatever we ask, we know that we *have obtained the requests made of him* [my italics].' As far as I'm aware the Greek here is in the *aorist*, i.e. the continuous present, meaning, 'you have begun to receive your request (in the present) and will go on receiving it (in the future).'

The evangelist adds a final point in Mk 11:25. Unforgiveness is a block to this kind of gratuitous faith. While God's merciful love is always available to the believer it can only be appropriated and experienced in the heart if she or he is willing to show that same merciful love of an unmerited kind to others. To withhold forgiveness, for whatever reason, is to lose the inner witness of God's immediate presence and inspirations, upon which the prayer and word of expectant faith both depend.

Some implications for evangelisation
Mark's gospel, as we have seen, stresses such things as the importance of petitionary and intercessory prayer, expectant faith, and deeds of power in the Christian life. At a time when there is such an urgent need for the new evangelisation called for by Popes John Paul II and Benedict XVI, Mark's short but nuanced teaching on prayer is highly relevant.

There are three main ways in which we can bear witness to Christ: 1) by preaching and teaching, 2) by one-to-one evangelisation, 3) and by performing charismatic deeds of power such as healings, exorcism and miracles. As a result of the revival of charismatic activity in the church, many Catholics, clerical and lay have been empowered to do similar things. As Paul VI observed, such gifts 'make the church fruitful, beautiful and splendid, and enable it to win the attention and astonishment of the profane and secularised world.' Mark's teaching on the prayer of expectant faith in 11:22-25 shows that it can be the gateway to the deeds of power, mentioned by the Pope, which are performed, in and through believers, by the God to whom nothing is impossible. However, Mark tempers that message with a complementary one in Mk 14:36 which will be dealt with in the next chapter. It shows that, while it is OK to pray that suffering might be alleviated by means of deeds of power, God will not always answer prayers as we would wish. As he did in Christ's life, he may use our sufferings for a greater redemptive purpose. The Pauline author of Col 1:24 wrote perceptively when he declared: 'In my flesh I am completing what is lacking in Christ's afflictions for the sake of his body, which is the church.' That sentiment is implicit in the prayer, said at the well known Jesuit Novena of Grace: 'If what I ask is not in accordance with your will or for your glory, grant me what is in accord with both.'

Conclusion
In par 72 of his encyclical *Catechesis in Our Time,* Pope John Paul

CHAPTER EIGHTEEN

II seemed to echo that balanced point of view when he said that evangelisation: 'will be authentic and will have real fruitfulness in the church, not so much according as it gives rise to extraordinary charisms, but according as it leads the greatest possible number of the faithful, as they travel their daily paths, to make a humble, patient and persevering effort to know the mystery of Christ better and better and to bear witness to it.' Happily, we do not have to choose between Christian fidelity or charisms. We can have both.

CHAPTER NINETEEN

St Mark on Learning from Gethsemane

All of us have to endure suffering in our everyday lives. It may be personal as a result of afflictions of our own, or it may be indirect because of the trials and tribulations of people we care about. There is another dimension which is caused by more widespread problems such as natural disasters and wars. For example, there is reason to believe that the difficulties we are experiencing during the current worldwide recession may get worse. There are prophetic intimations that they could lead to social disintegration and unrest, together with violence in the future. Here are some prophetic words which were spoken to a group of German Catholics in 1980, by Pope John Paul II. He said, 'We must be prepared to undergo great trials in the not-too-distant future; trials that will require us to give up even our lives, and a total gift of self to Christ and for Christ. Through your prayers and mine, it is possible to alleviate this tribulation, but it is no longer possible to avert it, because it is only in this way that the church can be effectively renewed. How many times, indeed, has the renewal of the church been effected in blood? This time it will not be otherwise.' In circumstances like these, how should we pray? Here is one suggestion.

The gospels make it clear that in his teaching on prayer, Jesus focused almost exclusively on the petitionary kind. It would be a mistake, however, to think that unlike praise and thanksgiving, petitionary prayer focuses primarily on human need and only in a secondary way upon the Lord. Instead of looking at God from the point of view of human needs, authentic Christian petition looks at human needs from the point of view of a trusting relationship with a benevolent and generous God. This was particularly obvious during the agony of Jesus in the garden of Gethsemane. On that occasion he implored: 'Abba, Father, everything is possible for you. Take this cup from me. Yet not what I will, but what you will' (Mk 14:36). This archetypal prayer can be looked at from four interrelated points of view: 1) Address: 'Abba Father.' 2) Declaration of divine omnipotence: 'Everything is possible for you.' 3) Petition: 'Take this cup away from me.' 4) Submission: 'But not what I will, but what you will.'

Address

The supplication of Jesus was God-centred, rather than self-centred. That is why he began with the words, 'Abba Father.' Jesus was vividly aware, not only that his Father loved him with an incomprehensible love, he was also conscious that his benevolent favour rested upon him, and that his Father was constantly assuring him that 'everything I have is yours' (Lk 15:31). As Jesus said to the disciples on one occasion, 'If you, then, though you are evil, know how to give good gifts to your children, how much more will your Father in heaven give good gifts to those who ask him?' (Mat 7:11). Jesus was well aware that imperfect parents can be extraordinarily generous to their children. Parental kindness, said Jesus, is only a pale shadow of the benevolent generosity of a perfect and loving God.

Omnipotence of God

In the first century the assertion that, 'everything is possible for God' was not widely accepted in either the Greco-Roman or Jewish world. For example, the Stoics not only believed that God was apathetic and unmoved by human suffering, they also maintained that the world was governed by inexorable and impersonal fate. For their part, the Jews were divided about the possibility of divine intervention. The Sadducees, for example, didn't believe that God could work miracles, while the Pharisees did (cf Acts 23:6-10). In our scientific age many people do not believe that God can do impossible things of a supernatural nature in people's lives. Echoing what the angel Gabriel had said to his mother at the annunciation, Jesus asserted his conviction on a number of occasions that nothing was impossible to God. For example, when the apostles observed that it would be impossible for rich people to enter heaven, Jesus responded, 'With man this is impossible, but with God all things are possible' (Mt 19:26). Time and time again, during his public ministry, he had demonstrated the soundness of that belief when he performed healings, miracles and exorcisms. In Gethsemane it was no different. Jesus stated once again that he was convinced that nothing was impossible to his Father.

Petition
From a human point of view, the prospect of having to endure the mind-numbing sufferings of passion week was almost too much for Jesus to contemplate. As the scripture recounts: 'During the days of his life on earth, he offered up prayers and petitions with loud cries and tears to the one who could save him from death' (Heb 5:7). In a way, this is surprising for two main reasons. Firstly, on a number of occasions Jesus had spoken about his impending passion as an expression of the divine will. We can recall how he reprimanded Peter when he tried to dissuade him from meeting such a fate in Jerusalem. He even went so far as to accuse him of being an agent of Satan! Secondly, it is possible that when Jesus was coming near the end of his life he was attracted by one of the Satanic temptations that he had experienced in the wilderness, the one which involved the possibility of his miraculous deliverance if he threw himself down from a tower. While in the past Jesus had resisted all such temptations, in the garden he didn't exactly reject the Father's will but he seemed to ask him to change his mind. In other words, Jesus expressed his anguished hope that the Father might be able to usher in his kingdom without him having to suffer. This would indicate that as man Jesus had a will and desires of his own, which seemed to be in conflict or tension with those of God.

Submission
Having poured out his human feelings, Jesus remained submissively God-orientated when he said: 'Yet not what I will, but what you will.' This was an echo of another prayer he had uttered some time before: 'Now my heart is troubled, and what shall I say? "Father, save me from this hour"? No, it was for this very reason I came to this hour' (Jn 12:27). While the Father often revealed his will to Jesus by means of inner inspirations, on this

occasion there was no apparent communication. Instead, God was silent. His purposes were only manifested to Jesus in and through the unfolding events of the passion. Our Lord courageously embraced God's saving plan. As he testified, 'For I have come down from heaven not to do my will but to do the will of him who sent me' (Jn 6:38). Afterwards, the author of Hebrews was to observe, 'Although he was a son, he learned obedience from what he suffered' (Heb 5:8).

Some Christian implications
I would suggest that all we need to know, either about petitionary or intercessory prayer, is contained in this poignant incident. Sooner or later, all of us have to endure sufferings of one kind or another. For instance, yesterday I received an email from a distraught woman who described the extreme physical sufferings which her aged mother has to endure and the stress which it is putting on her daughters who are trying to nurse her. The writer said that she believed in the power of a loving God and asked me to pray for her mother.

Conclusion
Needles to say, a believing Christian would want to affirm that God is our loving Father, that nothing is impossible to him and that it is good to pray to him in time of need, e.g. for the old lady's healing. But our attitude has to be like that of Jesus in Gethsemane. It is well expressed in the novena of grace in honour of St Francis Xavier. It could be adapted to read: 'Lord I ask you to grant the special favour I request. Although from a human point of view I ardently desire this favour, I am fully resigned to your loving and benevolent will. I pray and desire to obtain only that which is most conducive to your greater glory and the greater good of my soul, or the soul of the person I care about. If it is your mysterious will that I, or the person I love, continue to endure this suffering, give me the strength to embrace your will in the knowledge that we fill up in our flesh what is still lacking in your afflictions, for the sake of your body, which is the church' (cf Col 1:24).'

CHAPTER TWENTY

Rediscovering the Power of Praise

I don't quite know why, but recently I have felt a strong impulse to focus on the importance of praise in private and public worship. This has been helped, firstly by remembering the wonderful praise sessions in which I participated during the early days of renewal, and secondly, by rereading books on the subject such as Merlin Carothers' *Power in Praise* (1972), Judson Cornwall's *Let us Praise* (1973), and Paul Hinnebusch's *Praise a Way of Life* (1976).

The New Testament strongly encourages us to praise God. In Eph 1:12 we read: 'We who have first hoped in Christ, have been destined and appointed for the praise of his glory.' Heb 13:15 adds: 'Through Jesus, therefore, let us continually offer to God a sacrifice of praise – the fruit of lips that confess his name.' Again in 1 Pet 2:9 we are told that: 'You are a chosen people, a royal priesthood, a holy nation, a people belonging to God, that you may declare the praises of him who called you out of darkness into his wonderful light.'

In the *Divine Office* there is a short responsory: 'I will praise the Lord at all times, his praise will always be on my lips.' This sentiment is biblical. In Ps 34:1 we read: 'I will bless the Lord at all times; his praise shall continually be in my mouth.' In other words, there is something unconditional about this form of prayer. Whether life is going well or badly we should praise the Lord, in the belief that God's benevolent providence embraces all the circumstances of our lives and that God can bring good from evil. St Paul conveyed something of that conviction when he said in Rom 5:20: 'Where sin increased, grace increased all the more.' It would probably be true to say that the prayer of praise helps us to escape the gravitational pull of morbid self-absorption to become engrossed in God and in the victory Christ has won over Satan, sin and death. As the scriptures show, the prayer of praise can take many complementary forms.

CHAPTER TWENTY

Anticipatory praise – the festal shout

In this chapter I intend to focus in on one biblical form of praise known as the festal shout of victory. In the Old Testament there were frequent references to battles. Over and over again, the people of God had to contend with armies that were larger and better equipped than their own. But the Israelites had one great advantage. They had confidence that if they were following the will of the Lord, God would fight with them, so no matter what odds were stacked against them, they would be victorious. As they marched into battle they would utter the *teruwah Yahweh*. It was a blood curdling war cry that was intended to strike terror into the hearts of their enemies. It was also a liturgical chant which was meant to express their unshakable confidence in the One who would give them victory. There are many examples of this form of anticipatory praise. I will focus on one. It is to be found in 2 Chron 20.

King Jehoshaphat had received news that his kingdom was about to be attacked by formidable armies. From a military point of view the position looked hopeless. Not surprisingly, the king was filled with fear and anxiety. But instead of wrestling with the problem, he nestled by faith in the Lord by means of prayer and fasting. Having poured out his heart to the Lord, Jehoshaphat waited for a divine response. It came through one of his priests who spoke a word of prophecy. 'Your majesty,' he said, 'and all you people of Judah and Jerusalem, the Lord says you must not be discouraged or afraid to face this large army. The battle depends on God and not on you.' (2 Chron 20:15).

We are told that: 'Early in the morning ... As the army set out, Jehoshaphat stood and said, "Listen to me, Judah and people of Jerusalem! Have faith in the Lord your God and you will be upheld; have faith in his prophets and you will be successful".' After consulting the people, Jehoshaphat appointed men to sing to the Lord and to praise him for the splendour of his holiness as they went out at the head of the army, saying: 'Give thanks to the Lord, for his love endures forever.' In other words, the priests and musicians led the soldiers in shouting the *teruwah Yahweh* as they marched into battle. The scriptures tell us what happened next: 'As they began to sing and praise, the Lord set ambushes against the men of Ammon and Moab and Mount

Seir who were invading Judah, and they were defeated.' (2 Chron 20:20-22).

Later in the Old Testament we find that when the chosen people had settled down in Palestine there were fewer wars. But they remembered with nostalgia the battle cry of victory. They modified it for use in their temple worship. It became the 'festal shout' that is sometimes mentioned in the psalms. For example in Ps 47:1-8 we read: 'Clap your hands, all you nations; shout to God with cries of joy ... God has ascended amid shouts of joy, the Lord amid the sounding of trumpets. Sing praises to God, sing praises; sing praises to our King, sing praises. For God is the King of all the earth; sing to him a psalm of praise.' However, Ps 89:15 sums up the biblical attitude when it declares: 'Blessed are the people who know the festal shout.' There are a number of examples of the festal shout in the Old and New Testaments, e.g. Josh 6:1-20; Dan 3:24; Jonah 2:9-10.

Jesus' festal shout of victory as he died
On Palm Sunday, the praises of the people constituted a festal shout that anticipated the victory of Jesus by means of his saving death and resurrection. As Jesus said on that occasion, if the people didn't utter the festal shout 'the very stones would cry out' (Lk 19:40). I firmly believe that Jesus uttered the festal shout of victory as he died. We know that when he hung on the cross he quoted the first line of Ps 22: 'My God, my God, why have you forsaken me?' Scripture scholar Albert Gelin points out that, as a devout Jew, Jesus would have gone on to recite the rest of the psalm in his mind. At one point it suddenly switches from complaint to praise.'I will praise you to all my brothers; I will stand up before the congregation and testify of the wonderful things you have done. Praise the Lord, each one of you who fears him' (Ps 22:22-25). So when Jesus cried out on the cross: 'Father, into your hands I commit my spirit' (Lk 23:46) it was the culminating festal shout of victory which anticipated his vindication when his Father would raise him from the dead. I associate the Lord's dying words with the following verse, 'The Lord goes forth like a hero, like a warrior he stirs up his ardour; he shouts out his battlecry, against his enemies he shows his might. (Is 42:12). In view of the christological significance of the festal

Anticipatory praise and deliverance

Luke recounts a marvellous incident in Acts 16:16-34. As a result of an inspired vision, Paul had travelled from Asia to Philippi in Europe. There he preached the good news. But he was often interrupted by a young girl, who was oppressed by an evil spirit. 'This girl started following Paul and the rest of us and shouting, "Here are the servants of the Most High God; they have come to tell you how to be saved!" She did this day after day until Paul became exasperated and turned round and said to the spirit, "I order you in the name of Jesus Christ to leave that woman." The spirit went out of her then and there' (Acts 17:17-18). The girl's handlers were furious. They couldn't use her anymore to make money by means of her fortune-telling. So they had Paul and his companion Silas, arrested, sentenced, flogged, and imprisoned.

What did the two disciples do? They had broken no law. As Roman citizens they shouldn't have been flogged. Yet they had been unjustly and harshly dealt with. Did they get angry and rant and rave at their oppressors? No. They were in great pain, and bound in a dark and dank prison. Did they feel sorry for themselves as people who had been victimised? Not a bit of it. They rejoiced to be found worthy to participate in the sufferings of Christ (cf 1 Pet 4:13). 'In the middle of the night Paul and Silas were praying and singing God's praises, while the other prisoners listened' (Acts 16:25).

When Paul and Silas praised the Lord in this way, 'Suddenly there was an earthquake that shook the prison to its foundations. All the doors flew open and the chains fell from all the prisoners' (Acts 16:26). As it says in Ps 22:3-4: 'You are enthroned in the praises of your people. In you our fathers put their trust; they trusted and you delivered them.' In other words, unconditional praise of God delivers us, from a spiritual point of view.

Praise and healing

Those who engage in the praise of God know from personal experience that it creates a firewall against the power of the evil one. When we move from magnifying our problems, by concentrating on them, to magnifying Jesus and his Father, by concentrating on them, God helps us. The Lord does so in answer to the prayer, 'Search me, O God, and know my heart' (Ps 139:23) by helping us to recognise the roots of those problems. In his book, *Riding the Wind*, scripture scholar George Montague shared a prophetic word he received from the Lord: 'My son, my praise is the only mirror in which you can see rightly yourself and all that is in you, and all that is. For years you have stood, like a sentry at the gate of your dark depths, checking, analysing, and sometimes repressing these things within you. I have been leading you to see that in my presence you must let go of that pretended control and simply pour out my praise. If anxieties, problems, or even questionable thoughts or desires surface as you pray, turn them all over to me in praise. For as you let them go toward me, you will for the first time see their back side, you will begin to see their root. Till now you have been cutting off only the surface growth – and they have grown back as quickly as you cut. But when you turn totally to me, you can begin to see them totally, and this seeing is the beginning of your healing.' While this prophecy is personal in nature, surely when groups praise the Lord they will be enabled in one way or another to see the roots of their communal and personal problems and subsequently to experience healing and greater peace.

The work and the weapons are praise
My conviction about the importance of the festal shout of praise was nurtured during the troubles in Northern Ireland. Because ecumenically minded Christians seemed to face impossible odds we had to rely on God. For example, an inter-denominational conference was held in Belfast during the general strike of 1977. There was the threat of violence in the streets and of power failures. Nevertheless, over a thousand Protestants and Catholics gathered in Church House in the centre of the city for a 'Festival of Praise.' It was a remarkable experience. There was an outburst of strong, sustained praise such as I had never heard before. God's anointing fell upon us and we were graced with the festal shout, the kind that anticipated in praise the liberating action of God which was to come to fruition twenty-one years later with the Good Friday agreement. In a prophecy the Lord

called upon us to be united as his army. 'The work and the weapons are one,' he said, 'they are praise.' At a time when we face so many problems both inside and outside the church, those words are as relevant now as they were in the seventies.

Conclusion

I feel that those who lead worship, e.g. at charismatic prayer meetings and conferences, need to encourage praise that is loud and long. It seems to me that praise leaders need to explore the nature, motives and different means of praising God. The Lord has said through his modern day prophets, notably John Paul II, that a Christian springtime is on the way. No matter what difficulties we face in the meantime, we should anticipate the harvesting of a great number of souls for God with faith-filled praise.

CHAPTER TWENTY-ONE

Group Intercessory Prayer

While there is a good deal of overlap between petitionary and intercessory prayer, they are distinct. In the former people pray about personal needs. In the latter they pray about the needs of others. This chapter, which follows from the nineteenth one, reflects on the nature of biblical intercession, the reasons we have for engaging in it, and some practical ways in which groups can get involved in this important ministry.

Jesus our Advocate

Many of the great religious figures of the Old Testament such as Abraham, Moses and Jeremiah were intercessors, men who stood in the breach to pray on behalf of the people (cf Ezech 22:30). The ministry of intercession in the New Testament centres around two great advocates, Jesus and the Holy Spirit. As our one time intercessor on earth and now in heaven (cf 1 Jn 21; Heb 7:25; Rom 8:34), Jesus is our primary advocate. The word has a legal background. It refers to a lawyer who acts on a client's behalf, by expertly and effectively pleading his or her cause. There are a number of examples of Jesus' intercessory prayer such as Luke 22:31-32; Jn 17:20-21; Luke 23:34. During his ministry Jesus promised that he would send the Holy Spirit. 'I will ask the Father,' he said, 'and he will give you another Advocate to be with you always, the Spirit of truth' (Jn 14:16).

The Spirit as our Advocate

When people intercede in the Spirit they often express their longings in articulate ways such as remembered, written and vocal prayers. But there will be times when the inarticulate longings of their hearts cannot be put into words. Sometimes these inchoate longings can only be expressed in the form of tears, groans and sighs (cf Rom 8:26-27). Those who have received the gift of praying or singing in tongues – which is a form of pre-conceptual prayer expressed in unintelligible words – can intercede with their lips even when their understanding is shrouded in a cloud of unknowing. They believe that the Spirit within is praying to the God beyond, in accordance with the mind and heart of the Lord.

When St Paul wanted to describe this form of prayer, he compared it to the travail of childbirth. Compassionate intercession of this kind is like a painful movement of the spiritual womb which longs to give birth to new life in others. As St Paul says: 'We know that the whole creation has been groaning as in the pains of childbirth right up to the present time. Not only so, but we ourselves, who have the first fruits of the Spirit, groan inwardly' (Rom 8:22-23). In the light of this passage, it is not surprising, that women have a particularly deep insight into the nature, purposes and dynamics of intercession.

Mary as our gracious advocate
Our Catholic faith tells us that we have two divine advocates in the persons of Jesus and the Holy Spirit. However, our Blessed Lady, who is mother of Jesus and spouse of the Spirit, is our third advocate. She is the only human being who has been assumed body and soul into heaven. There she intercedes with her Son on our behalf. St Bernard said of her: 'Our heavenly Father who wants to show all possible mercy, gives us Jesus Christ as our principal advocate, and then gives us Mary as our advocate with Jesus.' Writing in 1805 Pope Pius VII said: 'While the prayers of those in heaven have, it is true, some claim on God's watchful eye, Mary's prayers place their assurance in a mother's right. For that reason, when she approaches her divine Son's throne, as Advocate she begs, as Handmaid she prays, but as Mother she commands.'

Spiritual Warfare
Those who are familiar with the ministry of intercession are well aware that anyone who wants to get deeply involved in it needs to appreciate the fact that it takes place within a context of spiritual conflict. As St Paul once warned: 'For our struggle is not against flesh and blood, but against the rulers, against the au-

thorities, against the powers of this dark world and against the spiritual forces of evil in the heavenly realms' (Eph 6:12). As a result, those who engage in intercessory prayer need to ascertain what spirit is at work, their own, the evil spirit, or the Spirit of God. As St John says: 'Do not trust every spirit but test the spirits to see whether they belong to God' (1 Jn 4:1). Because the evil one knows that intercession is so effective in advancing God's kingdom, it is not surprising that he tries to undermine the intercessors through such things as misfortune, ill-health, and temptations. On other occasions he will try to do this as an angel of light, e.g. under the guise of an apparent good such as a false inspiration (cf 2 Cor 11:14). Intercessors need to become aware of these tactics and to pray for protection against them. In Eph 6:16 Paul assures us that 'the shield of faith puts out all the fiery darts of the evil one.' So if the person/s under attack nestles in the Lord through faith, e.g. by means of praise and worship, instead of trying to wrestle with the evil one, they will be protected.

Discernment of Spirits
Discernment of spirits also enables intercessors to become aware of what to pray against in external situations of need. For instance, if they are praying about a war in another country, they need to recognise that the murderous, lying spirit of the accuser may well be at work (cf Jn 8:44). In this context 2 Cor 10:3-5 states: 'For though we live in the world, we do not wage war as the world does. The weapons we fight with are not the weapons of the world. On the contrary, they have divine power to demolish strongholds. We demolish arguments and every pretension that sets itself up against the knowledge of God, and we take captive every thought to make it obedient to Christ.' Intercessors can authoritatively command evil spirits, in the name of Jesus Christ, to yield to the liberating power of God.

Fasting and intercession
It is a striking fact that when Jesus was led into the wilderness, there to be tempted by the evil spirit, he fasted for forty days. In all probability this kind of mortification not only heightened his awareness of the presence and malignity of the devil he would have to contend with throughout his ministry, it also helped him

to recognise his false inspirations and to reject them. It is not surprising, therefore, that when the apostles asked Jesus why they hadn't been able to expel an evil spirit from an epileptic boy, Jesus replied: 'This kind can only come out through prayer and fasting' (Mk 9:29). In par 26 of his document *Some Aspects of Christian Meditation*, Pope John Paul II has written: 'The Christian fast signifies, above all, an exercise of penitence and sacrifice; but, already for the Fathers, it also had the aim of rendering man more open to the encounter with God and making a Christian more capable of self-dominion and at the same time more attentive to those in need.' Realising this to be true, many people who engage in intercessory prayer become involved in discreet and prudent fasting. Some live on bread and water on a designated day, others abstain from all food for part of a day, or for a few days. Many of those who fast in these ways find that they are not only more alert and perceptive from a spiritual point of view, their physical hunger acts as a symbol of their radical need for God's help. As the *Magnificat* says: 'He fills the hungry with good things' (Lk 1:53).

Prayer Walks
Intercessors can volunteer to go on prayer walks around the parish. I arranged for this to be done in Detroit when I was an acting pastor. Some men walked in twos on different roads within the parish boundaries. As they walked they prayed the rosary and also said spontaneous prayers of intercession for all the people living in the vicinity. They asked the Lord to bless all the homes, the people who lived in them and to deliver them from any evil which would try to prevent them from responding to the gospel message.

In this regard it is worth recalling what Jesus said about the role of the devil in the parable of the sower in Lk 8:11-13. Our Lord warned that Satan will do all in his power to prevent people from accepting the kerygma in faith. St Paul made the same kind of point in a striking passage in 2 Cor 4:3-4, 'If our gospel is veiled, it is veiled to those who are perishing. The god of this age has *blinded the minds of unbelievers* [my italics], so that they cannot see the light of the gospel of the glory of Christ, who is the image of God.' Although the *New Jerome Biblical Commentary* says that the phrase, 'the god of this age' may refer to a demon named Beliar rather than Satan, or 'the god who is this world,' (cf Phil 3:19), I believe that it does refer to Satan, the enemy of God, the power behind all unbelief. Jesus referred to him as 'prince of this world' in Jn 11:15; 14:30; 16:11.

Intercession is necessary whenever Christians are engaging in evangelisation. It is particularly appropriate in the period before a parish mission or evangelistic outreach such as Alpha. It is worth mentioning that in every parish there are sick and housebound people of faith. They could be asked not only to offer their sufferings and diminishments for the sake of effective evangelisation, but also to offer prayers of intercession for renewal in the parish, deliverance from evil influences, and for those who are committed to evangelisation. Here is a prayer they might agree to say each day.

New Evangelisation Rosary
  Opening Prayers
  1. Using a rosary beads, with the cross in hand say:
  'Jesus Christ himself, the good news of God.'
  2. On the first large bead, recite the Our Father …
  3. On the next three beads say the following
  1st) Grant me faith, hope and love to live your word today.
  2nd) Lead me to proclaim your loving mercy.
  3rd) Blessed Virgin Mary intercede for me.
  4. On the large beads say: Father, Son and Holy Spirit, I believe in you and I trust in you.

  For Each Decade
  Offer each decade for the following intentions:
  1st Decade) Renew within me the grace of Pentecost
  2nd Decade) Set my heart on fire that I may proclaim the good news with wisdom
  3rd Decade) Give me courage and strength
  4th Decade) Teach me ways to make you known and loved by all
  5th Decade) Let my life be a channel of your love today
  Alternatively, instead of saying the Hail Mary ten times one can repeat the aspirations above, ten times.

CHAPTER TWENTY-ONE

Concluding Prayer
Lord, with gratitude I acknowledge your grace and blessings, in the name of Jesus Christ.
Mary, star of the New Evangelisation, Pray for us.
Amen.

Group Intercession
Recently, the members of the New Springtime Community which is devoted to evangelisation and the formation of evangelisers have concluded that intercession for a new springtime in the church is particularly important. They recommend their associate members to follow these guidelines.
1. Appoint someone to take responsibility of leading the intercessory session by keeping these guidelines in mind, suggesting when to move from one point to another, and keeping the meeting within a specified time limit.
2. Make a conscious act of faith in the presence and power of God.
3. Ask the Holy Spirit to fill you and to guide your time of intercession.
4. Spend some time in worship by thanking, praising and worshipping the Lord. As Ps 144:2 assures us: 'He is my loving God and my fortress, my stronghold and my deliverer, my shield, in whom I take refuge.'
5. In Eph 6:18 we read: 'Pray in the Spirit on all occasions with all kinds of prayers and requests. With this in mind, be alert and always keep on praying for all the saints.' It is quite possible that when St Paul urges people to 'pray in the Spirit,' he has the gift of praying and singing in tongues in mind. Speaking about communal intercession, pars 45-46 of the *General Instruction of the Roman Missal* say: 'In the general intercessions ... it is appropriate that this prayer be included in all Masses celebrated with a congregation, so that petitions will be offered for the church, civil authorities, those oppressed by various needs, all young people, and for the salvation of the world. As a rule the sequence of intentions is to be:
- For the needs of the church
- For public authorities and the salvation of the world

- For those oppressed by any need
- For the local community.'
6. Pray for any intentions which you may have been asked to pray for, especially for those involved in evangelisation.
7. Allow the issues and concerns that are consciously in your heart to surface. Express your feelings and desires to the Lord.
8. Then blank your mind, pray in tongues for a while and ask the Spirit to guide your prayer by means of the charisms of revelation such as inspired thoughts, intuitions, a vision, word of knowledge, or scripture reading. As Gal 5:18 says 'Be guided by the Spirit.'
9. If no charismatic guidance seems to be forthcoming, intercede in an agnostic way by praying and singing in tongues, in the belief that the Spirit within is praying to God above. As Paul said in Rom 8:26-27: 'The Spirit himself intercedes for us with groans that words cannot express. And he who searches our hearts knows the mind of the Spirit, because the Spirit intercedes for the saints in accordance with God's will.'
10. As the time of intercession comes to an end, thank God in the belief that he is doing immeasurably more than you can ask or think through the power of his Spirit at work within you (cf Eph 3:20).

Many of those who are involved in the ministry of intercession will testify that it is one of the deepest, most demanding, mysterious and worthwhile forms of prayer .

SECTION FIVE

Pastoral

CHAPTER TWENTY-TWO

False Images of God and Resistance to Change

When we sing, 'I have decided to follow Jesus ... the world behind me, the cross before me, no turning back,' the sentiment may be sincere, but surely it is often a tad unrealistic due to a lack of self-awareness. Spiritual directors are well aware that Christian behaviour is influenced by conscious and unconscious factors. Firstly, there is *professed spirituality*, i.e. what we think and feel about God at a conscious level, and *operative spirituality*, i.e. our primal feelings and gut instincts about God which are largely unconscious and formed in childhood.

Dr Ana-Maria Rizzuto, a Catholic psychoanalyst, has described how a parish priest came to see her. His presenting symptoms were chronic fatigue and insomnia which compromised his ability to be available to his parishioners. A thorough examination revealed that there was nothing wrong with him physically. However, when Rizutto asked the priest about his family it became clear from his tone of voice that, although he admired his father, he also feared him because he was stern, strict and punitive. When she asked the priest about his relationship with God his reply was equally ambiguous. As Rizutto observed, the God of the priest was loving, patient and gentle (i.e. *professed spirituality*). However, the God of the man was critical, stern and demanding (i.e. *operative spirituality*). The God of the theologian was updated (i.e. *professed spirituality*), but the God of the man was anachronistic and disturbing (i.e. *operative spirituality*). Dr Rizutto went on to describe how she helped the priest to consciously recognise the conflict between his professed idea and his operative image of God, and how the former was the fruit of his education and the latter a result of his childhood experience of paternal authority. As soon as he became aware of these conflicting aspects of his relationship with God, he was able to revise his image of the Lord and to overcome his feeling of resistance.

From consolation to desolation of Spirit
The clash between these two forms of spirituality can be at work when we pray. For example, a Catholic woman called Joan went to see her spiritual director. When Sr Agnes asked, 'Did you feel particularly close to the Lord at any time since last we met?' Joan replied, 'As you know, I like *Lectio divina*. Some time ago I focused on the story of how Jesus met the Samaritan woman at the well. I read, reflected upon, and prayed about the passage as usual. But then at one point I had a vivid sense of the Lord's unconditional acceptance and love for me. It was so strong, it brought tears to my eyes.' 'How did you feel,' asked Sr Agnes, 'when you had that experience?' 'Great relief and joy,' replied Joan, 'and I also felt that I should tell other people about Jesus just as the Samaritan woman did.' But on the next two occasions when Joan met Sr Agnes she had to admit that instead of feeling the closeness of the Lord, she had endured nothing but dryness and a sense of alienation.

Quite often aridity and desolation of spirit is due to what is known as resistance, i.e. a backing away from intimate relationship. It is often due to negative feelings, e.g. fear, shame, unworthiness, anger, mistrust and resentment, which have been evoked by negative but unconscious images, e.g. that God is demanding, distant, hard to please, harsh, punitive or apathetic. When Joan felt accepted and loved by Jesus she reacted at first with spontaneous feelings of joy and consolation of spirit. But then negative images of God began to kick in when she sensed that she was being called to tell others about Jesus. Those images evoked feelings of anxiety and mistrust within her. At an unconscious level of awareness she felt that if God were to continue to relate to her in such a loving way, she would have no control over what he might say. He could say anything. Call her to anything. He could undermine her attitudes toward herself, challenge her emotional preoccupation with her work, overturn her basic social assumptions. She could be left without integration and confidence. As a result, she backed away from having a closer relationship with Jesus in the belief that if she kept him at arm's-length, she could avoid the scary prospect of having to make demanding changes in her life such as witnessing to others about him.

From negative to positive images of God
Spiritual directors are skilful in helping directees not only to recognise resistance but how to overcome it. For example, on a subsequent visit, Sr Agnes said, 'Joan, I know you feel far from Jesus at the moment, but can you recall the joyful experience you told me about a few weeks ago? What was it that you noticed about Jesus that evoked your feelings of consolation?' Joan replied, 'I was filled with joy when I realised how loving and accepting Jesus was when I mediated on his meeting with the Samaritan woman.' That would be a description of her positive image of God. Then Sr Agnes said, 'Joan try to stay with the feeling of closeness you had with Jesus. Did you have any other feelings afterwards?' Joan didn't say anything for a moment or two. Then she replied, 'At first there was the feeling of joy. But the next day when I was thinking about the call to tell others about Jesus, joy gave way to a feeling of apprehension.' Then Sr Agnes asked, 'Was there anything you noticed about Jesus that evoked your negative reaction?' Joan replied, 'I am a shy person. I don't think I have the courage to tell others about Jesus. Not only that, ever since childhood I have had an impression that the saints who get close to Jesus seem to suffer a lot and are asked to undertake very demanding tasks in their lives. I find life hard enough as it is. I don't think I could cope with any more hassle or demands.' In saying this Joan was admitting that she had an image of the Lord as a kill-joy, spoil sport or demanding taskmaster. Then Sr Agnes responded, 'Well Joan, you seem to have met two Lords in recent weeks, one who loves and accepts you as you are, and the other who is demanding and unreasonable in his expectations. Which of the two do you think is the real Jesus?' After pondering a moment the truth dawned on her, and Joan replied, 'It is the Jesus who reassured me of his unconditional acceptance and love.' In this way, Sr Agnes helped Joan to identify the fact that a negative, but unconscious image of God, had caused her resistance and therefore her aridity. I should say in passing that negative images of God are not the

only cause of resistance. Sometimes it is due to the fact that the change that the Lord is inviting the person to makes requires a degree of self-sacrifice that he or she is not willing to make.

Conclusion
Spiritual directors know that there is no growth in the spiritual life without preceding desire. The deeper and stronger the desire, the greater the openness to subsequent blessing. So whenever we ourselves or people we care about, experience resistance in their Christian lives, besides helping them to identify negative images of God, we can ask the question that Jesus asked the two disciples of John: 'What do you want?' (Jn 1:38). Once people get in touch with their deep down spiritual desire they are in touch with the activity of the Holy Spirit within them. As Paul assured us in Phil 2:13: 'It is God who works in you [e.g. by means of holy desires] to will and to act according to his good purpose [e.g. as an answer to heartfelt prayer].' Whereas, negative images and their associated feelings may move us away from surrender to the Lord, our spiritual desires not only have the power to overcome resistance, they will move us towards a more intimate relationship with the person and will of Jesus. The more we get to know Jesus as he is, the more false images of God are revealed and replaced.

CHAPTER TWENTY-THREE

Power Encounters in Ministry

There is a need to train lay people how to share the core teachings of Christianity with those they come in contact either on a one-to-one basis, in the course of casual, everyday conversations, doing house to house visitation, or engaging in street evangelism where one talks to people about meaning of life issues. They can be taught to see such encounters as divine appointments which were intended by God, e.g. like the conversation of Jesus with the woman at the well of Samaria, or the meeting between Philip the evangelist and the Ethiopian eunuch in the desert. They can be encouraged, no matter how well or badly the encounter has gone, to end it by asking the person they were talking to, whether he or she would like a prayer for any intention. Experience teaches that even those who are sceptical about Christianity will often reveal a need. It could be a driving test they are due to take, a relative who is sick, or some personal need of their own such as physical or emotional ill health. The revelation of such a need is significant because it is a revelation of material or spiritual poverty and therefore a certain openness to the grace and power of God. Remember the beatitude, 'Blessed are those who know their need of God, albeit in an inchoate way, the kingdom of heaven is theirs' (cf Mt 5:3).

The person who is ministering can be taught to ask, 'Would you mind if I said that prayer for you right now?' The person being asked this question will usually say that it is OK. Then the Christian can say, 'Do you mind if I place my fingers on your forehead?' Again, they will often say that it is OK. People have often asked, 'Why do you want to put your finger on the person's forehead?' In Hab 3:3-4 we read: 'God's brightness was like the sun; rays came forth from his hand, where his power lay hidden.' During his public ministry Jesus used his hands to express what was in his heart. For example, once a leper asked

Jesus to heal him. In response: 'Jesus stretched out his hand, touched him, and said, "I will do it. Be made clean"' (Lk 5:13). On another occasion Jesus said, 'If I drive out demons by the finger of God, then the kingdom of God has come to you' (Lk 11:20). We believe that these hands on times of ministry are divine appointments and power encounters, God's *kairos* moments (Greek for sacred as opposed to chronological time) when the Holy Spirit will be active. When I am praying for people in this way, I keep a number of interrelated points in mind:

a) Because of justification by grace God is at work within

Firstly, when I am praying for a person, I reject any exaggerated feelings of unworthiness by regarding them as a temptation from Satan, the accuser, the one who opposes the purposes of God. I believe that as a result of being justified by grace through firm faith in Christ's saving work on the cross, I am qualified to be a channel of his blessing to others (cf Col 1:12). As Paul assures us in Rom 8:1: 'There is now no condemnation for those in Christ Jesus.' They are declared not guilty and acquitted by the grace of God. So I affirm that the benevolent power and peace of God is about to flow into the person with whom I'm praying, in a mighty and effective way.

b) In the person of Christ

Secondly, when I am ministering to someone I believe that I am acting in the person of Jesus Christ (cf Phil 2:13). This point is made in par 521 of *The Catechism of the Catholic Church*, 'Christ enables us to live in him all that he himself lived, and he lives it in us.' As St Teresa of Avila stated: 'Christ has no body but yours, no hands, no feet on earth but yours. Yours are the eyes with which he looks with compassion on this world, yours are the feet with which he walks to do good, yours are the hands with which he blesses the world.'

c) The benevolence of God

Thirdly, I usually say silently, or out loud: 'God is love, Jesus loves you; because he loves you, he wants what is best for you. His love is the answer to your deepest need.' I affirm the fact that the Lord is benevolent. In other words he wills what is best for the person. Jesus referred to the benevolence of God, when he said to parents: 'If you, then, though you are evil, know how to give good gifts to your children, how much more will your Father in heaven give good gifts to those who ask him?' (Mt 7:11). I heard a moving story on radio which illustrated this point. A man described how, as a boy in Derry, he had been hit on the bridge of his nose by a rubber bullet. It blinded him in both eyes. When he was brought to Altnagelvin area hospital, he heard his father ask a doctor, 'Can you save my son's sight?' to which he replied, 'I'm afraid we cannot, the damage is too great.' Then the boy heard this father say, 'Could you not take my eyes and give them to my son?' to which the doctor responded, 'Unfortunately, that will not be possible either.' St Paul echoed that point when he said, 'He who did not spare his own Son but gave him up for us all, will he not also give us all things with him?' (Rom 8:32). If, like that father in Northern Ireland, a mere mortal with many faults wants what is best for his son, that is but a mere shadow compared to God's benevolent desire for his sons and daughters.

d) In the power of the Spirit

Fourthly, I affirm the fact that the Holy Spirit, the Lord and Giver of Life, is active in and through me. I focus on the fact that it is the same Spirit that raised Jesus from the powerlessness of death to triumphant and glorious new life. St Paul speaks eloquently about this in Eph 1:17-20: 'I keep asking that the God of our Lord Jesus Christ, the glorious Father, may give you the Spirit of wisdom and revelation, so that you may know … his incomparably great power for us who believe. That power is like the working of his mighty strength, which he exerted in Christ when he raised him from the dead and seated him at his right hand in the heavenly realms.' The Holy Spirit is the Lord and giver of life. I believe that not only is that power within me, it flows out through my hands in an authoritative way during times of ministry.

e) Praying within the will of God

Fifthly, I strive to pray in accordance within the will of God for the person and with the measure of faith I have received (cf Rom 12:3). Sometimes that is made easy because either before or during the time of ministry the Lord can give the praying person a word of knowledge. It not only reveals God's specific will, but it also evokes expectant faith, because as Paul told us in Rom 10:17: 'Faith comes from hearing the message, and the message is heard through the word of Christ.' Although that verse refers primarily to the *kerygma* (the core Christian teaching), it is also true of words of knowledge. One thing that really helps me when I'm praying for people in evangelisation situations is the belief that even if I do not know what God's specific will is for the person, I'm utterly convinced that God wants the person to experience his peace in some way or other, i.e. blessing, wholeness, harmony, and healing of either body, mind or spirit. It is significant that when the risen Jesus appeared to the disciples, he repeatedly said to them, 'Peace be with you.' So, more often than not, I pray for God's peace in the firm belief that God is granting it, in one way or another.

Testimony
I can share an amusing story about this. Some time ago I gave a short talk at Mass about praying in the way I have been trying to describe in this chapter. At one point I looked to my right, spotted an American man who I knew was not shy, and impetuously beckoned him to come up a number of steps to the altar. I wanted to demonstrate the stages involved in praying for others. Firstly, I asked Don if there was anything he wanted prayer for? He said that he was very tired and needed energy. Secondly, when I asked him if he minded if I prayed for him right there and then, he said it was OK. Thirdly, I asked is it all right if I put my fingers on his forehead? He told me to go ahead. I should emphasise that this was supposed to be a role play. But as soon as I began to pray for him I felt as if an energy had come upon me and was flowing through my hands. Don began to sway as if he was drunk, and I thought, my God he is going to fall backwards down the steps, he will be injured and we will have to pay thousands in compensation! So I stopped praying and grabbed his shoulders with my two hands in order to support him. Then spontaneously, Don said into the microphone, 'I could hardly stand because I felt a power coming upon me.' As many of us know, the power of the Spirit can be so strong during prayer that many people fall back and catchers lower them safely to the

ground. Those kinds of manifestations and their beneficial effects can convince people whose faith is weak or non-existent that God is alive and active in the modern world.

A few weeks after this incident, another occurred which went beyond being a role play to the real thing. A priest colleague and I had concluded a concelebrated Mass and had returned to the sacristy. When we finished divesting my colleague left and a woman approached me. She asked if she could discuss something. Although I was in a hurry to do something else, I said, 'Of course you can.' She explained that she had read a book of mine a few years before, one in which I had described how a clergyman had prayed for me so that I might be filled with the Holy Spirit. Then the woman asked, 'Father, will you say a similar prayer for me?' 'I would be delighted to,' I responded, 'There is nothing that the Lord wants more for you, than that you would be filled with his Spirit. As Paul said in Eph 3:18, "Be filled with the Spirit".' Then I said to her, 'You can have great confidence because you know that I will be praying within the will of God. He is a God of love. He loves you and wants what is best for you. His Spirit of love will be his answer to your deepest need.' Then I put my hands gently on the woman's head and prayed in faith. I had an inner conviction that the Lord was blessing her. Then spontaneously, I began to pray in tongues. As soon as I did so the woman began to fall backwards under the power of the Spirit. Fortunately, I was able to catch her and helped to break her fall. As she lay on the floor, she wept quietly. It was clear that she was inwardly touched by a heartfelt sense of the loving presence of the Lord. I knelt beside her, and said in a whisper, 'You may find that you can pray in tongues.' Immediately, she began to pray in the language of the angels. After a few minutes, I helped the woman to her feet. 'You have been truly blessed,' I said, as we gave one another a hug. With a big smile she responded, 'What a lovely birthday present. I'm seventy tomorrow.' At that moment of grace she looked years younger than her chronological age.

Conclusion
I am convinced that ministry in the power of the Spirit is a powerful and effective way of evangelising. There was a saying

which was attributed to Hanina Ben Dosa, a contemporary of Jesus: 'He whose actions exceed his wisdom, his wisdom shall endure, but he whose wisdom exceeds his actions, his wisdom shall not endure.' Not surprisingly, the apostles said similar things. For instance, St Paul testified: 'My message and my preaching were not with wise and persuasive words, but with a demonstration of the Spirit's power' (1 Cor 2:41).

CHAPTER TWENTY FOUR

The Occult, Reiki and Yoga Evaluated

In modern Ireland there has been a noticeable decline in church attendance and belief. When people stop believing in God, it is not that they believe in nothing, they tend to believe in anything. True religion is inclined to give way to superstition and the occult. The word 'occult' means secret knowledge about the spirit world. There has been a noticeable rise of interest in occult phenomena such as horoscopes, palmistry, mediums, clairvoyance, the Ouija board, channelling, angelology, use of crystals, fortune telling, witchcraft and many other bizarre beliefs and practices. For example, there have been many adds on TV encouraging people to ring such things as the Psychic Tarot Line to discover the secrets of happiness, love, money and destiny.

The Judeo-Christian religion has always opposed this kind of divination. In Ezek 21:21 we get some inkling of how people in Old Testament times engaged in divination: 'For the king of Babylon will stop at the fork in the road, at the junction of the two roads, to seek an omen: He will cast lots with arrows, he will consult his idols, he will examine the liver.' In Deut 18:10-12, however, these and similar activities are condemned: 'Let no one be found among you who ... practices divination or sorcery, interprets omens, engages in witchcraft, or casts spells, or who is a medium or spiritualist or who consults the dead. Anyone who does these things is detestable to the Lord.'

Needless to say, the New Testament is equally opposed to the occult. In Acts 16:16-18 we are told how Paul delivered a young fortune teller from an occult spirit. Rev 21:8 warns that: 'Those who practice magic arts, the idolaters and all liars – their place will be in the fiery lake of burning sulphur. This is the second death.' These sentiments were echoed in the early church. For example in par 3 of the *Didache* (130 AD) we read: 'Do not be always looking for omens, my son, for this leads to idolatry. Likewise have nothing to do with witchcraft, astrology, or magic; do not even consent to be a witness of such practices, for they too can all breed idolatry.'

Not surprisingly the contemporary church is also opposed to

CHAPTER TWENTY-FOUR

any involvement with the occult. As the *Catechism of the Catholic Church* says in pars 2116-2117, this kind of false religion 'conceals a desire for power over time, history and in the last analysis, other human beings, as well as a wish to conciliate hidden powers. They contradict the honour, respect and loving fear that we owe to God alone.' Clearly, involvement in the occult is sinful because it is opposed to the virtue of religion as complete dependence on the providence and provision of God.

In recent years I have noticed a marked increase in the number of disturbed and tormented people who seek to be released from spiritual oppression. While many cases are psychological in nature, there are some which can only be explained in terms of spiritual oppression as a result of involvement in the occult. Recently, a Catholic woman rang me. She had attended a course which focused on the lost city of Atlantis. If my memory serves me correctly the participants were urged to get in touch with a goddess for help. When she followed that advice, thereby breaking the first commandment, the devil may have got a foothold on her inner life because she was tormented by strange, disturbing thoughts. A week later another woman contacted me about a similar problem. She had attended a course where the participants were encouraged to consult angels as spirit guides. It was clear to me that the role of these angels had nothing to do with the service of Jesus Christ. As a result of dabbling in this kind of channelling, the woman felt she had become oppressed by evil spirits and needed deliverance. Like many nominal Christians, these women were naïve, and seemingly unaware of the fact that those who become involved with occult beliefs and practices, even if they are expressed in Christian terminology, do so at their peril. Once evil spirits make an entry, believe me, they are very hard to expel.

A number of points follow from this. Firstly, baptised and confirmed Christians should not attempt to incorporate occult elements into their spirituality. Secondly, if you, or anyone you know has done so out of ignorance, renounce those things which are incompatible with Christian belief and confess that sin in the sacrament of reconciliation. It will bring about forgiveness, healing and protection. Thirdly, if you have reason to believe that you are spiritually oppressed as a result of what you have done, you should ask a mature and experienced Christian for discernment and if needs be to pray a deliverance prayer for you. Fourthly, if you have any doubt about some belief or practice that you have come across, you would be well advised to consult a knowledgeable priest or lay person to discover the Catholic perspective. Fifthly, all believers should warn fellow Christians, especially young people, about the dangers of getting involved in occult practices. Sixthly, all of us should protect ourselves against the wiles of the evil one who 'prowls around like a roaring lion looking for someone to devour' (1 Pet 5:8). St Paul tells us how in Eph 6:16-17: "Take up the shield of faith', he says, 'with which you can extinguish all the flaming arrows of the evil one.' The shield is our unshakable trust in the person and name of Jesus Christ.

Reiki

Over the years a number of people asked me what I thought about Reiki. I admitted that I didn't know a great deal about the subject, but suggested that it sounded like a New Age form of healing. Recently, I was pleased to find that, in March of 2009 the doctrinal committee of the American hierarchy had published a lucid and helpful document entitled *Guidelines for Evaluating Reiki as an Alternative Therapy*.

It begins by saying there are two kinds of healing: natural and divine. On the one hand, we can be healed by human means such as surgery, psychotherapy and pills, while on the other hand, God can heal us by means of such things as the anointing of the sick and the charism of healing.

The Origins of Reiki

A Zen Buddhist monk, Mikao Usui, discovered Reiki in the mid-nineteenth century as a result of a religious awakening. He taught his disciples how to attune to the universal life-force. According to Reiki, sickness is ultimately due to an imbalance of that energy in the human body. So a Reiki practitioner brings about healing by placing his or her hands on the patient's body in order to facilitate the flow of Reiki. Rather than being the ultimate source of this energy, the healer is merely a channel for something that exists everywhere and in everything.

CHAPTER TWENTY-FOUR 211

Is Reiki a natural means of healing?
When one reads books and articles on Reiki it becomes clear that its beliefs are mainly expressed in spiritual and religious terms of a pantheistic kind. Such literature is filled with references to God, the Goddess, the 'divine healing power', and the 'divine mind'. Furthermore Reiki uses non-Christian symbols and it is referred to as a way of living governed by five ethical precepts. As the bishops point out, in some respects Reiki is similar to a religion.

That said, many practitioners such as nurses use Reiki as a purely natural form of healing. However, there is little or no empirical evidence to show that this form of alternative medicine has any good effects. In fact it lacks credibility in so far as the universal life energy that Reiki talks about is unknown to modern science. As the bishops observe, the justification for this form of therapy must necessarily come from something other than science.

Reiki and the healing power of Christ
As I know from personal experience, some modern day Christians such as priests, nuns and lay people, try to harmonise Reiki with Christian healing. To do so they have to accept, at least in an implicit way, the central tenets of the worldview that underpins Reiki. Many of them are incompatible with Christian belief. For example, Christians see divine healing as a free gift of God's grace, which is not within human control, whereas Reiki practitioners believe that healing can be reliably experienced as a result of human insight and effort.

Apparently, some practitioners of Reiki consult with spirit guides. This practice can leave them and their clients open to sinister spiritual influences. The American bishops wrote: 'This introduces the further danger of exposure to malevolent forces or powers.' This point may explain why I have heard quite a number of people say that, having received Reiki healing, they developed all kinds of problems ranging from depression to headaches. Indeed, a man who had been a Reiki master, ie someone who had advanced training in the subject, rang me some time ago. He told me that he had heard me warning about the dangers of this form of therapy in one of my recorded talks.

He said that he had come to see the truth of my words from his personal experience. I was glad to hear that he had given up Reiki because he recognised that it could have a dark, negative side.

While some practitioners attempt to Christianise Reiki by adding a prayer to Christ and using Christian symbols, the American bishops point out that these cosmetic changes do not alter the essentially non-Christian nature of this form of therapy. For these reasons, Reiki cannot be identified with what Christians call healing by divine grace.

Some Implications
The bishops conclude by observing that 'for a Catholic to believe in Reiki therapy presents insoluble problems'. They say that a Catholic who puts his or her trust in Reiki ends up 'operating in the realm of superstition, the no-man's land that is neither faith nor science.' The bishops warn that superstition corrupts the person's worship of God by turning religious feeling and practice in a false direction. They explain that while 'sometimes people fall into superstition through ignorance, it is the responsibility of all who teach in the name of the church, to eliminate such ignorance as much as possible.'

The document ends with these salutary words... 'Since Reiki therapy is not compatible with either Christian teaching or scientific evidence, it would be inappropriate for Catholic institutions, such as Catholic health facilities and retreat centres, or persons representing the church, such as Catholic chaplains, to promote or provide support for Reiki therapy.' I do hope that the practitioners of Reiki will accept what the bishops have said without trying to water it down, explain it away, or reject it.

Yoga
Over the years many people have been asked what I think about yoga. The word is associated with meditative practices in Hinduism, Buddhism and Jainism. Clearly, Christians cannot subscribe to the ideas that inform these religions. But besides its religious beliefs, yoga contains practices which in themselves are neither good or bad from a Christian point of view. A Letter to the Bishops of the Catholic Church on *Some Aspects of Christian Meditation*, was published by The Congregation for the Doctrine

of the Faith in 1989 by Cardinal Ratzinger. In par 2 he wrote: 'The ever more frequent contact with other religions and with their different styles and methods of prayer has, in recent decades, led many of the faithful to ask themselves what value non-Christian forms of meditation might have for Christians. Above all, the question concerns eastern methods.' The first footnote in the document says: 'The expression "eastern methods" is used to refer to methods which are inspired by Hinduism and Buddhism, such as "Zen," "Transcendental Meditation" or "Yoga". Par 16 of the same document goes on to say: 'Just as the Catholic Church rejects nothing of what is true and holy in these [non-Christian] religions, neither should these ways be rejected out of hand simply because they are not Christian. On the contrary, one can take from them what is useful so long as the Christian conception of prayer, its *logic and requirements are never obscured* [my italics].' Par 28 adds: 'That does not mean that genuine practices of meditation which come from the Christian East and from the great non-Christian religions, which prove attractive to the man of today who is divided and disoriented, cannot constitute a suitable means of helping the person who prays to come before God with an interior peace, even in the midst of external pressures.'

I was interested to see that in his book, *Deliverance From Evil Spirits: A Practical Guide*, Frank McNutt says that while a person might intend to only use the exercises involved in Yoga without buying in the beliefs that inform them, this is hard to do in practice. He says, that in his experience involvement in pagan beliefs, whether intentional or unintentional, can leave a person vulnerable to oppression by evil spirits. It is a cautionary comment worth noting.

Conclusion

For Catholics, the principles applied to the evaluation of Reiki and Yoga seems to be relevant for the evaluation of things such as reflexology, the enneagram, aromatherapy and the like. Although they are used by practitioners of New Age spirituality, in some circumstances they can be used with prudence and discretion by believers in so far as they are merely techniques for improving physical health or self awareness. However, if those using them buy into the unChristian beliefs and values that sometimes underpin them, they should either stop using them altogether, or consciously reject any non-Christian thinking that informs them.

CHAPTER TWENTY-FIVE

Private Revelation Assessed

In late August 2008, an Iraqi woman, who lives in Detroit, Michigan, discovered that one of her pictures of Mary was oozing oil. Sometime later, other religious objects in the same room also began to ooze oil. By 2011 hundreds of pounds of the oil had been collected in jars and used for blessing people. When it was analysed by a chemist it was found that while it was like olive oil, it is not the same. It is not as viscous, and has a different but pleasant odour. The woman receives messages from Mary in a modern form of Aramaic. She also claims that three messages have been associated with apparitions of the Blessed Virgin Mary. The messages can be viewed at http:// www.divinemercy radio. com. Here are two examples which have a similar theme. The first was given on 03/01/2009: 'My daughter, cruel days are coming upon the world, such as wars that have no comparison, if they do not seek refuge in my son. Many people say that they are returning to him; but they wound his heart like the crown of thorns which pierced his head.' In the second message received on 04/08/2010, Mary said: 'The people are not returning to the faith. Enough my beloved children; return to the faith. Let go of evil deeds. Come and return to my son. Difficult days are coming. Many difficulties will befall this world, such as wars, shedding of blood and floods. Return, O listeners, O people.' Currently, the diocese of Detroit is examining the woman's private revelations to see if they are truly from God or not.

Public and Private Revelation
The word revelation in English is derived from Latin and means, 'to disclose, unveil, or to make known something to a person by means of a divine or supernatural agency.' While I believe that post New Testament Christians can receive private

revelation from God, it is very difficult to know whether the revelations received, one's own or those of others, are true or false. This chapter will briefly assess statements such as: 'The Lord said to me by means of a word of knowledge ... a prophecy ... a picture or vision about so and so.' It is also very hard to know whether the many revelations of so-called mystics, visionaries and seers, which are in circulation in Catholic circles nowadays, are truly from God or not. As St Paul once advised in this regard: 'Test everything. Hold on to the good. Avoid every kind of evil' (1 Thess 5:21). Sometime later St John wrote: 'Test the spirits to see whether they are from God, because many false prophets have gone out into the world' (1 Jn 4:2).

The term 'public revelation' refers to the revealing action of God directed to humanity as a whole which finds its literary expression in the Old and New Testaments. Public or official revelation ended with the death of the last apostle. Ever since then, however, people have claimed to have received 'private revelation.' Speaking about this phenomenon, St Thomas Aquinas said: 'At all times there have not been lacking persons having the spirit of prophecy, not indeed for the declaration of any new doctrine of faith, but for the direction of human acts. Thus Augustine says (*De Civ. Dei* v, 26) that "The emperor Theodosius sent to John who dwelt in the Egyptian desert, and whom he knew by his ever-increasing fame to be endowed with the prophetic spirit: and from him he received a message assuring him of victory".'

Pope Benedict spoke about the relationship of the scriptures to private revelation in par 14 of his post-synodal apostolic declaration on *The Word of God*. Because of the authority of that declaration it is worth quoting from it at some length. 'The Synod pointed to the need to "help the faithful to distinguish the word of God from private revelations" whose role is not to "complete" Christ's definitive revelation, but to help live more fully by it *in a certain period of history* (my italics). The value of private revelations is essentially different from that of the one public revelation: the latter demands faith; in it God himself speaks to us through human words and the mediation of the living community of the church. The criterion for judging the truth of a private revelation is its orientation to Christ himself. If it leads us away from him, then it certainly does not come from the Holy Spirit, who guides us more deeply into the gospel, and not away from it. Private revelation is an aid to this faith, and it demonstrates its credibility precisely because it refers back to the one public revelation. Ecclesiastical approval of a private revelation essentially means that its message contains nothing contrary to faith and morals; it is licit to make it public and the faithful are authorised to give to it their prudent adhesion.' The Holy Father lists the positive aspects of private revelation.

1. A private revelation can introduce new emphases.
2. It can give rise to new forms of piety.
3. It can deepen older forms of piety.
4. It can have a certain prophetic character (cf 1 Thess 5:19-21).
5. It can be a valuable aid for better understanding and living the gospel at a certain time.

The Holy Father goes on to say: 'Consequently private revelation should not be treated lightly. It is a help which is proffered, but its use is not obligatory. In any event, it must be a matter of nourishing faith, hope and love, which are for everyone the permanent path of salvation.' Similar points are made in par 67 of *The Catechism of the Catholic Church*.

Inspiration and private revelation
Some time ago, a lay man of my acquaintance made a useful distinction between inspiration and revelation. When I asked him how he understood the two, he said that inspiration relies on natural knowledge, intelligence and experience, whereas revelation does not do so. There is a continuum between inspiration and revelation and it is hard to discern when one becomes the other. Both inspirations involving the gifts of wisdom and knowledge (cf Is 11:2) and revelation involving the charism of prophecy (cf 1 Cor 12:9) are both made possible by the Holy Spirit. However, there is reason to think that whereas the former is a grace which is given mainly for one's own sanctification, the latter is a charismatic grace which is given for the sanctification of others.

There seems to be a spectrum of private revelation ranging from prophecy, including words of knowledge which are sometimes exercised in the Charismatic Renewal, to special revelations which are often addressed to the church by seers like St Margaret Mary Alacoque, St Faustina Kowalska, Anne Catherine Emmerich, Fr Stephano Gobbi, Mrs Vassula Ryden and Anne the Apostle, in Ireland. Speaking about these inter-related kinds of revelation par 90 of a *Directory on Popular Piety and the Liturgy* says: 'Popular piety has always been interested in extraordinary happenings and events that are not infrequently connected with private revelations. While not confined to Marian piety alone, this phenomenon is particularly involved with "apparitions" and "messages".'

Inspiration in prayer
As was noted in an earlier chapter, St Teresa of Avila stated in her *Autobiography* that prayer is 'an intimate friendship, a frequent, *heart to heart conversation* [my italics] with the God by whom we know ourselves to be loved.' When they pray, Christians openly and honestly disclose their deepest thoughts, feelings, experiences and desires to the Lord. Having done so, they can expect the Lord to reveal the divine presence, loving mercy, and purposes to them. However, many Christians frankly admit that they can't recall an occasion when they experienced any communication from God. Some will even say to those who claim such inspiration in prayer, 'Surely you are not claiming to have a hot-line to God?' One could respond by asking, 'Are you actually saying that God has never revealed his presence, word or will to you in prayer? Didn't Jesus say, "I have yet many things to say to you, but you cannot bear them now. When the Spirit of truth comes, he will guide you into all the truth; for he will not speak on his own authority ... He will glorify me, for he will take what is mine and declare it to you"' (Jn 16:12-14). Sometime later St Paul spoke about the way in which Christ's promise was fulfilled: 'The Spirit searches all things, even the deep things of God ... We have not received the spirit of the world but the Spirit who is from God, that we may understand what God has freely given us ... "For who has known the mind of the Lord that he may instruct him?" But we have the mind of Christ' (1 Cor 2:10-16). Something similar is said in 1 Jn 2:27: 'As for you, the anointing you received from him remains in you, and you do not need anyone to teach you.

But his anointing teaches you about all things.'

Whenever we receive some inspiration in prayer we need to use something like St Ignatius of Loyola's rules for the discernment of spirits to establish whether the inspiration was prompted by our own spirit, the evil spirit, or the Spirit of God. As a general rule of thumb, one can say that if an inspiration is from God it usually begins in, and continues in, a sense of consolation of spirit, i.e. it is associated with feelings such as joy, peace, and hope. If not, it will end in desolation of spirit, i.e. feelings of restlessness, anxiety, dryness and lack of hope.

Prophetic Revelation

There is another related kind of revelation. As Paul says: 'To one there is given ... the gift of prophecy' (1 Cor 12:10). This charism is a special ability given to some Christians to receive and communicate a message from God to the community or to an individual, in the form of an anointed utterance. Writing about this gift St Thomas said: 'Prophetic knowledge relies on God's light in which all things are visible, human and divine, bodily and spiritual, so that anything whatever can be the subject of prophetic revelation ... So it is in the revelation of future events that prophecy above all consists and to which it owes its name. But in a broad sense the subject of prophecy is whatever man knows by God's revelation. It differs from other charisms such as wisdom and knowledge and understanding of speech, the subjects of which man can know by natural reason, though not as perfectly as by God's light.' Over the years I have heard and read many prophecies which have been spoken in the Charismatic Renewal. Clearly there is a need to establish whether they come from God, the person who spoke them, or an evil Spirit. The charism of the discernment of spirits mentioned in 1 Cor 12:10, is first and foremost a God-given ability to distinguish true from false prophecy. Genuine prophecies sometimes have considerable authority because of the circumstances in which they were spoken, the giftedness of the people who spoke them, and the answering amen they evoked in the hearts of those who heard them.

Words of knowledge are a particular manifestation of the prophetic gift whereby one person is enabled to know what God is doing in another person's soul or body, or of knowing the secrets of his or her heart (*kardiagnosis*), in a way that often evokes expectant faith thereby enabling the person to receive a blessing from the Lord. There are many examples of such words of knowledge in the lives of the saints. In his biography of St Francis of Assisi, St Bonaventure tells us that he possessed the 'spirit of prophecy and foretold things to come, and beheld the secrets of hearts, and knew things absent as if they were present.' Bonaventure says that: 'He foresaw the ruin of many who appeared likely to persevere; and on the contrary, predicted with assured certainty the conversion of many sinners to Christ.' He gives many examples. For instance, two friars came to visit Francis. While on the way, the elder one gave scandal to the younger. When they arrived, Francis asked them how the journey had gone. The younger friar said, 'Very well,' but Francis responded: 'Take heed, brother lest you tell a lie under the semblance of humility, for I know what I know, but wait a while and you shall see.' The young friar was astonished to see that the Spirit had revealed to Francis what had really happened. Apparently, a few days later, the elder man who had given scandal, departed 'in contempt of religion'. Bonaventure concluded: 'In the ruin of this one man two things were made manifest – the divine justice, and the prophetic gift of St Francis.' There is a simple test for words of knowledge. Are they accurate? Do they lead to blessing?

Revelation addressed to the church
Commenting on special revelations, St Alphonsus Liguori wrote: 'The revelations of secret or future things, such as the mysteries of the faith, the reading of consciences, the predestination of certain persons, their death, their elevation to some dignity, and other similar things, may occur in three ways: by visions, by locutions [i.e. hearing an inner or outer voice] and by a simple apprehending of the truth.' Many saints such as Catherine Labouré (1806-76), Bernadette Soubirous (1844-79), and the children of Fatima, have claimed that either Jesus, Mary, or God has given them a message in one or other of the ways described by St Alphonsus. Writing about this phenomenon in an article entitled, 'Private Revelations: Some Theological Observations,' Karl Rahner SJ, observed: 'To say that private revelations never con-

tain anything but truths which one could know through the common revelation and, hence, independently of these revelations – for example, the possibility and utility of a new devotion – this is to pose yet another question: Why then does God reveal it, and not rather leave to the intelligence of theologians the concern of making explicit this new aspect of revelation?'

When messages are reported the question arises, are they truly from heaven or not? The following questions may prove to be helpful: Is the person who uttered the prophecy leading a holy life? Is he or she humble and God-centred? Is the person emotionally and psychologically balanced? Is there anything in the message which seems to be opposed to the scriptures or church teaching? Does the person hope to gain status, influence or material benefits as a result of the revelation? It is a matter of public record that the church has withheld its approval for a number of private revelations which have been widely disseminated, such as those of William Kamm, also known as *The Little Pebble*, who lives in Australia. That said, it is good to recall the Latin adage, *abusus non tollit usum*, 'abuse of anything does not invalidate its right use.'

Should Christians seek inspiration and private revelation?
Should a Christian seek inspiration? Yes, Christians should seek inspiration from God. It is quite legitimate to expect the Lord to reveal himself and the divine word and will to us in prayer. That is why the Lord says: 'Call to me and I will answer you and tell you great and unsearchable things you do not know' (Jer 33:3), and St Paul says such things as: 'We have not stopped praying for you and asking God to fill you with the knowledge of his will through all spiritual wisdom and understanding' (Col 1:9-10) and 'be guided by the Spirit'(Gal 5:18).

When St Paul said in 1 Cor 14:1, 'eagerly desire spiritual gifts, especially the gift of prophecy,' I suspect he was addressing the Christian community rather than individuals. Speaking of the charisms, including prophecy, in 1 Cor 12:8-10, the dogmatic constitution on *The Church* said in par 12: 'These charisms, whether they be the more outstanding or the more simple and widely diffused, are to be received with thanksgiving and consolation for they are perfectly suited to and useful for the needs of the church. Extraordinary gifts *are not to be sought after* [my italics].' It seems to me that the Christian community, as the body of Christ, desires the gifts, but individuals leave it up to God which, if any, of the gifts the Lord wants to bestow upon them for the common good. As John Paul II observed in par 72 of *Catechesis in Our Time*, 'Renewal in the Spirit will be authentic not so much according as it gives rise to extraordinary charisms, but according as it leads the greatest possible number of the faithful, as they travel their daily paths, to make a humble, patient and persevering effort to know the mystery of Christ better and better, and to bear witness to it.'

Not surprisingly, a number of saints have echoed church teaching in their writings. Although St Vincent Ferrer believed as a result of personal experience that a person could receive a genuine revelation in a gratuitous way from God, he wrote: 'Be thoroughly persuaded that true revelations, and the extraordinary means by which God's secrets are known, are not the result of the desire, nor of any diligence or effort on the part of the soul itself; but that they are solely the effects of the pure goodness of God communicating itself to a soul filled with humility, who respectfully seeks for him and sighs after him with all its strength.' Nevertheless he is wary of private revelation because he was so aware that people could be subject to illusions and false inspirations. In his *Treatise on the Spiritual Life*, he wrote: 'The first remedy against spiritual temptation which the devil plants in the hearts of many persons in these unhappy times is to have no desire to procure by prayer, meditation or any other good work, what are called revelations, or spiritual experiences, beyond what happens in the ordinary course of things.' St Teresa of Avila echoed that point when she wrote in her *Interior Castle*: 'I will only warn you that, when you learn or hear that God is granting souls these graces, you must never beg or desire him *to lead you by this road* [my italics]. Even if you think it is a very good one ... there are certain reasons why such a course is not wise.' She went on to explain why. Firstly, such a desire shows a lack of humility. Secondly, one thereby leaves oneself open to 'great peril because the devil has only to see a door left a bit ajar to enter.' Thirdly, there is a danger of auto-suggestion: 'When a person has a great desire for something, he convinces himself that he is seeing or hearing what he desires.' Fourthly, very heavy trials usually go with these favours: could we be sure of being able to bear them? Fifthly: 'You may well find that the very thing from which you had expected gain will bring you loss.'

Conclusion

We can expect to experience a kind of private inspiration in prayer, particularly prayer of the charismatic or contemplative kind. However, when followers of popular devotion have spoken to me over the years about the private revelations that either they themselves or seers have claimed to have received, it has often occurred to me that, firstly, the so-called revelations were questionable in themselves, and secondly, that those who believed in them seemed to base their spirituality more upon these questionable experiences than on the scriptures and the teachings of the church. It is quite likely that in the uncertain and anxious times in which we life, when the authority of the church has been weakened by things such as secularisation and scandals, there will be a great increase in the numbers of people claiming to have received revelation from God. Like St Vincent Ferrer who lived in similar circumstances in the fourteenth century, we have to remember that all that glistens is not gold.

CHAPTER TWENTY SIX

Being a Loyal Catholic

The word Catholic is derived from Greek and means universal. The term was first used by St Ignatius of Antioch in his *Letter to the Smyrnaens*. He said, 'Where the bishop is present, we have the Catholic Church.' The church is Catholic because, among other things, it embraces a rich diversity of twenty three liturgical rites and many different spiritualities and theologies. Ever since the Reformation, the word Catholic has been commonly used to describe those who are not Protestant. That has raised a problem. Are Catholics those people who are in communion with Rome, i.e. Roman Catholics, or just plain Catholics? Some argue that the designation Roman is important because there are Anglicans, Orthodox and Protestant believers who regard themselves as Catholic. There are other Catholics who object to the use of the adjective Roman on ecclesiastical grounds. It is not the Roman primacy that gives Catholicism a distinctive mark of identity, but rather the Petrine primacy.

Who exactly is a Petrine Catholic? Par 837 of *The Catechism of the Catholic Church* gives a succinct answer. Catholics are those who are: 'Fully incorporated into the society of the church ... who, possessing the Spirit of Christ, accept all the means of salvation given to the church together with her entire organisation, and who – by the bonds constituted by the profession of faith, the sacraments, ecclesiastical government, and communion – are joined in the visible structure of the church of Christ, who rules her through the Supreme Pontiff and the bishops.'

From authority to experience
In modern culture there has been a discernible shift from authority to the primacy of experience. This trend has also had an impact on the Catholic Church where the centre of gravity has been shifting from the experience of religious authority to the

authority of religious experience. Nowadays, instead of emphasising the objective teachings of the Pope, councils and bishops, there has been an increasing tendency to adopt those beliefs and practices which seem meaningful and relevant at a subjective level. As John Paul II observed: 'People today trust more in experience than in dogma.' As a result of this kind of subjectivism, Catholics sometimes adopt ideas from different sources, both Christian and non-Christian. Some of the latter are not really compatible with Catholic belief. The technical name for this kind of approach is syncretism, i.e. the combination or synthesis of different and often incompatible forms of belief and practice.

The Catholic faith is universal in the sense that it is open to all truth. Quoting St Thomas Aquinas, Pope John Paul II said in par 44 of his encyclical *Faith and Reason*: 'Whatever its source, truth is of the Holy Spirit.' Just like the biblical authors, the church has absorbed ideas from many sources over the centuries, including non-Christian ones, when they were compatible with Christian revelation. For example, St Thomas Aquinas often quoted Greek philosopher Aristotle with approval. However, the church has always avoided syncretism, i.e. combining non-Catholic beliefs with Catholic ones even if the former are not really compatible with the teaching of the church. As we know from personal experience, when we go to eat in a restaurant there is usually a choice between a set menu and an *à la carte* version, i.e. a menu which enables a person to pick and choose what he or she likes from a list of individually priced items. In modern Catholicism there is an increasing number of people who seem to pick and choose what they want to believe, rather than accepting the fixed beliefs and values of the religion they profess. Here are three examples:

a) New Age Spirituality

A few years ago I was asked to teach a course on contemporary spirituality in a theological college in Dublin. There were about thirty adults in the class, all of whom were either practising or non-practising Catholics. I decided to begin with a sort of experiment. I talked about New Age beliefs, but did so entirely in terms of Christian language. When I had finished my presentation I asked for reactions. By and large the students were very positive and enthusiastic. A number of the men and women in the class said that I had put into words what they themselves already believed. They got a shock when I revealed that what I had been describing in Christian terminology were the pagan beliefs of New Age religion. In a document published by the Pontifical Council for Culture and The Pontifical Council for Inter-religious Dialogue entitled *Jesus Christ Bearer of the Water of Life: A Christian reflection on the New Age*, section 2.3.3 says that despite the immense variety within New Age, there are some common points:

1) The cosmos is seen as an organic whole.
2) It is animated by an Energy, which is also identified as the divine Soul or Spirit.
3) Much credence is given to the mediation of various spiritual entities.
4) Humans are capable of ascending to invisible higher spheres, and of controlling their own lives beyond death.
5) There is held to be a 'perennial knowledge' which predates and is superior to all religions and cultures.
6) Devotees follow enlightened masters.

For more on this subject, see the final chapter.

b) Liberalism

Many liberal Catholics like scripture scholar John Dominic Crossan, and theologian Roger Haight SJ, have been influenced by Enlightenment and post-Enlightenment ideas such as those of Friederich Schleiermacher (1768-1834) and Immanuel Kant (1724-1804). They tend to demythologise the supernatural aspects of the Christian faith, e.g. belief in the virgin birth, the existence of the devil, miracles, hell, and the bodily resurrection of Jesus. To a greater or lesser extent, they reinterpret traditional Christian doctrines in a more humanistic way which is more acceptable in the scientific culture in which we live. There is also a tendency in the liberal approach to adopt a certain relativism e.g. as regards the uniqueness of the revelation given in and through Jesus Christ. For example, the Vatican criticised the understanding of religious pluralism in the writings of Tissa Balsuriya, Paul Knitter and Jacques Dupuis SJ, because they seemed to propound views which called into question the fact that Jesus and his church are necessary for salvation. For more on this topic see the final chapter.

c) Evangelicalism

In par 55 of *Faith and Reason,* Pope John Paul II said that orthodoxy in the Catholic Church rests on three pillars of authority. 'Scripture is not the church's sole point of reference. The supreme rule of her faith derives from the unity which the Spirit has created between sacred tradition, sacred scripture and the magisterium of the church in a reciprocity, which means that none of the three can survive without the others.' Commenting on Catholic evangelicals, Protestant theologian Alister McGrath says that they display four characteristics. The first is a strong theological and devotional emphasis on the bible. Secondly, Evangelical Catholics stress the life, death, and resurrection of Jesus Christ as the cause of salvation for all mankind. Thirdly, they stress a personal need for interior conversion. Fourthly, they have a deep commitment to evangelisation. None of these points are inconsistent with the Catholic faith.

That said, there are evangelical Catholics, who like their Protestant counterparts, tend to rely on scripture alone as the sole pillar of orthodoxy, and some of them do so in a fundamentalist way. That is why we read in the document, *Teaching Authority and Infallibility in the Church*: 'Lutherans think that Catholics have overconfidently identified the locus of the work of the Spirit with a particular person or office.' Because of their reliance on scripture alone, many Anglicans hold a similar view. For instance, the final report of the Anglican-Roman Catholic International Commission (ARCIC) says: 'Anglicans find grave difficulty in the affirmation that the Pope can be infallible in his teaching ... special difficulties are created by the recent Marian dogmas, because Anglicans doubt their appropriateness, or even the possibility of defining them as essential to the faith of believers.'

I have found that some evangelical Catholics can sometimes adopt beliefs and attitudes which are not consistent with the Catholic faith, e.g. to do with teachings such as mariology, the role of tradition, praying for the dead, the interpretation of scripture, the importance of papal infallibility, etc. Surely, history shows that when Christians rely solely on their own understanding of scripture, no matter how sincere and spiritual they may be, they can become victims of illusions and false inspirations. As St Paul warned, the devil can deceive well-meaning people by appearing as an angel of light (cf 2 Cor 11:14). If subjective experience is not assessed in the light of tradition and the teaching of the church, it can lead to all kinds of unedifying splits and divisions, as the history of Protestantism and Pentecostalism has demonstrated.

A Catholic crisis of faith

The current crisis of faith in the Catholic Church, to which I have briefly adverted, is weakening unity of mind in the body of Christ and compromising its ability to witness effectively to the truth of the gospel, as understood and taught by the church. Like the first disciples, modern day Catholics should seek to be one in mind and heart. Unity of mind has to be founded on the teachings of Christ and the apostles as taught by the church. Unity of heart has to based on the unconditional love that the members of the church have for one another. There is a reciprocal relationship between doctrinal truth and loving relationships. As Pope Benedict XVI reminds us in par 3 of *Love in Truth*: 'Only in truth does charity shine forth, only in truth can charity be authentically lived. Truth is the light that gives meaning and value to charity ... Without truth, charity degenerates into sentimentality. Love becomes an empty shell, to be filled in an arbitrary way.'

Over the years I have been disappointed to find that many Catholics, who are highly educated and well informed where secular knowledge is concerned, are surprisingly ignorant of the teachings of the Catholic Church. Surely, all Catholics have an obligation to have a knowledge of their faith which is somewhat commensurate with their secular knowledge. Furthermore, conscientious Catholics have a duty in charity, to gently challenge their co-religionists who have inadvertently drifted away from orthodox Catholic belief. They can do this in private conversation; by urging them to attend catechetical and theological courses; or by giving them relevant reading material or DVDs. If, having heard or read what the church teaches, they still reject or doubt that teaching, one would hope that they would continue to seek the truth in a prayerful and open-minded way.

The Catholic Faith
Many years ago I heard Cardinal Cahal Daly make a helpful observation. He explained that the English word 'dogma,' was derived from Greek and means, 'that which seems good'. In other words the teachings of the church can be used as a means of discernment. Dogmas can be utilised to establish whether the theological views, private revelations or beliefs adopted by an individual or a group, are in harmony with the public and definitive revelation that has come to us from Christ and the apostles. As par 100 of *The Catechism of the Catholic Church* points out: 'The task of interpreting the Word of God authentically has been entrusted solely to the magisterium of the church, that is, to the Pope and to the bishops in communion with him.' More recently, in par 17 of his post-synodal apostolic declaration *The Word of God*, Pope Benedict wrote: 'The living tradition is essential for enabling the church to grow through time in the understanding of the truth revealed in the scriptures'

In recent years the Catholic Church has made a number of notable attempts to state its essential dogmatic beliefs. In 1968 Pope Paul VI published his *Creed of the People of God*. In the introduction the Holy Father said: 'We have wished our profession of faith to be to a high degree complete and explicit, in order that it may respond in a fitting way to the need of light felt by so many faithful souls, and by all those in the world, to whatever spiritual family they belong, who are in search of the Truth.' In 1992, Pope John Paul II published *The Catechism of the Catholic Church*. At the time of its publication he explained in the apostolic constitution, *The Deposit of Faith*: 'The principal task entrusted to the Council by Pope John XXIII was to guard and present better the precious deposit of Christian doctrine in order to make it more accessible to the Christian faithful and to all people of good will. For this reason the Council was not first of all to condemn the errors of the time, but above all to strive calmly to show the strength and beauty of the doctrine of the faith.' A little later, John Paul said, that the *Catechism* was universally authoritative and 'a sure norm for teaching the faith,' and thus 'a valid and legitimate instrument for ecclesial communion.'

a) The church on New Age religion

As already mentioned, *Jesus Christ the Bearer of the Water of Life: A Christian Reflection on the New Age* was published in the Vatican. While it acknowledged that there were some good points in New Age thinking, it concluded that it was a modern form of Gnosticism and therefore unacceptable from a Christian point of view. Firstly, God is not an impersonal energy as New Age thinking suggests. Secondly, when the New Age says that Jesus Christ is not uniquely God, but one of the many historical manifestations of cosmic and universal divinity, it is quite mistaken. Thirdly, whereas the New Age movement believes that we save ourselves by raising our levels of consciousness by using man-made techniques, Christians believe that we are justified by grace through faith in Christ and not by our own unaided efforts. Fourthly, Christians reject the New Age notion of sin as merely an imperfect form of knowledge which can be redressed by means of New Age methods.

b) The church on liberalism

Ever since St Pius X introduced the oath against the errors of Modernism in 1910, the Catholic Church has rejected the anti-supernatural bias of some liberal Christian thinking. Just to take two examples: Many Catholics say that the devil is only another word for the darkness in the human unconscious and a code word for the systemic evil involved in the unjust and oppressive structures of society. That, however, is not the church's view. For example, Pope Paul VI said in the course of a long address which was published in *L'Osservatore Romano* in 1972: 'Why do we not speak of the influence of Satan anymore? We do not speak about it because we lack a visible experience. We believe that what we do not see does not exist. Instead, we fight against evil. But, what is evil? We are speaking of evil as a deficiency, a lack of something. If someone is ill, he lacks health. If someone is poor, he lacks money. And so on. This is not the case when we speak about the devil; that is why this is a terrible reality. We are not dealing with a deficiency, an evil caused by the lack of something. We must realise that we face an efficiency that is evil in itself; an existing evil, an evil that is a person; an evil that we cannot classify as corruption of goodness. We are speaking of an affirmation of evil, and if this does not frighten us, it should.' In par 12 of the constitution on *The Church*, of Vatican II, there is an affirmation of the edifying role of the supernatural charisms mentioned in 1 Cor 12:8-10. Among them are the charisms of healing and miracle working. The church still requires two authenticated miracles for the canonisation of saints. So it is quite clear that the Catholic Church rejects any liberal agenda which seeks to ignore the supernatural dimension of religion.

Secondly, before his election as Pope, Benedict XVI wrote the declaration *The Lord Jesus* (2000), in which he argued against the liberal, relativist view that the great religions of the world provide equally valid ways to God and salvation. Christ is acknowledged as a great man who taught wisely as a person full of godliness. But so were Budda, Confucius, Lau Tzu, Zoroaster, and Mohammed. In other words, Christ is not seen as being the unique son of God. In par 5 of *The Lord Jesus* he said: 'As a remedy for this relativistic mentality, which is becoming ever more common, it is necessary above all to reassert the definitive and complete character of the revelation of Jesus Christ. In fact, it must be firmly believed that, in the mystery of Jesus Christ, the Incarnate Son of God, who is "the way, the truth, and the life" (Jn 14:6) the full revelation of divine truth is given.' In saying this he is echoing an important line in 'For there is only one ... mediator between God and mankind, himself a man, Christ Jesus, who sacrificed himself as a ransom for them all.'

Although par 16 of the constitution on *The Church* affirms that people of goodwill, who have never heard of Christ through no fault of their own, and who live by their conscience, can be saved. Although they do not know it, the grace they receive comes to them in virtue of the saving death and resurrection of Jesus Christ. It is the duty of Christians to tell them about Christ and to assure them that he fulfills all that is best in their way of life.

c) The church on evangelical beliefs

The Catholic Church is irrevocably and passionately committed to ecumenism. But as John Paul II said in par 18 of *That They All may be One*: 'The unity willed by God can be attained only by the adherence of all to the content of *revealed faith in its entirety* [my italics]. In matters of faith, compromise is in contradiction with God who is Truth. In the Body of Christ, 'the way, and the truth, and the life' (Jn 14:6), who could consider legitimate a reconciliation brought about at the expense of the truth? While there has been a great deal of theological agreement between Catholics and Protestants in recent years, e.g. the joint declaration on justification which was published by the Lutheran World Federation and the Catholic Church in 1999, there are still many doctrinal points that divide the Christian churches. For example, in his *Credo*, Paul VI (1968), reiterated the church's belief in the Immaculate Conception and Assumption of Mary, the existence of purgatory as a state of purification after death, and therefore the value of praying for the dead. As was noted in chapter nine, the church also rejects any fundamentalist form of scripture interpretation that excludes the role of tradition or the teaching authority of the Church.

So a Catholic is a person who in a spirit of humility is willing to reject anything in his or her personal beliefs which is not consistent with the authoritative teaching of the church. A loyal Catholic is one who believes what the church believes. In Gal 1:8-9, St.Paul said: 'But even if we or an angel from heaven should preach a gospel other than the one we preached to you, let him be eternally condemned! As we have already said, so now I say again: If anybody is preaching to you a gospel other than what you accepted, let him be eternally condemned!'

An instructive historical incident
Following his conversion experience, Ignatius of Loyola became absolutely convinced that God wanted him to live out his life following Christ, the poor man, in the Holy Land. As a result, Ignatius set off for Jerusalem. There he accidentally met the provincial of the Franciscans whose friars administered the holy places. Ignatius tells us in his *Autobiography* that when he spoke to this priest about his sense of calling, he told him in no uncertain terms that he should return home and that, if he didn't do so, he would excommunicate him. Ignatius was caught on the horns of a dilemma. As a layman he was persuaded, as a result

of his own discernment of spirits, to follow Christ the poor man by serving pilgrims in the holy places. On the other hand, as a person with legitimate church authority, the Franciscan provincial had told him, albeit in an unreasonable way, that he could not remain in the Holy Land.

What did Ignatius decide? As he himself recounted, 'It was not God's will for him (Ignatius) to remain in the holy places.' For Ignatius it came down to a choice between obedience to the inner voice of God, which would have led him to being separated from the church, or obedience to the properly constituted authority of a church official, even if he was exercising it in a questionable way. He concluded that there must have been something lacking in his own discernment of spirits, no matter how sincere and conscientious it was. He decided to return home. But that left him with a dilemma: if he wasn't to follow Christ in the Holy Land, where would he do so? Ultimately, providence led him, by a process of trial and error, to France where he founded the Society of Jesus in 1540. In retrospect, the incident in Jerusalem was a matter of a *felix culpa*, i.e. a happy fault which led, in a providential way, to subsequent blessing. Arguably, if Ignatius had refused to obey the Franciscan provincial there would be no Jesuit order in the church today.

Conclusion
Although the incident from the life of Ignatius did not concern doctrinal truth, the founder of the Society of Jesus would have argued that whenever there is a clash between private judgement, to do with doctrinal or ethical truth, a Catholic is bound to obediently submit his or her mind and will to the teaching of the church, in the belief that in doing so he or she is submitting to the Lord. So it is not too surprising to find that Rule one of Ignatius' *Rules for thinking with the church* said: 'Always be ready to obey with mind and heart, setting aside all judgement of one's own, the true spouse of Jesus Christ, our holy mother, our infallible and orthodox mistress, the Catholic Church, whose authority is exercised over us by the hierarchy.' Rule thirteen added: 'That we may be altogether of the same mind and in conformity with the church herself, if she shall have defined anything to be black which to our eyes appears to be white, we

ought in like manner to pronounce it to be black. For we must undoubtedly believe that the Spirit of our Lord Jesus Christ, and the Spirit of the orthodox church, his Spouse, by which Spirit we are governed and directed to salvation, is the same.' What Ignatius was asking for is an aspect of the obedience of faith spoken about in par 5 of the dogmatic constitution *On Divine Revelation*: 'The "obedience of faith" is to be given to God who reveals, by which man freely commits his total self to God by offering "the full submission of intellect and will to the God who reveals," and by assenting willingly to the revelation given by him.' This principle applies to revelation as it is reliably interpreted by the church. In this way, a true unity of mind and heart is maintained and deepened among Catholics as the indispensable prerequisite of effective evangelisation in the modern world.

CHAPTER TWENTY-SEVEN

The Devil's Advocate and Mother Teresa of Calcutta

Blessed Teresa of Calcutta's was born in 1915. Her Albanian name was Gonxha (Agnes) Bojaxhu. Her father died when she was nine. She and her two sisters were raised by their mother Drana. Evidently, Drana had a genuine love for the poor. For instance, she looked after an alcoholic by washing and feeding her twice a week. When a local widow died, Mrs Bojaxhu raised her six children in her own home. Surely, this example of Christian charity made a deep and lasting impression on young Agnes. She left home at age 18 to join the Sisters of Loreto as a missionary. She never again saw her mother or sisters. Agnes initially went to the Loreto Abbey in Rathfarnham, Ireland to learn English, the language the Sisters of Loreto used to teach in India. We know that when she was living in a Loreto school in Calcutta, Teresa's mother Drana used to encourage her daughter, by letter, to be mindful of the poor.

Founded the Missionaries of Charity
Teresa took her mother's example and advice to heart. She often visited the local hospitals and slums. These experiences made a deep impression on her. At one point she made a retreat during which she felt that God was asking her to leave the Loreto sisters, to live with, and help the poorest of the poor. She said: 'It was an order, a duty, an absolute certainty. I knew what to do, but I did not know how.' So at the age of thirty-eight she donned a sari and began to serve the least of her brothers and sisters (cf Mt 25:40). Some time later she founded the Missionaries of Charity to assist her in her work. The rule encapsulated the essence of Mother Teresa's spirituality. It stated that the sisters should freely devote themselves to the service of the poorest of the poor with a view to living and spreading the gospel.

There were other formative influences on her spirituality.

The following are worth mentioning: Firstly, from her childhood years onwards, as a long-time member of the Legion of Mary, Mother Teresa had a heartfelt devotion to the Virgin Mary as the one who would lead her to Jesus. Secondly, Teresa's spirituality was eucharistic in focus. It was a matter of contemplating Christ, firstly under the appearance of bread and wine, and then in the 'disturbing disguise' of the poor. Thirdly, she was intensely prayerful. She encapsulated her thinking in these words: 'The fruit of silence is prayer, the fruit of prayer is faith, the fruit of faith is love, the fruit of love is service, and the fruit of service is peace.' Fourthly, as a Loreto sister, she was familiar with the Ignatian notion of desolation of spirit, whereby God withdraws all consolation, such as a felt sense of the divine presence, in order to purify the person's commitment to God. Fifthly, at the time of her profession, she took the name of Teresa as a mark of respect for St Thérèse of Lisieux.

Canonisation process initiated
A few weeks after Mother Teresa's death in September 1997, Pope John Paul II stated: 'I hope she will be a saint.' Eighteen months later he agreed to dispense with the normal five-year waiting period before the formal canonisation process could be initiated, by giving the Archbishop of Calcutta the go-ahead. Until 1983 the process was like a trial. The person's cause would be promoted by a postulator and queried by the devil's advocate. While the procedure has now been streamlined, and the role of devil's advocate abolished, in this chapter, I would like to propose, and respond to, four arguments which could be used to oppose the canonisation of Mother Teresa.
1. Although Mother Teresa and her collaborators engaged in deeds of mercy, they neglected action for justice which has been advocated in the post Vatican II era.
2. Mother Teresa, adopted a rather liberal, unscriptural attitude to the subject of salvation and the need for conversion to Christ who, as scripture assures us, is our only way, truth and life (cf Jn 14:6).
3. While one would expect a holy person to feel close to God, Mother Teresa admitted that there were times when she didn't pray and seemed to have no faith.

4. If Mother Teresa was truly a holy woman why did she need to be exorcised a year before her death?

Deeds of mercy, action for justice
Since the Second Vatican Council, the church has stressed the fact that, while it is good to help the poor, it is also important to identify and change the unjust and oppressive structures of society that lead to that poverty. This point was clearly made in the post-synodal document, *Justice in the World* (1971). In par 6 of the introduction it said: 'Action on behalf of justice and participation in the transformation of the world fully appear to us as a constitutive dimension of the preaching of the gospel.' The tie in between evangelisation and action for justice was endorsed in pars 29-38 of Pope Paul VI's encyclical, *Evangelization Today* (1976). Furthermore, John Paul II wrote in 1986: 'Search out more than ever, with boldness, humility and skill, the causes of poverty and encourage short and long term solutions . By doing so, you will work for the credibility of the gospel.' In spite of these clear teachings, Mother Teresa said repeatedly, 'We are not concerned about the cause of a problem, we look after the effects.'

It can be said in Mother Teresa's defence that her congregation was formed in the pre-Vatican era, when the church did not yet fully appreciate the connection between evangelisation and action for justice. Not only that, Sr Teresa had been led by God to engage in works of mercy for the poorest of the poor. She saw her sisters and other collaborators like fire men and women trying to put out the flames of extreme hunger and need. It was up to the fire inspectors, i.e. other church groups to establish what caused the flames and to recommend how to avoid them in the future. In other words, she subscribed to the New Testament notion that different but complementary gifts are given to different individuals and groups within the church (cf 1 Cor 12:4-11; Eph 4:7-13).

Non-Christians and salvation
While Protestant evangelicals of a fundamentalist hue admire and applaud what Mother Teresa and her followers did for the poorest of the poor, they argue that she was not a true Christian for two reasons. Firstly, she didn't try to convert members of

other religions to the Christian faith in the belief that 'there is only one mediator between God and men, the man Jesus Christ' (1 Tim 2:5). On one occasion she was asked by Naven Chawala, one of her biographers, 'Do you convert people?' She replied: 'Of course I convert them. I convert them to be a better Hindu, or a better Muslim or a better Protestant. Once you have found God it is up to you to decide how to worship him.' Secondly, she believed that non-Christians could be saved. When asked whether those who believed in the Hindu Gods, Shiva or Ram, would go to heaven, she replied: 'Yes, that is their faith. My own faith will lead me to God ... So if they have believed in their God very strongly, if they have faith, surely they will be saved.'

It is my belief that Mother Teresa's point of view was correct for two main reasons. Echoing the teaching of par 16 of the dogmatic constitution on *The Church*, par 1260 of *The Catechism of the Catholic Church* says that many of those who have been born into other faiths have received baptism of desire. It says: 'Every man who is ignorant of the gospel of Christ and of his church, but seeks the truth and does the will of God in accordance with his understanding of it, can be saved.' Furthermore, commenting on the parable of the last judgement in Mt 25:34-40, Joachim Jeremias once asked: by what criterion will non-Christians be judged, are they lost? He maintained that Jesus replies in effect: 'Non-Christians have met me in an anonymous way in my brothers and sisters, for the needy are family to me, the one who shows love to them has shown it to me, the friend of the poor.' Furthermore he argues that implicit in that kind of love is the justifying faith mentioned by St Paul, 'the only thing that counts is faith working through love' (Gal 5:6).

Dark Night of the Soul
You would think that someone living a good Christian life would feel close to God. However, since her death, Mother Teresa's private letters have revealed that all had not been sweetness and light in the life of the 'messiah of love'. While her public utterances were beautiful, uplifting and positive, her private correspondence, especially in the 1950s and 60s, Brian Kolodiejchuk's book, *Mother Teresa: Come Be My Light*, indicates that she often experienced desolation of spirit, and severe

CHAPTER TWENTY-SEVEN

temptations against faith. For example, she wrote: 'When I try to raise my thoughts to heaven, there is such utter emptiness that those very thoughts return like sharp knives and hurt my very soul. I want God with all the power of my soul, and yet between us there is terrible separation. *I don't pray any longer* [my italics].' On another occasion she wrote privately to her spiritual advisor: 'People say they are drawn close to God, seeing my strong faith. Is this not deceiving people? Every time I have wanted to tell the truth, that *I have no faith* [my italics], the words just do not come, my mouth remains closed.'

There was nothing unusual in what Teresa had to endure. Scripture warns: 'If you want to serve the Lord, prepare yourself for an ordeal' (Sir 2:1). As a former Loreto sister, Mother Teresa was quite familiar with *The Spiritual Exercises* of St Ignatius of Loyola. Like many other spiritual classics, it warns that those who are advancing in the Christian life sometimes experience desolation of spirit, whereby God withdraws all consolation, such as a felt sense of the divine presence. This is done in order to purify their commitment to God. Like her namesake, St Thérèse of Lisieux, Mother Teresa had to walk through the valley of darkness (cf Ps 23:4; 139:11-12). In this way she learned at a very deep level of her personality to be devoted to the God of consolation rather than the consolations of God.

Teresa's Exorcism
It came as a surprise to me and many others to hear that Mother Teresa had been exorcised. Apparently, a year before her death, she had been admitted to a hospital in Calcutta for an angiogram and angioplasty. Afterwards she had been very agitated at night-time. She had tried to pull out the intravenous drips and to pull off the electrodes attached to her body. When Archbishop de Souza of Calcutta, who also happened to be a patient in hospital at the same time, heard about this, he suspected that she was under diabolical attack. 'It struck me,' he said, 'that there could be some evil spirit which was trying to disturb her ... because of her weakened physical state.' He added, 'I wanted her to calm down and asked a priest ... an old Italian missionary who was very holy ... in the name of the church, to perform an exorcism prayer on her.' The priest was a 79-year-old Sicilian,

named Rosario Stroscio. The archbishop instructed him: 'You command the devil to go if he is there. In the name of the church, as archbishop, I command you to go and do it.' Apparently Mother Teresa was happy to submit to what the archbishop proposed. The deliverance prayer lasted about half an hour. Afterwards, the archbishop explained that a solemn exorcism to expel the devil from Mother Teresa's personality had not been necessary.

In an article entitled, 'Mother Teresa's Dark Night of the Soul' which was published in *Doctrine and Life* (November 2001) I suggested that the archbishop may have been mistaken in his discernment. I think it is true to say that sometimes when older people have an angiogram and dye is put into their veins it can cause them to be quite agitated afterwards. I'd suspect that Mother Teresa's rapid recovery following the deliverance prayer may have been partly due to the fact that the dye was no longer affecting her. In any case, when he was asked whether the simple exorcism would hinder the cause for Mother Theresa's beatification, the archbishop said it would have the opposite effect. He stated that: 'It would be an indication of the holiness of Mother.' In the Christian life, it is common for the saintly friends of God to be attacked in this way. This was the way with saints like Thérèse of Lisieux, Gemma Galgani, and Padre Pio. It would seem that Mother Teresa had been allowed to share in Christ's feeling of being abandoned by God and harassed by the evil one. Like her Saviour, she triumphed, with God's help, over every adversity.

Conclusion
In spite of the best efforts of would-be devil's advocates, there is clear evidence that Mother Teresa led a life of heroic Christian virtue. The church acknowledged her sanctity when it beatified her in 2003. Now the church waits for two first class miracles which will confirm her heroic sanctity and thereby lead to her canonisation.

CHAPTER TWENTY-EIGHT

Who Do Men Say I Am?

In Mt 16:13-19 we read: 'When Jesus came to the region of Caesarea Philippi, he asked his disciples, "Who do people say the Son of Man is?' They replied, "Some say John the Baptist; others say Elijah; and still others, Jeremiah or one of the prophets." "But what about you?" he asked. "Who do you say I am?" Simon Peter answered, "You are the Christ, the Son of the living God." Jesus replied, "Blessed are you, Simon son of Jonah, for this was not revealed to you by man, but by my Father in heaven. And I tell you that you are Peter, and on this rock I will build my church, and the gates of Hades will not overcome it. I will give you the keys of the kingdom of heaven; whatever you bind on earth will be bound in heaven, and whatever you loose on earth will be loosed in heaven".'

This incident occurred at a turning point in the ministry of Jesus when he decided to stop working in his native Galilee in order to head South to Jerusalem, to his eventual passion and death. Caesarea Philippi was an entirely Gentile city founded by Philip the Tetrarch, a brother of Herod the Great. It contained many pagan temples devoted to such divinities as Pan, Caesar, and Baal. It was at this significant time and place that Jesus asked the disciples, 'Who do people say the Son of Man is?' They responded by mentioning a number of opinions that were current at the time. Some said that Jesus was John the Baptist, Elijah, Jeremiah, or one of the other prophets who had returned. It goes without saying that, while there was a grain of truth in these different responses, they were all incorrect.

Down the centuries, Jesus could have asked the same question time and time again and there would have been many heretical answers. I will briefly refer to three of them.
1. Arianism maintained that Jesus was the highest of all creatures but lesser than God.

2. Adoptionism maintained that Jesus was purely human but adopted as the Son of God.
3. Nestorianism stressed the humanity of Christ. It said he was a mixture of two persons, one human, the other divine.

In the contemporary world many heretical answers are still being given in response to the question, 'Who do men say that the Son of Man is?' I will refer to four influential but mistaken replies.

1) The naturalist response of atheists and agnostics
The naturalist view of the world rejects the supernatural. It sees God as a code word for human potential, and the devil as a code word for the darkness of the human unconscious. When naturalists are asked who Jesus was, they answer that he was a great man, a remarkable teacher of ethics and spiritual values, such as the Golden Rule in Mt 7:12. However, atheists and agnostics reject any claim that Jesus performed healings or miracles. Needless to say, they do not believe that Jesus rose from the dead. Albert Einstein, the best known scientist of the 20th century espoused a naturalist point of view. Speaking about Jesus he said: 'As a child I received instruction both in the bible and in the Talmud. I am a Jew, but I am enthralled by the luminous figure of the Nazarene ... No one can read the gospels without feeling the actual presence of Jesus. His personality pulsates in every word. No myth is filled with such life.' Although it is clear that Einstein revered Jesus the man, he did not believe he was divine.

2) Non-Christian responses
Some of the great world religions have interesting things to say about Jesus. For example, Islam accepts that the Old Testament was inspired. It believes that Jesus was born of the virgin Mary, and was one of God's greatest prophets who performed healings and miracles. That said, Islam teaches that Jesus was raised into heaven at the end of his life, but it neither accepts that he was divine or that he died on the cross for the forgiveness of sins. It also believes that although the New Testament was inspired when it was written, its interpretation was subject to

corruption from the beginning. According to Islam, the revelation made to Mohammed, the last and greatest of the prophets superseded the teachings of the New Testament.

Some Hindus also reverence Jesus as a person who manifested the presence of God to an unusual degree. They see Jesus as either an Avatar, i.e. a bodily manifestation of the Supreme Being, or a Guru, i.e. a wise teacher. Mohandas Gandhi, the well known Hindu leader, stated: 'What then does Jesus mean to me? To me, he was one of the greatest teachers humanity has ever had. To his believers he was God's only begotten son ... Is all the grandeur of his teaching and of his doctrine to be forbidden to me? I cannot believe so. To me it implies a spiritual birth. My interpretation, in other words, is that in Jesus' own life is the key to his nearness to God; that he expressed as, as no other could, the spirit and will of God.' While this is a great testament to Jesus, it is clear that Gandhi did not believe in the divinity of Jesus as the unique Son of God.

3) A pagan New Age response
In recent years so called New Age spirituality has had considerable influence in the Western world. As you may know Catholic bishops asked the Vatican to publish a document on the subject. A few years ago it published *Jesus Christ Bearer of the Waters of Life: A Reflection on the New Age*. The document offers a well-informed, balanced and sympathetic description of the worldview informing the New Age movement. For example, speaking of its beliefs, it says succinctly:
1. The world, including the human race, constitutes an expression of a higher, more comprehensive divine nature.
2. Hidden within each human being is a higher divine self, which is a manifestation of the higher, more comprehensive divine nature.
3. This higher nature can be awakened and can become the centre of the individual's everyday life.
4. This awakening is the reason for the existence of each individual life.

A few points are worth noting here. Firstly, New Age spirituality is pantheistic. It maintains that everything that exists, including ourselves is God. In other words, there is no transcendent God separate from the world. Secondly, New Age spirituality does not believe in a creator. Thirdly, New Age spirituality does not see God as a Person, but rather as an energy. New Age spirituality says that human beings can get in touch with the divine energy that is in all things by looking into the deepest recesses of human consciousness. It uses all kinds of psychological techniques in order to do this, such as Transcendental Meditation, Jungian methods of introspection, and the use of mantras. As a result, New Age spirituality believes that it becomes aware of God within.

Some time ago, I got into theological conversation with a Catholic I know. When I heard what he had to say about Jesus I could see that it owed a lot to New Age thinking. He felt that Jesus was merely a highly gifted person who had developed his divine potential, a potential we all share. He saw him as a spiritual pioneer like Buddha, Confucius, Lao Tzu, Zoroaster, Mohamed, and the like. He could not agree that Jesus was uniquely divine by nature, or the sole mediator between God and man. Needless to say, he also rejected the claim of the Catholic Church to be the one true church founded by Christ. In a relativistic way, he felt that all the great religions were equally valid ways to God. He believed there is one great river of religious experience, and many wells in the form of different religions.

4) The liberal Christian response

Many liberal scripture scholars offer their own mistaken response to the question, 'Who do men say that I am?' Perhaps the most influential of them all in the 20th century was Rudolf Bultmann. He was well aware of the scientific, and rationalistic approach of modern culture. He felt that the bible should be stripped of its supernatural and mythical elements if it was to make sense to the people of our time. In *Mythology and the New Testament* he wrote: 'Man's knowledge and mastery of the world have advanced to such an extent through science and technology that it is no longer possible for anyone seriously to hold the New Testament view of the world.' Bultmann maintained that the gospels tell us what the early church believed about Christ, but that we know very little about the historical Jesus. Bultmann seemed to deny that Jesus was divine. He also rejected the doctrine of the virgin birth, the existence of good and bad angels, and accounts of Jesus' healings, miracles and exorcisms. They were a mythological way of understanding purely natural events. Bultmann maintained that if Jesus healed people, those accounts could be understood as psychosomatic cures; if he exorcised people, it was merely a primitive form of psychiatry.

Bultmann and his followers have had a big impact on theological colleges. Many of the lecturers are influenced by his de-supernaturalised interpretation of Jesus and his message. For example, I can remember a particular Sunday when the gospel reading was about the multiplication of the loaves and fish. The homilist explained in the college chapel that the story should not be interpreted in a literal way. He explained that many of the people in the crowd had food but they were not prepared to share with those who had none. But when Jesus blessed the five loaves and two fish, people were deeply touched and shared what they had. This kind of liberal interpretation, which is the result of an anti-supernatural bias, has no basis in the text.

5) An Orthodox Catholic response

So far we looked at some of the ways that different groups of people have wrongly answered the question, 'Who do men say the Son of Man is?' Now we go on to look at the following few verses which read: 'What about you?' he asked. 'Who do you say I am?' Simon Peter answered, 'You are the Christ, the Son of the living God.' Jesus replied, 'Blessed are you, Simon son of Jonah, for this was not revealed to you by man, but by my Father in heaven. And I tell you that you are Peter, and on this rock I will build my church, and the gates of Hades will not overcome it. I will give you the keys of the kingdom of heaven; whatever you bind on earth will be bound in heaven, and whatever you loose on earth will be loosed in heaven.'

Whereas a number of the disciples had responded to Jesus' first question, only Peter responded to the second. The gospels of Mark, Luke and Matthew have Peter declare that Jesus is the Christ, i.e. the promised Messiah who is anointed by God, and empowered by God's Spirit to deliver his people, and establish his kingdom. Christ understood his messianic identity in terms of Isaiah's prophecies about the Suffering Servant who would be afflicted and die for the people. In Matthew's gospel, Peter goes on to say that Jesus is 'the Son of the living God'. It is a declaration that as the anointed one of God, Jesus is divine. As Pope Benedict has pointed out, the post-resurrection belief that Jesus was divine had already been intimated during the public ministry of Jesus. For example, in Lk 5:1-10 we read about the miraculous catch of fish. Peter was overawed. He fell at the feet of Jesus in an attitude of adoration and said: 'Depart from me, for I am a sinful man, O Lord' (Lk 5:8). It is significant that Peter referred to Jesus as Lord, because in doing so he used the designation for God in the Old Testament.

Jesus was deeply impressed by Peter's profession of faith. He stated that it wasn't flesh and blood, i.e. human knowledge or reason, that revealed his identity and mission to him but rather his Father in heaven. This a vital point. We can only get to know who Jesus really is by a revelation from God. St Paul testified that this is what happened in his own case. In Gal 1:11-12 he wrote: 'I want you to know, brothers, that the gospel I preached is not something that man made up. I did not receive it from any man, nor was I taught it; rather, I received it by revelation from Jesus Christ.' Paul's case was unusual.

All of us of us were taught about the faith either as children or adults. I had the advantage of both. I was raised in a devout Catholic family and studied scripture and theology for four years before my ordination. As a result, I knew a lot about the Lord. However, as I explained in chapter three, until I was 29 I was still a prisoner of statements and words about Jesus, but I couldn't go beyond them to experience the mysterious Person they signified. Intimate knowledge of the Lord was only made possible by the gifts of wisdom and knowledge which were granted to me by the Holy Spirit. As Jesus promised in Jn 14:26: 'The Counsellor, the Holy Spirit, whom the Father will send in my name, will teach you all things and will remind you of everything I have said to you.' Anyone who has been baptised in the Spirit can truly answer the question, 'But who do you say that I am?'

Conclusion

CHAPTER TWENTY-EIGHT

The question Jesus posed to the disciples about who men say that he is, has produced many well meaning but mistaken answers. We need to recognise what is true and false. For example, although Napoleon Bonaparte was raised as a Catholic he was an agnostic. When asked who did he think that Jesus was, he responded: 'Everything in Christ astonishes me. His spirit overawes me, and his will confounds me. Between him, and whoever else in the world, there is no possible term of comparison ... I search in vain in history to find the similar to Jesus Christ, or anything which can approach the gospel. Neither history, nor humanity, nor the ages, nor nature, offer anything with which I am able to compare it or to explain it. Here everything is extraordinary. The more I consider the gospel the more I am assured that there is nothing there which is not beyond the march of events, and above the human mind.' It is an impressive answer, but is it orthodox? I don't think so. Notice how he says nothing about the divinity of Jesus or the fact that by faith in his death and resurrection we are saved from our sins. Novelist Fyodor Dostoyevsky, who belonged to the Russian Orthodox Church, did know the Lord. He wrote: 'I believe that there is nothing lovelier, deeper, more sympathetic and more perfect than the Saviour; I say to myself with jealous love that not only is there no one else like him, but that there could be no one ... There is in the world only one figure of absolute beauty: Christ. That infinitely lovely figure is as a matter of course, an infinite marvel.'

This book ends with the authoritative response of Paul VI to Jesus' question, 'Who do you say that I am?' In his Credo he wrote:

> We believe in our Lord Jesus Christ, who is the Son of God. He is the Eternal Word, born of the Father before time began, and one in substance with the Father, and through him all things were made. He was incarnate of the Virgin Mary by the power of the Holy Spirit, and was made man: equal therefore to the Father according to his divinity, and inferior to the Father according to his humanity; and himself one, not by some impossible confusion of his natures, but by the unity of his person.
>
> He dwelt among us, full of grace and truth. He pro-

claimed and established the kingdom of God and made us know in himself the Father. He gave us his new commandment to love one another as he loved us. He taught us the way of the beatitudes of the gospel: poverty in spirit, meekness, suffering borne with patience, thirst after justice, mercy, purity of heart, will for peace, persecution suffered for justice sake. Under Pontius Pilate he suffered – the Lamb of God bearing on himself the sins of the world, and he died for us on the cross, saving us by his redeeming blood. He was buried and, of his own power, rose on the third day, raising us by his resurrection to that sharing in the divine life which is the life of grace. He ascended to heaven, and he will come again, this time in glory, to judge the living and the dead: each according to his merits – those who have responded to the love and piety of God going to eternal life, those who have refused them to the end going to the fire that is not extinguished. And his kingdom will have no end.'

Index

Abelly, Bishop Louis, 69, 76
Abraham, 105
Adoptionism, 242
Alpha, 9, 42, 56, 151, 152
Argyle, Michael, 45
Arianism, 241
Aristotle, 22, 23, 225
Balsuriya, Tissa, 226
Barth, Karl, 134
Bellah, Robert, 149
Belonging, 56, 148, 150, 151
Benedict XVI, 8, 17, 19, 21, 60, 64, 87, 88, 91, 92, 94, 96, 101, 106, 112, 116, 120, 125, 135, 136, 137, 139, 140, 145, 178, 216, 228, 229, 231
Blake, William, 59
Boethius, 27
Bolt, Robert, 93
Bonaparte, Napoleon, 247
Brown, Raymond, 94, 116
Bultmann, Rudolf, 111, 244
Cantalamessa, Raniero, 127
Carothers, Merlin, 184
Cessationism, 120
Charismatic Renewal, 7, 20, 219
Charisms, 75, 115, 120, 123, 179, 221
Cicero, 111
Civil religion, 149
Compassion, 27, 68, 108, 191
    Defined, 107
Community, 33, 147, 162
Conn, Walter, 47

Consolation of spirit, 199
Continuationism, 120
Cornwall, Judson, 184
Coste, Pierre, 69, 71
Contemplation, 46, 63, 89, 129, 132
    Characteristics, 61
    Defined, 60, 61
Conversion, 36, 43, 238
    Definition, 36
    Stages of, 37, 38
Crises, 55
Crossan, John Dominic, 226
Daly, Cardinal Cahal, 229
Danneels, Cardinal Godfried, 76
Davis, Charles, 128
de Chardin, Teilhard, 51
de Castillejo, Irene,
Desire/s, 56, 125, 201
Desolation of spirit, 199, 239
Devil, 13, 16, 55, 182, 184, 219, 222, 230
Didache, 17, 161, 208
Discernment of spirits, 130, 192, 219
Docetism, 141, 142
Dostoyevsky, Fyodor, 247
Donahue, John, 170
Douglas, Mary, 149
Duff, Frank, 57
Durkheim, Emile, 148
Dupuis, Jacques, 226
Dowd, Sharon, Echols, 176
Ecumenism, 154
Einstein, Albert, 242
Eliot, T. S., 147
Eucharist, 132, 137, 138, 143, 145, 160, 206
Evangelisation, 33, 36, 39, 46, 51, 63, 65, 75, 152, 206
Evangelicalism, 227, 231
Exorcism, 239
Faith, 47, 84, 107, 126, 174, 234
    Charism, 123-4, 168, 169, 175

INDEX 251

    Steppingstones to, 50, 51
Fasting, 192
Fatula, Mary Ann, 34
Forgiveness, 177
Friendship, 22-35, 159
Fundamentalism, 93-5
Gandhi, Mohandas, 243
Gelin, Albert, 186
Girard, Rene, 101-2
Haight, Roger, 226
Harrington, Daniel, 170
Hay, David, 51
Healing, 187, 211
Hinnebusch, Paul, 184
Historical critical method, 95-7
Holiness, 65, 74, 75
Holy Spirit, 8, 9, 26, 28, 32, 43, 82, 120-1, 133, 190, 204, 246
    Baptism in the Spirit, 120-1
Hopkins, Gerard Manley, 60
Hunt, Kate, 51
Huxley, Aldous, 53
Images of God, 200
Inculturation, 50
Inspiration, 217, 221
Islam, 242
Jamison, Abbot Christopher, 53
Jaspers, Karl, 52
Jeremias, Joachim, 81, 238
John Paul II, 8, 16, 18, 19, 24, 25, 34, 35, 36, 41, 43, 48, 49, 50, 51, 53, 54, 62, 64, 65, 87, 88, 106, 108, 132, 135, 136, 138, 151, 154, 158, 161, 178, 189, 193, 222, 225, 227, 229, 231, 236
Julian of Norwich, 125
Jung, Carl, 149
Kant, Immanuel, 226
Kavanagh, Patrick, 62
Kerr, Cecil, 154, 155, 156, 157, 158
Keller, Helen, 126
Kelly, Larry, 156
Kelly, Matthew, 34

Knitter, Paul, 226
Kolodiejchuk, Brian, 238
Kulhman, Kathryn, 124
Lambertini, Bishop Prospero, 74
Lane, W. S., 174
Lectio Divina, 64, 88, 92, 135
Legion of Mary, 57, 86, 236
Lewis, C. S., 40
Liberalism, 111, 226
Lonergan, Bernard, 46
Louf, Andre, 172
Marriage, 24, 25
Maloney, Francis, 119
Maloney, Newton, 47
Mann, C.S., 174
Marsh, John, 110
Marshall, Christopher, 169, 174, 176
Marrion, Malachy, 168, 169
McGrath, Alister, 227
McKee, David, 156
McNutt, Francis, 115, 213
Meier, 173
Montague, George, 44, 78, 175, 188
Nehemiah, 13-19
Nestorianism, 242
New age, 213, 225, 226, 230, 243-4
New evangelisation, 8, 19, 37, 76, 106, 194
Newman, Cardinal John Henry, 41, 112
New Springtime, 7, 8, 21, 76, 92, 189, 195
Occult, 52, 208
O'Conner, Edward, 176
Origen, 88
Paul VI, 12, 16, 19, 41, 48, 50, 60, 123, 178, 229, 230, 232, 237, 247
Pentecost, 8, 32, 121
Perini, Piri, 152
Perkins, Pheme, 119
Person, 27
Pius VII, 191
Postmodernism, 51

INDEX

Potter, Christopher, 49
Pradel, Andrew, 68
Prayer, 18, 64, 89, 104, 114, 135, 138-9, 171, 174, 176
    Definition, 166
    For others, 202
    Intercession, 20, 190, 194, 195-6
    Petition, 180, 182
    Praise, 19, 184
    Walks, 193
Prince, Derek, 175
Prophecy, 7, 12, 13, 188, 219
Pujo, Bernard, 72
Pythagoras, 33
Radar, Rosemary, 33
Rahner, Karl, 51, 52, 128, 220
Ratzinger, Cardinal Joseph, 36, 213
RCIA, 9, 152
Reiki, 210-12
Religious desires, 201
Religious experience, 53, 60, 62, 65, 66, 225
Repentance, 37
Revelation, 176, 215-
    Defined, 215
    Private, 130
    Public, 216
Rizzuto, Ana-Maria, 198
Roman, Jose Maria, 72
Rosary, 64
Rousseau, Jean Jacques, 149
Sanders, E. P., 111
Schleiermacher, Friedrich, 226
Schnackenburg, Rudolf, 117-8
Secularism, 48, 49, 158
Sepulveda, Mario, 55
Shaw, Russell, 34
Signs and wonders, 108-10, 115, 121
Silence, 53
Southard, Samuel, 47
Spirituality, 198

Operative, 198
Professed, 198
Spiritual combat, 18, 191
St Aelred of Rievaulx, 30
St Albert the Great, 22
St Alphonsus, 220
St Ambrose, 161
St Anselm, 90
St Antonious, 74
St Augustine of Hippo, 9, 22, 28, 29, 54, 111, 113, 216
St Basil, 23
St Bernadette, Soubirous, 220
St Bernard of Clairvaux, 61, 191
St Bonaventure, 220
St Catherine Laboure, 220
St Collette DeBoilet, 68
St Cyprian of Carthage, 40
St Francis of Assisi, 13, 14, 113, 220
St Francis Xavier, 183
St Gregory of Nazianzen, 23
St Ignatius of Antioch, 140-6, 224
St Ignatius of Loyola, 79, 129, 219, 232, 233, 239
St Irenaeus, 110
St Joan of Arc, 70
St John Chrysostom, 160
St John Damascene, 166
St John Eudes, 122
St Justin Martyr, 39, 134
St Pius X, 230
St Teresa of Avila, 166, 203-5, 218, 222
St Therese of Lisieux, 239
St Thomas Aquinas, 22, 23, 29, 30, 63, 67, 89, 90, 107, 111, 113, 168, 216, 219, 225
St Thomas More, 93
St Vincent de Paul, 63, 68-9, 91, 127
    The Little Method, 73
St. Vincent Ferrer, 8, 66-8, 72, 222, 223
Suenens, Cardinal Leo Joseph, 123
Teresa of Calcutta, 235

INDEX

Tribulations, 180, 183
Trinity, 9, 22, 26, 29, 122, 140, 142
    Economical, 27-28
    Immanent, 28-29
Tshudin, Verena, 62
Urban IV, 112
Virgin Mary, 8, 25, 64, 105, 106, 191
Von Goethe, Wolfgang, 78
Wallis, Ian, 169
Wesley, John, 164
Wigglesworth, Smith, 7
Williamson, Peter, 118
Witness, 59, 126, 157
Woodhead, Harry, 156
Word of God/scripture, 78, 80, 101, 129, 134, 216
    Allegorical sense, 98, 99
    Anagogical sense, 98, 100
    Full sense, 100-1
    Literal sense, 98-9
    Liturgical, 134
    Moral sense, 98, 99
    Promises, 177
    Spiritual sense, 97
Wycliffe, John, 70
Yoga, 212